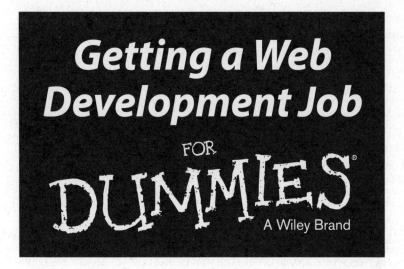

Getting a Web Development Job

FOR

DUMMIES®

A Wiley Brand

by Kathy Taylor and Bud E. Smith

FOR

DUMMIES®

A Wiley Brand

Getting a Web Development Job For Dummies®

Published by: **John Wiley & Sons, Inc.,** 111 River Street, Hoboken, NJ 07030-5774, www.wiley.com

Copyright © 2015 by John Wiley & Sons, Inc., Hoboken, New Jersey

Published simultaneously in Canada

No part of this publication may be reproduced, stored in a retrieval system or transmitted in any form or by any means, electronic, mechanical, photocopying, recording, scanning or otherwise, except as permitted under Sections 107 or 108 of the 1976 United States Copyright Act, without the prior written permission of the Publisher. Requests to the Publisher for permission should be addressed to the Permissions Department, John Wiley & Sons, Inc., 111 River Street, Hoboken, NJ 07030, (201) 748-6011, fax (201) 748-6008, or online at http://www.wiley.com/go/permissions.

Trademarks: Wiley, For Dummies, the Dummies Man logo, Dummies.com, Making Everything Easier, and related trade dress are trademarks or registered trademarks of John Wiley & Sons, Inc. and may not be used without written permission. QuickBooks is a registered trademark of Intuit, Inc. All other trademarks are the property of their respective owners. John Wiley & Sons, Inc. is not associated with any product or vendor mentioned in this book.

LIMIT OF LIABILITY/DISCLAIMER OF WARRANTY: THE PUBLISHER AND THE AUTHOR MAKE NO REPRESENTATIONS OR WARRANTIES WITH RESPECT TO THE ACCURACY OR COMPLETENESS OF THE CONTENTS OF THIS WORK AND SPECIFICALLY DISCLAIM ALL WARRANTIES, INCLUDING WITHOUT LIMITATION WARRANTIES OF FITNESS FOR A PARTICULAR PURPOSE. NO WARRANTY MAY BE CREATED OR EXTENDED BY SALES OR PROMOTIONAL MATERIALS. THE ADVICE AND STRATEGIES CONTAINED HEREIN MAY NOT BE SUITABLE FOR EVERY SITUATION. THIS WORK IS SOLD WITH THE UNDERSTANDING THAT THE PUBLISHER IS NOT ENGAGED IN RENDERING LEGAL, ACCOUNTING, OR OTHER PROFESSIONAL SERVICES. IF PROFESSIONAL ASSISTANCE IS REQUIRED, THE SERVICES OF A COMPETENT PROFESSIONAL PERSON SHOULD BE SOUGHT. NEITHER THE PUBLISHER NOR THE AUTHOR SHALL BE LIABLE FOR DAMAGES ARISING HEREFROM. THE FACT THAT AN ORGANIZATION OR WEBSITE IS REFERRED TO IN THIS WORK AS A CITATION AND/OR A POTENTIAL SOURCE OF FURTHER INFORMATION DOES NOT MEAN THAT THE AUTHOR OR THE PUBLISHER ENDORSES THE INFORMATION THE ORGANIZATION OR WEBSITE MAY PROVIDE OR RECOMMENDATIONS IT MAY MAKE. FURTHER, READERS SHOULD BE AWARE THAT INTERNET WEBSITES LISTED IN THIS WORK MAY HAVE CHANGED OR DISAPPEARED BETWEEN WHEN THIS WORK WAS WRITTEN AND WHEN IT IS READ.

For general information on our other products and services, please contact our Customer Care Department within the U.S. at 877-762-2974, outside the U.S. at 317-572-3993, or fax 317-572-4002. For technical support, please visit www.wiley.com/techsupport.

Wiley publishes in a variety of print and electronic formats and by print-on-demand. Some material included with standard print versions of this book may not be included in e-books or in print-on-demand. If this book refers to media such as a CD or DVD that is not included in the version you purchased, you may download this material at http://booksupport.wiley.com. For more information about Wiley products, visit www.wiley.com.

Library of Congress Control Number: 2014948513

ISBN 978-1-118-96776-8 (pbk); ISBN 978-1-118-96778-2 (ebk); ISBN 978-1-118-96797-3 (ebk)

Manufactured in the United States of America

10 9 8 7 6 5 4 3 2 1

Contents at a Glance

Table of Contents

Introduction

•••

*W*eb development is a big bright spot in the world of work. Web development jobs include graphic designers, visual designers, front-end software developers, back-end software developers, content developers, and user experience people. All of these jobs tend to be interesting and high-paying. Most important, they make up a large and fast-growing part of the economy.

Although web development represents a passel of new opportunities, getting a job in the web development area can be a nerve-wracking prospect. The web area is changing fast, and the web needs of organizations change rapidly too. Large companies hire scores or hundreds of people for a big project, then let most of them go when the project is over. Or they hire a web development company, which staffs up when times are good, and then downsizes the moment they get a little difficult.

Web development people are also quick to change jobs to pursue new opportunities and to keep their skills sharp. So, as a web developer, you're likely to spend less time in each job than people in other kinds of careers, and to be looking for a job more of the time.

This book helps you get a web development job, keep a web development job, and then get your next web development job. It helps you understand what your immediate colleagues with the same or similar job title do for a living, and what your not-so-immediate colleagues who fill out all the related positions on a web development team do as well.

With this book, you can become more valued, more employable, better paid, and easier to hire.

About This Book

Getting a Web Development Job For Dummies introduces you to the world of web development and to employment in web development. With this book as your guide, you'll learn

  ✔ How web development got to be such a big and important area

  ✔ Why companies care so much about their web-development efforts

  ✔ How to make yourself valuable within the web development world

- ✔ What the major categories of web development jobs are
- ✔ Which web development jobs you can position yourself for, given your interests and skill set
- ✔ How to position yourself if your core abilities are graphical and artistic
- ✔ How to position yourself if your core abilities are technical (related to writing code of some kind)
- ✔ How to teach yourself what's needed to offer the best of both worlds — and to get hired easily and paid accordingly
- ✔ How the web development needs of small companies, big companies, educational institutions, governments, and non-profits differ — and how that affects your employment prospects
- ✔ How to choose from among full-time employment for a traditional organization, full-time employment for a web development organization, and self-employment
- ✔ Why a web portfolio matters so much
- ✔ What the key concepts of web design jobs are
- ✔ How to get formal education for web development
- ✔ How to get on-the-job training — the famous OJT — for web development
- ✔ What the major web development tools are
- ✔ How to work for different kinds of companies
- ✔ How to network effectively in web development
- ✔ How to use online job boards and LinkedIn
- ✔ How to ace the interview
- ✔ How to create a portfolio site that will help you get the job you want, over and over again
- ✔ How to keep and grow within your ideal job when you find it

After you decide you want a web development job — or, once you have one, and decide that you want to keep working in web development — how do you move forward?

That's what this book is here for. It empowers you to understand the web development landscape and get the job you want, and then build the skills you need and the career you deserve.

The web development world is different from most other kinds of work: jobs, technologies, tools, and standards are changing all the time. This book is your guide to keeping up.

Many people got web development jobs — and some even kept them — without this book in hand. But, using this book as a reference, you can get jobs more easily, negotiate a better package for yourself, and build a career that you're proud of.

Foolish Assumptions

Getting a Web Development Job For Dummies is written in a way that's fully accessible for beginners, for people who don't currently hold a web design job and are looking to get their first one. However, we do have to make a few assumptions in writing this book because we wouldn't have enough space to help you with the key parts of getting a job if we had to explain what a web page is! Here are our assumptions:

✔ You are familiar with computers, such as Windows PCs or Macintosh computers. We assume you can work with icons, the keyboard, and a mouse, and that you know the basics of using your computer for things like using the Internet or writing letters.

✔ You are familiar with using web pages for common tasks such as searching the web, looking for a job, and buying items such as books and movie tickets.

✔ You have a smartphone or a tablet computer and have used apps, and that you've used an app store to find and download new apps. If you do not have a smartphone, get a friend who has one to show you around the smartphone and how to find and download a new app.

✔ You know something about the basic mechanics of getting a job. If not, please see *Job Hunting For Dummies,* 2nd Edition, by Max Messmer (Wiley) to get up to speed.

Icons Used in This Book

If you've read other *For Dummies* books, you know that these books use icons in the margin to call attention to particularly important or useful ideas in the text. In this book, we use four such icons:

The Tip icon highlights expert shortcuts or simple ideas that can make life easier for you.

Arguably, the whole book is technical stuff, but this icon highlights something that's particularly technical. We've tried to avoid unnecessary jargon and complexity, but some background information can give you a better understanding of what you're doing, and sometimes we do need to get techy. Sections highlighted with this icon might be worth re-reading to make sure you understand, or you might decide that you don't need to know that much detail. It's up to you!

Although we'd like to think that reading this book is an unforgettable experience, we've highlighted some points that you might want to particularly commit to memory. They're either important takeaways, or they are fundamental to the project you're working on.

As you would on the road, slow down when you see a warning sign. It highlights an area where things could go wrong.

Beyond the Book

- ✔ **Cheat Sheet:** This book's Cheat Sheet can be found online at www. dummies.com/cheatsheet/gettingawebdevelopmentjob. See the Cheat Sheet for information about the switch from tables to CSS, as well as the rocky introduction of the CSS standard in the late 1990s and early 2000s.

- ✔ **Dummies.com online articles:** Companion articles to this book's content can be found online at www.dummies.com/extras/ gettingawebdevelopmentjob. The articles deal with creating an online portfolio, tips for searching for a job online, and how to get up to speed on specific tools.

- ✔ **Bonus *Getting a Job For Dummies* content:** Like all books in the *Getting a Job For Dummies* series, this book offers additional bonus content on the web. Sample resumes, a resume template, and videos about the web developer role can be found at www.dummies.com/extras/ gettingawebdevelopmentjob.

- ✔ **Updates:** If this book has any updates after printing, they will be posted to www.dummies.com/extras/gettingawebdevelopmentjob.

Where to Go from Here

Like other *For Dummies* books, *Getting a Web Development Job For Dummies* is a reference. That means you can read it in any order that you wish. You can page through the book for hot topics or use the Table of Contents and the Index to hone in on what interests you.

You can also read the book in order. This is especially valuable in two quite different situations. If you're new to the world of web development, reading the book through is a great way to pick up a lot of context about what web development people do, and how they work together.

Also, if you're moving up into some kind of leadership or management role, it's valuable to read the book all the way through at that time as well. You can use the book's descriptions as an opportunity to think about how all the different kinds of professionals on a web team work together, as well as to reflect on what you can improve in your organization's web development efforts.

If you're considering moving into web development, either as your first career or from another area of work, read Part III. It talks about how to get a web-development education. If you have some other kind of education, or don't have any higher education, you can use this Part to figure out what relevant background you do have, and how to fill in any gaps.

If you're looking for a job and you have experience already, read Part IV. It tells you how to build a portfolio site, or how to improve one if you have it already, as well as how to carry out your job search.

Part I

Getting a Job in Web Development

In this part . . .

✔ Understand why web development matters

✔ Explore web development career paths

✔ Understand organizations that hire web development professionals

✔ Learn about the web development jobs market in the U.S.

Chapter 1

Seeing the Big Picture of Web Development Jobs

*W*eb development is the largest and fastest-growing area of employment today. Web development includes technically oriented people who write computer programs, graphic designers who never see a line of computer code, content and marketing experts who concentrate on the visual and verbal appeal of a page, and many more experts and dabblers.

The ways in which people work in web development are as many and varied as the kind of work that is covered by the web development umbrella. Many people work traditional "day jobs," but you will also see just as many people in a garage startup working 80 hours a week, contractors, consultants, part-timers, and people who will give you crucial insights that save your project just because you were good enough to buy them lunch.

The reason for the many and varied job descriptions, and the many and varied ways of working, in web development is simple: The web is the greatest creative canvas in human history. The rapid and continuing growth of the web is driven by the appeal of simple combinations of words and pictures, abetted now by multimedia, laid out in easy to scan and attractive ways, and offering users functionality from the simplest task — reading a newspaper article, say — to a dashboard that displays the operational status of a multibillion-dollar factory (or a multibillion-dollar war). Art, music, photography, creative writing, commerce — almost anything that people do is delivered by the web, or supported by content and functionality delivered by the web.

Only some of the work roles that support the wonders of the web are considered "web development jobs." Here are a few descriptive phrases to help narrow down what we can consider part of the web development world:

- **Technical:** Web development jobs usually involve dealing with the technical considerations that are unique to the web — from the computer code that runs it, to the markup languages that control the delivery and display of words and images, to the hardware and software functionality that determines whether a web page appears quickly or slowly, to the often complex and demanding tools that are used to create websites and web content.

- **Creative:** The web is so new that there are relatively few rules in web development. The best way to do most things has usually not been found yet, let alone widely discussed, agreed, and set in concrete. Instead, a willingness to improvise, to try new things — and to search widely, and quickly, for the best of what other people are doing — is crucial to web development work.

- **Fast-changing:** The web development world is constantly and unrelentingly changing. Some things that used to be unreliable are now settled, such as the basics of HTML and even, dare we say it, CSS. (HTML, HyperText Markup Language, is the simple code that specifies parts of text, such as headlines or emphasized text, and that shows where to find an image file that will be displayed on the page. CSS, Cascading Style Sheets, is a newer kind of code that gives you considerable flexibility and control in onscreen page layout.) But more things are changing — new capabilities, new tools, new programming languages, and new best practices. ("Best" being a relative term here.)

- **Varied:** There are many specialists in web development, but people are expected to be multi-skilled, and to move away from less-needed or even obsolete skills to new abilities that are on today's cutting edge. As an example, many web developers made a good living tweaking HTML markup and CSS code to make a web page work well on different personal computer web browsers, such as Internet Explorer and Netscape Navigator. That area has largely settled down, and many of the same people are now making the same web page work well on desktops, laptops, tablets, and smartphones, using the new versions of the same standards — HTML5 and CSS3.

We could go on, but this list captures the wide and fast-changing world of web development as well as any brief description can. And this list helps us to identify the one common element that is the most important in distinguishing the web development world, and the most crucial characteristic of the many, many people who thrive in it.

The common element in web development is change; most areas of web development are changing quickly. Even where technical standards have settled down, how and even why we do things in web development continue to evolve. Styles come and go, such as web pages with big images and few words; needs change, as with the unrelenting growth of mobile.

And the most important characteristic of successful web development people is the secret to accommodating this rapid pace of change: a love of learning. It's great for a web developer to love change in and of itself, but what helps her thrive in that fast-changing world is the desire to swim better in these fast-flowing currents by picking up new information, new skills, new attitudes, and new ways of working.

The fact that you're reading this book shows that you probably have this core characteristic, this love of learning. You aren't happy with a top ten list or a brief video clip when you face a serious issue, and a big opportunity, such as moving over to, or moving up in, the world of web development. Of course, you will probably look at many top ten lists and video clips as well; there are several of each associated with or linked to from this book. But, as a reader of this book, you're willing to do some heavy lifting to understand this still-new world. Welcome!

Getting Why Web Development Matters

Web development matters because the web matters in so many ways that we could take this whole chapter just to briefly describe them all.

Here's one way of describing how important the web has become, and how quickly it has grown in importance. One of us, Bud Smith, was working for Apple Computer in 1994. (Which, luckily, was nothing like *1984* — that's an old Apple joke.)

Smith started hearing about something called the World Wide Web, and seeing Mosaic, an early web browser, on developers' screens. He quickly pulled together a book proposal, and he was soon the proud co-author of an early web book, *Creating Web Pages For Dummies* (Wiley). This book went to nine editions and is still in print more than 20 years later. That's about how long the web has been known to most people, as usage grew and grew and grew.

In that time, the web has become ubiquitous in the developed world, and commonly used in the developing world. Facebook alone, which started out as a website and is now powered by mobile apps, has more than 1.3 billion monthly average users.

The web is now a major source of information, entertainment, commerce, computing capability, and more, and growing fast in all these areas every year. About ten percent of all retail sales go through the web in the developed world, and steady growth continues. Websites change all the time, and many mobile apps — a very fast-growing area of software — are simply repurposed, and simplified, websites.

Books, magazines, newspapers, the telephone, movies, and television are all important communications and entertainment media today, and all of them, in their traditional forms, are being disrupted by the web. That is, all of them partly depend on the web as infrastructure and distribution — and all of them see the web as competition. And one can hardly emphasize enough that this disruption is continuing year after year after year.

Also, none of the other media listed is also a front end for software. Inventor and entrepreneur Marc Andreesen famously said, "Software is eating the world." This means that more and more of the things that people do are being converted to software. And more and more of that software is being presented to people through websites and apps. (See the sidebar "Is app development the same as web development?" for more.)

For an example, consider Amazon (`www.amazon.com`). Amazon stores and presents user reviews for an immense range of products. It displays a different version of its home page to you based on your past purchases. And it makes recommendations to you based on your past purchases and the content you're currently looking at. It also lets you buy with a single click, if you wish. (This feature is almost unique to Amazon, which protects its intellectual property zealously.)

All this functionality is based in software — often quite consequential software. Amazon's recommendation engine, for instance, is a major software engineering project in its own right, protected by patents and trade secrets just like other advanced technology.

What's important here is that all this technology is presented through a web interface and is considered to be part of this market-leading website. As a supporting point, making a website work better is causing new and improved technology to be developed on a rapid and constant basis.

So you have the fastest-growing medium ever, and one that is at least as consequential as any other medium, ever. And it was invented and became popular not much more than a couple of decades ago. The size and importance of the web, its innovative use and creation of technology, and its incredibly rapid growth are the core reasons why web development is so important.

Apps are also pretty specialized, given that they work on small screens and have limited functionality. Overall, app development is not the same as web development, but many apps are repurposed websites, including significant functionality, and web development jobs can include app development. Companies that specialize in app development are likely to hire people with web development backgrounds, and then teach them a few additional skills so they can help turn out killer apps instead.

Is app development the same as web development?

An app is a computer program that's sold as a product in an app store: Apple's iTunes App Store, the Google Play Store, or similar.

An app is, technically speaking, the same as an application — a computer program that's sold as a product. But apps were designed for small-screen devices, such as the iPhone and Android phones, then extended to tablets. They evolved to mostly be limited in purpose (one function, or a few closely related functions); very easy to use; and cheap, either free, or sold for a few dollars.

Many websites are a lot like apps (and vice versa). For instance, your bank's website probably lets you see your statements, pay bills, make deposits by photographing checks, and more. If your bank has a phone app or an iPad app, they probably do all of the same things.

However, apps are not exactly the same as websites. Many websites are information-only, or information-mostly, with just a little bit of functionality — such as a simple form that you fill in to join an email list. But Apple has recently moved to prevent apps that are information-mostly from being listed on the App Store.

Why There Are So Many Web Development Jobs

Web development jobs are one of the largest new categories, and one of the fastest-growing categories, in employment. For the U.S., the Bureau of Labor Statistics says that there are roughly 150,000 positions at this writing. Over the next decade, employment is expected to grow about 20 percent here. The main driver of job growth in web development is e-commerce. In many retail categories, about 10 percent of all sales are completed online. That percentage is expected to roughly double over the next decade.

However, there are more web development jobs in the job listings than for other kinds of positions, even those with more total employees. Why is this? A few reasons spring to mind:

- **Rapid growth:** Most job categories aren't growing by double digits per decade. Companies need to advertise constantly to support growing their roster of web development people.

- **Rapid change:** The skills needed in web development are constantly changing. For instance, Facebook recently introduced a new computer language called Hack. It's a version of the web scripting language PHP, but with strong *typing,* which is the capability to declare what kind of information a new variable holds in advance, such as text or integers (numbers without decimal points, such as –1, 0, and 42). If you can show that you have experience as a Hack developer, a company that wants to put the new language to use will probably hire you.

✔ **High conventional turnover:** There's high turnover in web development jobs, with people leaving one job for another job, or leaving the workforce for other kinds of jobs, family reasons, or retirement. It often seems that the only way to get paid fairly for hot or new skills is to leave one job and go to another. Two years can be a long stint at one company in web development!

✔ **New approach:** The emergence of mobile devices, now equaling conventional PCs for web access, has led to new needs. Responsive websites, which work well across a wide range of screen sizes, and mobile apps are among the new needs that drive growth.

✔ **High unconventional turnover:** In web development, people often move back and forth from regular employment to contracting (you get paid by the hour, without much in the way of benefits from the employer) or consulting (similar to contracting, but usually including giving advice on what to do, with perhaps some contracting-type hourly work included). This kind of turnover really gooses the job postings as employers struggle to keep people in conventional jobs.

✔ **Prospecting:** Companies are often not fully serious about job postings in general, and tech job postings in particular. That is, they don't have an open position right now that they'll fill if they find the right candidate. Instead, they'll get resumes in, interview people, and then have someone ready if an opening comes up — or move an existing employee out, even if he's fairly productive, and move someone who seems more promising, or less expensive, in.

✔ **More employer:** There are many new companies springing up to meet the needs of established companies, as well as startups with their own needs for standout web development. There's lots of greenfield work — developing brand-new websites that haven't existed before — as well as improvements and extensions to existing websites, especially changes to add to mobile functionality.

Why Do Companies Care about Web Development?

Companies care tremendously about web development. The reasons are complicated, numerous, and differ from one company to another, but there are many common themes.

Web development needs differ from organization to organization — and, within an organization, often from quarter to quarter. That's because the web is protean — it can do so many things.

Following is a brief and partial list of different types of websites. It's important that you recognize these types of sites because the types of job roles they require will vary significantly.

Basic company brochureware

Every company of any consequence today has at least basic "brochureware" website. This website does the same thing as a brochure that the same company might hand out at a trade show or a job fair, or give to investors or press people:

- ✔ **Describe what the company does:** People who learn of a company sometimes wonder what the company does — and, for some companies that are particularly complex, including those that have grown through multiple acquisitions, the people wondering can include managers of the company itself! A website will have an About section that describes what a company wants to say it does in the world.

- ✔ **Show where the company is:** A company uses its website to describe where it's located. This can be very simple, as with a single company office location, or very complicated, including not only multiple sites where the company has offices, but also the location of distributors, retailers, repair shops for a company's products, and more.

- ✔ **Announce who managers are:** Some companies put all their employees' descriptions up on the web, and companies with investors are compelled to put the names of certain legally defined officers. Most companies put up at least the top half a dozen or so employees, who are meant to be an impressive-looking group that will make you want to invest, go to work for the company, buy their products, and so on.

- ✔ **Show off what the company sells:** A website is a great place for photographs of any tangible products the company sells, whether it's knives for professional chefs, house plants, cars, or boats. Again, this is a classic brochure function, translated to the web.

- ✔ **Tell you where to buy the company's products:** A website helps you find out how to buy. This can mean everything from going to the nearest corner store to contacting the company's sales department.

- ✔ **Tell you how to get a job:** A website usually tells you how to look for work at a company. It will often have job listings and an email address or form for submitting your resume and a cover letter.

- ✔ **Keeping in touch:** Many companies will offer an email list that you can join for regular updates from the company.

Brochureware sites were developed because it's easier and cheaper to put this kind of information on a website than it is to write, lay out, and print up a brochure, and then get it in the hands of the person who needs it — which usually takes precious time. The people seeking information doesn't have to wait to get a brochure, try to remember where they put it, or worry about whether it's up-to-date. They just find the website and look for themselves.

Brochureware sites also serve another purpose — they allow a company to say, "Of course we have a website." Brochureware sites often reflect a company that hasn't thought through how it can really take best advantage of the web.

Figure 1-1 shows a discussion of brochureware sites on the National Institutes of Health site, where it compares them to interactive websites. You can visit it at `www.ncbi.nlm.nih.gov/pmc/articles/PMC3096269/`.

Websites are commonly used to sell, support, and arrange for service for products. If a typical company isn't looking to do these things online, it probably should.

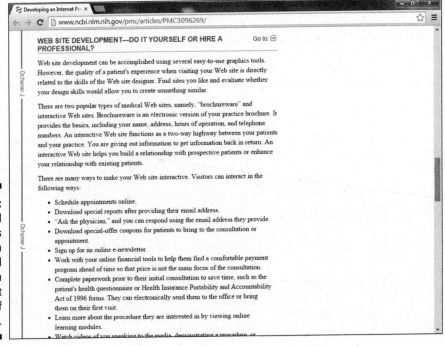

Figure 1-1:
The National Institutes of Health has a useful discussion of different types of websites.

When Marc Andreessen says that "software is eating the world," this is what he means. It's very often easier, cheaper, and more effective to do at least part of any function a company does online, supported by software and available to everyone. Just for one example: A company may have a product that's very hard to choose and fit online, such as shoes. (We know shoes are sold online, but they're still sold in person a lot too, for these reasons.)

So say that you've decided to only sell shoes in person. Well, you're not done. A customer who has purchased your great shoes and received your great service may want to buy another pair of shoes like the ones she bought before. If she hasn't grown or otherwise changed, the exact same shoes will work for her. A website is a great way to help her reorder them.

Or, perhaps the customer is really excited about her shoes and wants to join a club or have an ongoing discussion about them. The online world is a great place to do that.

Brochureware sites for large companies can be very extensive, with tons of information. But in these cases, it's even more likely that the company is missing opportunities to do more online.

If a company hires you to work on a brochureware site, think through whether it's missing opportunities to do more. You may be able to expand the job opportunity — but, if the company is too stuck in the mud, you may decide you don't want to work for the company at all.

What kinds of website developers are needed for a brochureware site? Here are a few descriptive characterizations, although one person can have more than one skill:

- **Website designer:** Usually, when most people refer to a website designer, they mean a generalist — relatively speaking — who can mock up the look of a website for approval, lay out the site using HTML and CSS, and put content in it.

- **Graphic designer:** A graphic designer will fine-tune the look of the website, possibly take and possibly edit photographs, help choose fonts, and so on. The website designer will often be, or hire in, the graphic artist.

- **Writer:** Often a writer will be hired to write and edit the words in a website. The task is often more about editing than writing, because the words are often adapted from existing materials, such as — you guessed it — a static, printed marketing brochure.

- **Analyst:** Often, after a website is up, companies will want to know who's looking at what pages, and what actions they take, where possible — clicking for more information, filling out a form to request information, and so on.

"Just go look on the website"

One of the most annoying things a potential customer can be told by a company employee when she has a question is "just go look on the website."

People today know that organizations have websites and that they can find all sorts of information on them. They also know that it can be hard to find information on websites, especially on a smartphone — which is all they're likely to have handy when they're asking an employee a question.

When people are talking to an employee, they want information now, and they may want more specific information than a website is likely to provide; they may want the newest information, which may not be on the website yet; they may have follow-up questions, so the easy one is just a starting point; and they may not want

to bother to search online, now (with their smartphone) or later (with a tablet or personal computer).

Recognizing these user needs, what can a web developer do? First, use questions that employees get from people, including questions that are asked live and in-person, as fodder for the website. The web indeed should answer all the questions that people commonly asked, and the information should be dead easy to find.

But, as a web developer, you should also recognize that people get information in many ways, not only through your precious site. Consider working with others in your organization to make sure that there's a free flow of information that gets on the website — and that customers can get directly from employees when they want it.

A database-driven site

A database-driven site can be almost any kind of site, but at minimum it's a step up in technical complexity from a brochureware site. In a database-driven site, each page that's shown in the site is generated from a database call.

Look at a site for a newspaper such as *The New York Times*. The *Times* has too many stories that change too fast to write separate HTML and CSS code for each web page that displays a new story. Instead, the story is placed in a database, and the data is then retrieved when someone wants to see the story.

With this kind of flexible web page, ads, recommended stories, and other content on the web page can also be generated from database calls. The website becomes far more flexible; at the same time, an entire new level of complexity is introduced because it becomes much harder to know, or track, just who among the visitors to your site has seen exactly what.

A database-driven site typically uses a content management system (CMS): a tool for people to enter and link information that will appear on the website. A good CMS makes a lot of people's jobs easier, but it's also the case that, between the CMS and the database functionality that makes pages appear, there's now a lot of complexity between the person who wants information to appear on a web page and the user who actually sees the information.

Figure 1-2 shows a web page promoting Go Gov!, a CMS developed for use by governments by the state of Oklahoma. You can visit the page at the following catchy URL: www.ok.gov/go.

Figure 1-2: Oklahoma offers Go Gov!, a CMS specifically designed for use by governments.

So who are some of the people you might see added to a database-driven site team, in addition to the people you see on simpler sites, such as website designers, graphic artists, writers, and analysts?

- ✔ **CMS manager:** Someone has to buy in or (shudder) create the CMS software, and someone else has to manage it. (Writing a CMS today would be hard, as there are a lot of demands on CMS software.) With about half of all new sites today being WordPress-based, the CMS manager role will be growing quickly.

- ✔ **CSS expert:** Whereas most website designers know something about CSS, a marketing site needs to generate many similar pages quickly. A reusable library of professionally designed CSS templates is a vital resource for this kind of work.

✔ **Database programmer:** This role might or might not be considered a web design job, but it's definitely an important role for a database-driven website team to have. This can be a whole bunch of people, one of whom might be considered part of the web design team, whereas others are considered "back-end" and more purely technical developers.

The URL challenge

Experienced users of the web often develop an eye for URLs, or Uniform Resource Locators — the description at the top of a web page that explains where a web page is retrieved from. Users can look to the URL for information about where they are on a site, where they might go next, and other information.

For instance, here's a URL generated when you're looking at Google Calendar:

```
https://www.google.com/
calendar/render
```

This URL at least tells you where you are on the web: at Google's Calendar site. The last part of the URL, render, refers to the process of generating the calendar that appears on the website — obviously, a database-driven page, but that's not obvious from the URL. The URL doesn't tell the user much, but it's not distracting or obnoxious.

Here's a mixed URL from Google:

```
https://www.google.com/search?
q=how+to+think+like+a+computer+
scientist&ie=utf-8&oe=utf-
8&aq=t&rls=org.mozilla:en-
US:official&client=firefox-a&
channel=fflb#channel=fflb&
q=%22how+to+think+like+a+co
mputer+scientist%22+python
+review&rls=org.mozilla:en-
US:official&start=20
```

Plainly, this is a Google Search result, but there's a lot of additional information too. The information after the question mark (?) is a set of *key-value pairs*. A key-value pair is a combination of a descriptive term — the key — and actual live data, the value. So the q that follows the question mark, in this case, is the key for the value the user entered; the value is the words the user entered, which happens to be the name of an article the user found online called "How to Think Like a Computer Scientist." This kind of URL is confusing to the casual user, even though with some dedication — and some knowledge of the history of the web — you can figure most of it out.

Now here's a URL from *The New York Times:*

```
www.nytimes.com/2014/06/29/
world/africa/libyan-suspected-
in-benghazi-mission-attack-
arrives-in-washington.html?h
p&action=click&pgtype=Homepa
ge&version=LedeSum&module=fi
rst-column-region&region=top-
news&WT.nav=top-news
```

We mentioned earlier that the *The New York Times* uses a database-driven website, and you can see that here. But the URL at least includes information about the date, category, and title of the story. Some websites hide the key-value information entirely and only display information that makes sense to the casual user in the URL, which is the user-friendliest way to display URLs of all.

A marketing site

A marketing site is a big step up from a brochureware site. The purpose of a properly designed marketing site, in our humble opinion, is to get leads. This is not "feel-good" marketing that makes visitors feel all warm and fuzzy, but doesn't ask them to do anything specific. It's a site that has goals and gathers hard evidence of success.

Many marketing sites build up a complete marketing lead from "bits and bobs" — pieces gathered from various sources. For instance, if you buy a list of leads, you can then compare that to people who have created a login for your website. The lead can now be extended to include information about the person's on-site activity and marketing involvement with the company, such as participating in a webinar.

These leads can supplement, or be the main source of, the information that a company uses to run its sales operation. The list of leads is the interface between marketing, which generates and augments the list of leads, and sales, which uses them to contact potential customers and sell.

Many brochureware sites would do a lot more good for their companies if they were converted to lead-generating marketing sites. This latter kind of site actually makes the website part of a profit center, sales, rather than a cost center such as a brochureware site, with results that can't easily be tied to sales revenue.

However, this is not an easy or necessarily an inexpensive transition. An example is the kind of software needed to manage this process. A company called Marketo automates much of the process of offering information, brochure downloads, webinars, and similar information online. Marketo software can track potential customers as they surf a company's website, building up a complete lead a piece at a time, using a name and email address to generate a webinar signup, and then using the webinar signup to complete the lead with full customer information. (And then augmenting that with data about the lead's participation in the webinar she signed up for.)

The difference between a brochureware site and an active marketing site is shown by something that happens only on the latter. If a potential Marketo software customer gives the company basic lead information and then checks the company's software pricing page, he gets a call from a pre-sales employee within five minutes because Marketo has determined that this was the optimal window for moving the sales process forward. A subscription to the company's software costs at least $500 a month, so it's worth investing some time from an actual employee to contact a hot lead who was more or less ready to buy.

Like a brochureware site, a marketing site will need a designer, an artist, and a writer. More than a brochureware site, it will need multiple analysts to track information generated by the site. (And Marketo, among others, sells specialized software for this purpose.)

Active marketing sites are highly likely to be database-driven, so they will also need roles such as CMS manager, CSS expert, and database programmer, as described in the previous section.

Here are some other roles you might need for an active marketing site:

- **Interaction designer:** A true marketing site is optimized to gather information from visitors, so an interaction designer — someone who studies how people actually use a product or service, such as a website — can be a vital part of the picture. (You can find interaction designers working on all kinds of websites, but active marketing websites have an especially strong need for them.)

- **JavaScript engineer:** Active marketing sites use JavaScript or other software technology to tie marketing emails to the lead database to what gets displayed to specific companies on the website. Marketo claims to automate this process, but if you're footing the bill for this kind of software, you're probably working with a lot of leads and a lot of emails and web pages, so you'll want an internal person managing the process and fixing problems. Someone who combines HTML, CSS, and JavaScript skills might be called a "front-end developer."

- **PERL engineer:** Active marketing websites use a lot of variable content in web pages, and tend to use web page URLs to pass information back and forth. (You will have seen this kind of information after the question mark [?] in a complex URL if you have been looking, which you should be.) PERL is a flexible programming language often used for developing web applications.

Figure 1-3 shows introductory notes to the PERL programming language from the U.S. National Institute of Standards. PERL is widely used in government for its facility with statistics, among other reasons. You can download the notes at www.ncnr.nist.gov/staff/nickm/perl/PerlIntroNotes.pdf.

An e-commerce site

Even simple sites can have an e-commerce capability, but this is usually an outsourced capability that's driven by a shared web page or small amounts of HTML and/or CSS that allow an external e-commerce capability to appear to be part of other sites.

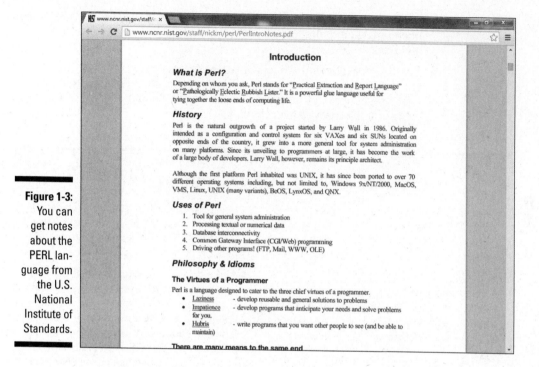

Figure 1-3:
You can get notes about the PERL language from the U.S. National Institute of Standards.

The e-commerce sites that most people are familiar with are database-driven sites that also have a marketing component built in. They can be exceedingly complex. The most well-known example of an e-commerce site is Amazon, which is so robust that it has spawned off a separate web software development platform, Amazon Web Services.

E-commerce sites support many functions at the same time. Their core capability, however, is the capability to complete a sale online.

As you can imagine, this puts a whole new kind of pressure on all the other capabilities included in an e-commerce website. Web pages showing products have to be easy to access, easy to use, and effective at gathering clicks from interested users to perform their part in online business. Similar considerations hold for the entire site.

In addition to the skills described in previous sections, and oftentimes a layer of management to supervise multiple contributors in a given role, job titles required for a robust e-commerce site are likely to include

> ✔ **UX designer (short for *user experience designer*, also called a *visual designer*):** This job goes beyond even the interaction designer role to

take responsibility for the user's entire experience on the website, which of course should often result in a sale where an e-commerce site is involved.

✔ **Art director (also known as a *design director*):** An art director is the boss of everyone who touches the look of the site, making sure it all works together and that there is a consistent visual appearance that evolves and improves over time.

What makes a sales lead valid?

A major purpose for websites today is generating valid sales leads; adding information to existing sales leads; and verifying that sales leads are still valid. In order to help gather this information, you need to know what it is.

A valid sales lead for a company has several pieces to it, which are different for different companies. Usually, a sales lead for a business-to-business site includes

✔ **Name:** People love the sound of their own names. If you want to contact people again, you really need to get this information, and to get it right.

✔ **Email address:** If only one piece of information can be gathered, this is it. Even without a name, the email address allows you to contact a person again and to detect when the same person enters his email address on your site again. In most cases, you want to be sure to get a company email address.

✔ **Phone number:** Most solid marketing sites prioritize phone number, along with name and email address. With the phone number, you can call a prospect to see if he's interested in buying.

✔ **Company name:** It's old-fashioned to ask people about their company — how many employees it has, what its sales revenues are, and so on. Instead, the modern approach is to just get the company name

(and perhaps division or department name), and then merge that information with a database that has current information about huge numbers of companies.

✔ **Address:** This may not actually be very important for reaching people by snail mail. It's more for geotargeting — for instance, identifying which prospects to invite to which of your events on a marketing tour, or identifying which division or department of a company a given company employee works for.

✔ **Job title:** Combined with company name, this is a crucial piece of information for identifying who from the leads database a company wants to contact for follow-up on a given product or within a given marketing campaign. CxOs may be invited to a special meeting at a trade show; middle managers might get a special offer. (*CxO* is a newish term covering CEOs, CFOs, and so on. This group is also sometimes referred to as the *C-suite*.)

There's lots more information that can be gathered, but it's important that the core fields for a sales lead be kept as few as possible; the fewer fields, the easier it is to get more leads. Find out what information is required for a valid sales lead in your organization and find out how the company website interacts with the leads database. ("Not at all" is not a very good answer.)

Educational institutions

Just about all colleges and universities, and a great majority of elementary schools and secondary schools, have their own websites. In some cases, the site is like a company's brochureware site — it provides basic information about the school and who's who in the school's administration. However, more and more sites, especially college or university sites, are quite advanced. Here are the core functions that most college and university websites, and a growing number of sites for younger students, offer:

- **Describe what the school's focus is:** People who learn of a school often wonder what makes that school stand out. Is it a somewhat generic school that provides needed educational services for its geographic area, or does it stand out in some way? The website will have an About section that allows a school to stake a claim as to how it's special, and those special characteristics will be reflected in other site content and functionality as well.

- **Show where the school is:** The website describes where the school is located. This can be a single building, an extensive campus, or multiple campuses — some schools even have study-abroad offices located in other countries.

- **Announce who administrators are:** Key administrators are listed online; often, there's a searchable directory of the entire staff.

- **Sell school-related stuff:** A school's website can include an online bookstore, for textbooks and possibly for other books, and all sorts of merchandise, often branded tchotchkes like fluffy toys representing the school's mascot.

- **Tell you how to apply:** Most schools have an application process, and the website is the place to find out about it.

- **Tell you how to get a job:** The school's website is a great place to go to find current job openings and how to apply.

- **Keeping in touch:** Many schools will offer subscriptions to an email newsletter to keep you up to date. (Don't be surprised if signing up results in your receiving fundraising emails.)

- **Signing up for courses, viewing assignments, turning in homework:** Many schools do a lot of academic support work online, which is expensive to set up and support, but ultimately less expensive than any other way of accomplishing the same things.

Like a company's brochureware site, the non-interactive parts of a school's website are developed largely to save money, while providing easier access, easier updating, and better ease of use. The interactive parts save money too.

How to make a career with Amazon Web Services

Amazon Web Services is easily the leader among cloud service providers. This new category provides a cloud platform — the capability to develop, test, and run software and database services in the cloud, completely away from the customer's premises.

Cloud service providers allow organizations to add capability without buying servers of their own. The catch is that Amazon offers its own technology bundle for creating new capabilities; developers can't simply run their own internal software on Amazon's servers.

Using Amazon Web Services is designed to be easy, but there are more than a dozen separate services included under the Amazon Web Services umbrella. Just learning what they are and how they work together is a chore. Figuring out how a business might use these services together, how that fits with the business's existing computing services, and what it might cost to provision and run a new capability internally versus on Amazon Web Services versus on competitors is a major headache. Of course, web development is full of people who take something that others see as a headache and make a fun challenge out of it.

But, to coin a modern proverb, in disorder, there is profit. If you become expert at creating web services on the AWS platform, or even specifying, overseeing the delivery of, and running such services, you may be set in your career direction for a long time to come.

What kinds of website developers are needed for an educational institution's site? The roles are similar to the brochureware site described earlier — a designer for the site, a graphic designer, a writer, and an analyst for site traffic. For the many school sites that support academic services such as signing up for courses and turning in homework, there may also be people for database access and interaction design.

Chapter 2

Exploring Web Development Career Paths

In This Chapter

▶ Discovering how the web developer role has splintered

▶ Exploring front-end jobs

▶ Getting to know other contributors

▶ Understanding why Photoshop is (still) key to web development

here are almost as many ways into web development as there are people with web development jobs. However, there are a few common elements among different "tribes" in web development that provide a kind of ladder for working your way into a career, and then making your way in the web development world.

An initial screen is what "bucket" of related areas your talents and interests fall into. If your skill is in making things look good, you are somewhere in the artistic and graphics areas. The key job title here is visual designer. In this chapter, we explain the difference, and more.

Distinguishing between Visual Designer and Web Developer

Web development jobs are thought of as technical, but the "looking good" area is really at the core of web development versus other career paths. The key job title here is visual designer, although people doing this work can be called graphic designers, web designers, and other titles as well. (The old, very broad term *webmaster* is still used sometimes.)

The first priority for a visual designer is creating a look and feel to the site. To do this, the designer uses a pretty standard toolkit — either tools from the Adobe suite, including Photoshop, Illustrator, and Designer, or alternatives such as GIMP for graphics. The designer will have a good understanding of color theory and how color works across digital platforms, as well as in print and other static media.

The initial goal for getting a website design approved is that a CEO, managing director, company president, marketing director, startup founder, or other leader likes the look and feels comfortable cruising around the site. These people typically weigh in at two stages in a project — and they are part of the first reason why these jobs are so difficult.

That's because the visual designer — and, with that person, the entire web development team — are at the mercy of the gut feel of people in upper management who often aren't that knowledgeable about any aspect of the project: what its goals are, who's working on it, how much effort has already occurred, how much more work has to be done in so little time, and so on.

They often are also lacking knowledge in branding, visual design (what's possible visually on the web), technical standards (what's possible technically on the web), or the needs of the user base. Yes, it's common enough that a key decision-maker has some part of the relevant skill set and knowledge base; it's rare indeed that they have most or all of it.

Yet senior managers have to approve website designs based on scanty information. They are being asked to make an important decision, perhaps even a bet-the-company decision in some cases, on their gut. So a gut check, rather than an informed decision, is what you're likely to get.

And, you're likely to go through two approval cycles: once near the beginning of the project, when you need a signature or verbal approval to get the project going; and once near the end, when you're looking for a sign-off for launch. This can be an anxiety-producing process, with lots of tweaks, or even a significant reset in the project.

In addition to a desire to make things look good, and nerves of steel, the visual designer also needs good technical skills. That's because website publishing demands that things look good, while making it very hard to actually carry that off consistently across different devices, screen sizes, and browsers.

Every visual designer needs to understand the technical barriers well enough to optimize his or her design work for what's actually possible. The best visual designers understand the technology well enough to actually implement the design, or lead the implementation of the design, themselves.

This is the hottest ticket in web development — the single individual who has mastered visual design and enough coding skills to carry the whole project forward alone, or to lead a project as the highly skilled professional at the top of two complementary teams.

The second major bucket after artistic/graphical skills for web designers is, of course, technical skills. This is the ability to work in various kinds of coding languages to Get. Things. Done. The main languages used are HyperText Markup Language (HTML), Cascading Style Sheets (CSS), and JavaScript.

A web designer who combines visual design skills with enough technical skills to implement his own designs is currently *the* hot ticket in the whole web development area and should be for a long time to come.

A web designer who knows about graphical appearances, but knows little about the technology, is likely to have a career that's frustrating, for all concerned, and possibly quite limited.

HTML is a markup language; commands such as <b> and </b>, to indicate the beginning and end of bolding, are inserted into normal text. CSS is a standard way of describing how a web page will be laid out. A general style sheet can set out the look and feel of an entire website, whereas more specific style sheets "cascade" from the more general ones to control the specific appearance details for specific pages. JavaScript is a sort of programming language called a *scripting language* because it's easy to write and because scripts are re-interpreted each time they're used. This is a slow but flexible way to write code.

These three coding standards (they aren't quite programming languages) are the core of the ability to make websites look great and appear to a typical user as easy to use. They also help you get desired results from a web page, such as visits to a particular page, signups for an event, sales of a product, or views of a video. In addition to being the major secondary skills for most visual designers, this is also the core skill set of most web developers who are expressly technical.

Getting to Know Front-End Roles

In addition to these "front-facing" technical capabilities, which affect things that users see and click or tap, there are back-end software development jobs as well. These typically use languages such as Python and SQL to manage the interface between users visiting a website and one or more databases which are accessed for content, and updated with user-generated information as a result.

Finally, there are many additional categories, including

- **Content developers,** responsible for creating words, images, and multimedia.
- **Usability professionals,** who make sure that users are able to accomplish the things they — and you — want to accomplish.
- **Interaction designers,** who also work in usability, but have a more precise focus on how the user works with the site even than usability people.
- **Data scientists,** who manage the large databases that are often the product of web interactions.
- **Traditional software developers,** whose work is increasingly caught up in web and app development.

Each of these categories is discussed in some detail in this chapter. Study the categories carefully to see where you might best fit in.

The prevalence of Photoshop skills in web development jobs

The often-frustrating search for approvals, go-aheads, budget sign-offs, and related "green lights" regarding the look, feel, and functionality of a site is the reason Photoshop skills have such a disproportionate role in web development. With Photoshop skills, designers can not only make a prototype that looks as good as the final site is going to look; they can make a prototype that looks *better* than the final site is going to look. It's common to see shades of color, fonts, and finely tuned layouts in a prototype that will never actually appear on a real website, at least for the vast majority of users.

Not only can a Photoshop-skilled designer create these Potemkin websites, but they can make new versions of them in a hurry. (A "Potemkin website" is a reference to a "Potemkin village." When Russian empress Catherine the Great toured a Russian region by boat in the 1700s, a government minister named Potemkin had attractive false fronts placed on huts an shacks along the riverfront. The empress approved heartily of what she was seeing.) More red in the design? More white space? Bigger headers, more figures, smaller body text? No problem.

The sign-off gate is frustrating, when you can't get a needed go-ahead for your project, but just part of the way the game is played. One common result is that executive input to a prototype is often made and accepted, even though it makes no difference in the actual final website that most people see. Websites are commonly very limited in the number of fonts they can display, for instance. (In certain viewing modes on a smartphone, the number of fonts available is approximately "one.") But that doesn't stop sophisticated font combinations from getting sold to executives for approval, even if they can't be reliably implemented online. Don't laugh — you'll probably do it too someday, if you have to.

The maestro: The visual designer

The lead role in web development is the role of visual designer. A visual designer has overall responsibility for the look, feel, and functionality of the website.

The reason for this somewhat of an historical accident. An organization's website is often the most important presentation of that organization to the world, and the idea that website creation usually needs to be led by someone with a graphics and artistic background — rather than, say, a technical person, a marketing manager, a general businessperson, or even a lawyer — is controversial, with good reason.

For many organizations, the stakes are even higher because their websites generate, or support, part or all of their revenues and profits. Website storefronts are substantial cash generators for many companies, the main customer service and support location for others, and the whole ball of wax for quite a few — handling all aspects of customer interaction. In these cases, there's even more reason for having the web effort led by a general business manager of some sort. Still, the justification for having a strong design background before you take on top web development jobs is quite strong.

Visual designers almost always have some formal education in art and design, and often have broad, interesting backgrounds, including work as painters, sculptors, filmmakers, print designers, or artists who work in advertising. Web design is very friendly to people who have a strong academic background and strong real-world experience outside the web world.

Even the most artistic visual designer, though, is going to be expected to know her stuff technically — what is and isn't possible online; how different devices display page layouts, content, and multimedia; and how to work productively with people who put their technical hat before their designer hat, or who don't wear a designer hat at all.

At best, the visual designer is himself a technical person; he can mock up a great design in Photoshop, tweak it until the budget holders involved are happy, and then implement a working site in a matter of weeks or, for large sites, a few months.

Check the next job area description, front-end developer, for a list of skills that any talented visual designer would be well served to master, or at least become competent in, alongside design.

Some visual designers go the other way, though. They leave the technical implementation completely to others and take on a range of projects beyond the website. A visual designer's work can grow to include apps, print, signs, shirts, and marketing stuff. In that case, the visual designer might be referred to simply as a designer.

Art directors create beauty

Making things beautiful might seem a high bar to set for a website, which has so many technical challenges to meet before it even works well for most users. But some organizations really try to maximize the attractiveness of everything they put in front of people, and such organizations are likely to have one or more art directors as part of the web development team, and possibly in other areas as well. (Another term for art director is "design director.")

Art directors can really focus on the look of a site and the impression it leaves on people. They can help enforce visual consistency — and,

yes, beauty — across a mind-bogglingly wide variety of digital and "meat space" media. (*Meat space* is a term that's been popularized in science fiction to refer to the non-online world.)

Art directors are likely to also be responsible for a company's bank of creative assets. As a simple example, an art director will try to ensure that a company has a high-resolution, printable version of any image it uses. That way, campaigns that start online — where low-resolution, compressed images are the norm — can easily move to print, billboards, and other media, where very high-resolution images are a must.

You will know that you're a potential visual designer if you have an arts background, love making things look great, care deeply about making them work well, and have a strong technical bent.

The visual designer is not quite the same as a web designer. Web designer is a broader term that can include all the job descriptions here, and others besides. A visual designer's job description is somewhat narrower and states clearly that the title holder has strong graphic design and even artistic skills.

Front-of-house manager: The front-end developer

A front-end developer is the logical complement to a visual designer. (When people use the broader term *web designer,* they are usually looking for someone who can do most of the work in both categories.) A front-end developer can take a visual developer's Photoshop mock-up of a web page and make it appear onscreen as part of a website.

There are three terms that you need to know really well for any kind of web development work, plus one that is nearly as vital in many organizations, which will be part of the meat and potatoes of your daily work if you become a front-end developer:

  ✔ **HTML:** HyperText Markup Language (HTML) is a strange coding standard that adds descriptive information about how to display things right into a stream of text. The invention and refinement of HTML, beginning in 1989 with the description of the coding standard by Tim Berners-Lee, were the basis for the launch and rapid growth of the web. (Clickable hyperlinks and the capability to easily put images onto the same page with text were key reasons for the insanely fast growth of the web.)

✔ **CSS:** Cascading Style Sheets (CSS) are an even stranger coding standard that manage the look and, to some extent, the interaction — the feel — of a website. A general, high-level style sheet might apply to an entire website, whereas a lower-level one adds to and overrides the general style sheet for specific web pages and groups of web pages. (That's where "cascading" comes from.) The ten or so years when CSS was being developed and implemented, unevenly, across web browsers, beginning in the late 1990s, were probably the most painful years to be a web designer, but also pretty lucrative ones as well. Many web designers swear by CSS, whereas others — including everyone who has to learn CSS for the first time — swear at it.

✔ **JavaScript:** JavaScript is a scripting language – that is, a programmer's tool that is only interpreted into the computer's language when the JavaScript code is executed. Its informality, lack of structure, and ease of use — including the ease of making mistakes — differentiate JavaScript from a "real" programming language. JavaScript is used to do things like create a pull-down menu, and it can also do a lot of the things CSS is used for. JavaScript was inconsistent during roughly the same decade that CSS was, but it too has settled down, and now occupies a proud place in most web developers' toolkits.

✔ **Python:** Python is another interpreted language, like JavaScript, but Python's greater structure and formality mean that it's considered a "real" programming language. Python is good for many things, but especially for writing code to interface to databases on the fly. Because most professionally developed sites today are database-driven, Python is often just as important as JavaScript in a web developer's toolkit.

Web designers used to be able to make a very good living indeed by being expert in the various versions of HTML, CSS, JavaScript, and mainstream Windows and Macintosh web browsers as standards grew steadily more capable and complex and as browsers grew ever more capable — and, for a while, inconsistent. Browsers are much more standardized today; now the challenge of making websites work across personal computer browsers is less, but the rise of smartphones and tablets, which mostly have smaller screens than personal computers, has replaced the old standards challenge with new challenges driven by the proliferation of different devices.

If you specialize in front-end development, you might come to be referred to as a front-end engineer. You could also become a JavaScript developer or JavaScript engineer. You could become known for your expertise in creating and managing libraries of CSS style sheets as well. The room for growth and development is endless.

What distinguishes front-end developers from traditional software developers can include an interest in working with people and not just computers; fascination with the web and its possibilities; and really, really, really liking rapid change — change in the technologies in use, change in projects, change in employers, and often all three at once.

Front-end developers usually study software development in school, but they can also be musicians, artists, writers, scientists, or come from almost any background. Demand for these skills is so high that those who have the right mindset and are willing to apply themselves can quickly find themselves working right alongside people with CS (computer science) degrees from prestigious universities.

Making things feel right: Usability professionals

Usability people make sure that websites work to specification, and then they try to improve the design to make it easy, obvious — almost inescapable — to go deeper and deeper into a website, until you buy something, download a white paper, watch a cat video, or whatever the site's developers want you to do. They tend to work using web design tools such as the Dreamweaver suite, although they will often know a smattering or more of the technologies described previously.

Usability people come from a wide variety of backgrounds. We've known teachers, writers, and actors who have moved into usability work successfully. Many usability people work as consultants because their skills are most needed at certain key points in a project.

The importance (and pitfalls) of user testing

The results of watching someone try to buy something, for instance, on an early version of a site can be hilarious if painful for the developers. It can be more painful than hilarious, though, in the non-digital world.

A large computer company once called in users to try upgrading the memory inside a personal computer. One test subject opened the computer case, reached into the innards, and cut her hand on a piece of sharp metal. The minor cut made her hand bleed all over the motherboard. The developers watched in horror as the woman, crying, started to apologize for ruining the computer, while she continued to try to add memory onto the motherboard. They stopped the test immediately, and then redesigned the computer's innards to prevent injury to users.

Usability-related titles include

- **User interface designer (UI designer):** This role is often similar to the role of the visual designer, although with less need for a design or artistic background. UI designers will go through a site with a fine-tooth comb, finding and fixing problems, and then have naïve users come in and try the site to unearth more problems yet.

- **User experience designer (UX designer):** A user experience designer focuses on what it's like for the users as they work their way around a site, trying to get tasks accomplished. UX designers are somewhat like psychologists, asking users, "How do you feel about this?" A UX designer is a very valuable role to have on a web development team, even if she's only brought in as a consultant at key points in a project.

- **Interaction designer:** An interaction designer focuses very specifically on what users read and where they click as they try to accomplish specific tasks. An interaction designer will help you place the Buy button on your selling page so it will get more clicks, and help you get the size, shape, color, and font on the button right as well.

Bringing in inexperienced users to try your site is called *user testing*.

Making things work right: The web developer

The term web developer can mean two things: any professional on a web development team, including the graphics-oriented and usability people; or only the more technically based people. In this section, we use the more technically oriented definition.

A web developer is a full-time software developer who usually works in web-friendly programming languages such as Python, Ruby, PHP, and so on. A web developer will usually be good with JavaScript, good at database work, and be able to get tasks done in HTML and CSS.

The web developer doesn't need to have any artistic or design background, although of course every web professional will do well to understand the outlines of, and have respect for, every role in the overall effort.

Many web development roles are extremely demanding. On a big web development project, all the pieces are moving at once, and a web developer has to do useful work that can adapt to changes in the front end, the back end, the project goals, and anything else you can imagine. This extends to the sudden cancellation of website features or entire projects — and just as suddenly reviving them months or years later.

The web developer title is a big umbrella that can include front-end developers and back-end developers. Used properly, it really refers to the middle and toward the back end of a project. Web developers definitely need to know what's going on within the user-facing website project, but their role is to work with the front-end developers to receive and send information from databases and other organizational resources. They aren't likely to directly concern themselves with the user interface, for instance.

Web developers who aren't front-end specialists tend to be a bit less concerned with the user's experience and more concerned with traditional CS concerns like security and structure. A good web developer will make the lives of back-end developers pretty easy.

We are not treating back-end developers as "web developers" for the purpose of this book. Back-end developers spend their time in traditional programming languages like C or C++ and doing database programming in languages like SQL. These developers often work on web-related projects, but their work is informed by, rather than determined by, the needs of any one web development project.

Contributors beyond the Front End

Front-end roles are focused on the look and feel that the user encounters. There are additional roles that are not back-end jobs (the site's underpinnings and technical interaction with websites), but that are somewhat separate from the front end's focus on what exactly a user sees and interacts with.

Prepping each piece: Content professionals

Given that one of us (Bud Smith) is a professional web content developer, let us say right here and now that this is one of the most underrated and misunderstood roles in web development or, really, any sphere of human endeavor, ever. Content professionals provide the words, images, and multimedia assets that people visit a website to experience in the first place.

Writing for the web is different than any other kind of writing. People who are reading online — which is "like staring into a light bulb," as some have described it — get tired more easily and are able to give less attention to detail than traditional print readers.

So fewer, more powerful, more action-oriented words are needed to get the point across quickly and move on. Bulleted lists and lots of headers give variety to the flow of text and help the reader find key facts and key points.

Images and multimedia for online are specialty areas as well. (Or, perhaps, they should be, as a lot of not-very-suitable stuff gets put up online.) Web video is, in its own right, a whole new area of human endeavor, and one that's attracting a lot of talent — including Hollywood writers, producers, and stars — to try their hand in a new medium.

Most web content professionals have backgrounds in a given area before the web. Web writers are well-suited to this work if their previous background includes advertising or marketing writing and a strong technical grounding, which is a rare combination indeed. Writers tend to have some formal education in writing, either as the focus of their bachelor's degree, or from a related area such as history.

Content written for the web usually goes into a content management system (CMS), where it can be edited, moved around, displayed, tallied, reused, and ultimately disposed of. There are several major CMSs, such as Drupal, Joomla!, and CushyCMS (we aren't kidding). Each has its own advocates and fans. Writers sometimes move into more or less technical roles as CMS experts.

WordPress is a quick and easy to use website development tool with a built-in CMS. You can't use WordPress strictly as a CMS — it controls the look and feel as well — but it has more users than any other CMS.

As with artistic assets, writing assets need managing. There is a whole industry around writing small chunks of easy-to-translate, easy-to-reuse content, and then combining the chunks for different purposes. The chunks are also easier to translate and reuse than long blocks of text. There's specialist work here for writers, content management professionals, translators, and others.

The marketing maven: Product manager

A *product manager,* like a writer, is an unusual beast. Product managers are marketing managers who are responsible for getting a product — in this case, a website — to market. Like writers, many product managers are former technical professionals who prefer to work in areas where they have, to a certain extent, an outsider's view of the project.

Product managers can be very strong — mini-CEOs, with budget responsibility and hiring and firing power or influence — or more like internal consultants who suggest, but can't require, user-friendly and sales-friendly ways of doing things. The skilled product manager can thrive across a wide range of job attributes as well as a wide range of technical challenges.

Although the roles are often confused, a *project manager* is different than a product manager. Project managers make the trains run on time. They help set the schedule, secure resources, and ensure that milestones are met. Project managers are sometimes also the boss of a project, but they are more often working at the middle level.

An *evangelist* is a specialized role which includes part of a product manager's job. An evangelist talks to people outside the project, selling the vision for the site to get people ready for it, and gathering information to help the project team meet customers' needs better. (Unlike in usability, money talks when an evangelist determines where to spend her time.)

Look for a product manager role if you have a chance to get a strong degree in business or marketing, or if you work in almost any other web development role and have strong business or people skills. If you have that same background, but are more detail-oriented than people-oriented, consider project management. And if you have great people skills, but don't yet have the business background for product management, try evangelism, brothers and sisters.

The SEO specialist

Some of us have a weak spot for search engine optimization (SEO) specialists. This is one of the most in-demand roles in the web development universe, and rightly so. It's a tremendously important role, and the people who fulfill it well have special skills indeed.

For most web development professionals, it's difficult to remember a time before Google, but Google changed the online world at a critical time. Before Google, the best way to find the content you needed was to work toward it through Yahoo!'s carefully curated lists of relevant sites. After Yahoo!, in the Google era, you just type in a couple of keywords off the top of your head, and bam! Usually, there's the content you need, or close enough to it so as to not make a difference, at the top of Google's list of search results.

But you want your website to appear at the top of relevant search results lists, and this is where the SEO specialist comes in. The first job of an SEO specialist is, oddly, to make sure your web page shows up exactly where it should. When a user types in your company or organization name,

the name of a recent blog post, or the name of an event your company has participated in, you will of course want your organization's name to appear near the top of search results.

This is part of an SEO specialist's job, but not the part that gets the most attention. The part that gets the most attention is the job of getting your organization's website at the top of competitive search engine results for widely used terms like *flowers*, *pizza*, and *fun*.

You will, of course, get huge kudos if your website appears at the top of the list for a generic search for *fun*, however briefly. But this is of limited value. If you sell Pez candy dispensers, and you appear at the top of a list of search results for *fun*, how many more Pez candy dispensers will you sell as a result? Whereas appearing at the top of a list for *Pez* or even *Pez San Francisco* may well result in big sales increases.

So look for an SEO specialist with business savvy as well as technical skills and, if she does the job well, be ready to replace her when another company hires her away.

Chapter 3

Understanding Where Web Designers Work

In This Chapter

▶ Discovering what it's like to work at a web development company

▶ Understanding how other organizations use web developers

▶ Knowing what to look out for when working for a company

*W*eb designers are everywhere. Every organization has a website — and there are many professional-looking websites that don't really have much of an organization behind them. So web work is ubiquitous; every organization has web developers working for it at least part of the time, whether they're full-time employees, contractors, or employees of a web services firm.

Most web designers take somewhat of a random walk into and through their careers. They get an initial job in web development, or they start doing web development work when they have an entirely different title and set of responsibilities. Then the technologies they use, the areas of expertise which they develop, and the people they get to know determine the next step in their career, and so on, perhaps for decades.

In this chapter, we provide you key information you need to use in deciding how to start your career — or how to continue it in a more interesting and rewarding direction. We describe the different types of organizations that web developers work in and how being employed by different types of organizations affects the way you work.

Finding Out about Work at a Web Development Company

One of the very best ways to kick-start your career in web development, or to energize a career that's started to run out of steam, is to find work with a web development company.

Web development companies are focused on web development as their only job. This has all sorts of implications, mostly good, for the job you'll be doing and for your career going forward.

In a web development company, you probably won't do much but web work, and you'll do a lot of it in a short period of time, hopefully to a high level of expertise — supported by other awesome professionals like yourself.

Oddly, web development work often doesn't pay all that well. In a web development company, you might experience the joy of being billed out to a client for a princely (or princessly) sum such as $1,000 a day, and seeing about 20 percent of that amount in your paycheck after deductions.

Also, the client rules the roost. Web services companies live and die on their clients' happiness, so, at the end of the day, the customer is always right. The good web service companies have rules, procedures, and structure that keep the client at least somewhat in line, or get a lot more money from them if they keep moving the goalposts during a project. A bad web services company tries to make up for its own missed deadlines and its clients' flightiness by sweating its assets — which means trying to get more work out of you without paying you any more money.

In a web services company, you'll work very hard, for relatively little money, but with brilliant people. You'll use the latest technology and be paid to live on the cutting edge. Your later career will benefit many times over from even a few years spent at a web services company.

The table below sums up the pros and cons of working for a web services company. Read and enjoy:

- **Pros:** Varied and interesting work. Latest technologies. Lots of travel. Bright, hardworking people. Respect from (the better) clients and peers in web development jobs.
- **Cons:** Long hours. Pay on the low side, demands on the high side. Lots of travel. The client is king.
- **Salary:** Often low for the role and responsibilities, and bordering on a minimum wage violation when you consider the number of hours you're likely to work.
- **Benefits:** Often solid, if the company is well-established.
- **Career path:** Get underpaid working for a web services company for a few years, then get overpaid to work half as hard, for twice the money, from a non-web services company that will be dead impressed by your background.

Web services companies are often pressure cookers. They're great places to have worked for, and difficult places to actually work.

Figure 3-1 shows a promotional blurb put on the Small Business Administration (SBA) site for a web services company (`www.sba.gov/community/discussion-boards/web-design-web-development-and-seo-small-businesses`). You can see that this company is a generalist firm without any one strong technological edge; the focus is helping small businesses. Other web development companies have any number of specialties.

Figure 3-1:
The SBA hosts a promotional paragraph for a web development company.

Finding Out How Companies Use Web Developers

Web development jobs at companies that do something besides web development as their main work — which means, most web development jobs — are pretty hit or miss.

First, the bad news. Web development work is inherently uneven in nature. When someone needs to do something new, whether a new site or a new approach to an existing one, there's a lot to do, and it's often creative and satisfying work — adding new capabilities, using new technologies, engaging with new customers.

Getting the clients to make up their minds

The most frustrating single thing in web development, as in many other creative endeavors that people do for money, has nothing to do with the actual work. It's getting the thrice-darned client to make up his mind.

Web work is protean — in both senses of the term. It changes frequently and easily, and, the results of the work are versatile, able to do many things. It is at least theoretically possible to build an entire website with one talented developer — and for that website to be more capable, more functional, and more attractive than a website that's had a team working on it for a long time. Of course, this kind of outcome is unlikely, but it is possible.

So web developers often spend most of their time trying to figure out the specification, finding out that there's no way the specification can work, dealing with changes in the specification, and so on. What's really happening is that the client is wanting to be wowed, to see amazing work done for very little money — so he keeps pushing the developers to do miracles as the deadline looms and the requirements list gets longer.

There is often no extra pay for the rework relating to this process, and the final deadline drives the project — everything will get done in a rush at the end, perhaps poorly, because that's what it takes for people to stop arguing and start supporting the completion of actual work. Working in a web services company is often valuable largely because successful web services companies have put a structure around this process; they insist on client commitment strong enough to ensure forward motion. If they're not getting it, overage fees start piling up, which is usually enough to force a quick decision in one direction or another.

The trouble is, most companies don't have enough personnel to do big projects well. So they overcommit their internal resources or hire in external specialists, who at best teach the internal folks new skills. At worst, the external company does the best bits, and leaves the meat-and-potatoes work to the internal people.

Worse, when an internal team is between big projects, its people can become layoff bait — people who are easy to let go when budgetary pressures hit. Then, when a bigger staff is needed for the next big project, there aren't enough internal people around to handle it, and the depressed and demoralized remaining staff may not feel super-energized to step up to the plate either.

Now, though, for the good news. Companies are in business to make money, so they need to "keep up with the Joneses" — or stay ahead of them. This competitive pressure can push the company to do some pretty interesting things online. A sophisticated company will manage its web development people well, getting them educated and letting them experiment during slow periods, so they're fully ready to go when the stuff hits the fan.

The difference between contractors and consultants

One of the most abused pairs of related terms in the English language is *contractor/consultant*. Here we attempt to bring clarity to these oft-confused words.

A *consultant* was originally a term used in England for a consulting physician: a doctor so eminent that he (it was always "he" at the time) was called in to consult on other doctors' tough cases. Today, the mainstream meaning of consultant is similar — a somewhat eminent man or woman who is called in to advise other, perhaps less experienced, practitioners on what to do next. Consultants may also pick up a scalpel and join in the actual work at hand, but they're being paid for their strategic insight and next-level expertise more than for any actual work they turn out.

A *contractor* is simply an individual contributor (usually) working under contract instead of as an employee. It actually sounds, and often is, somewhat less prestigious than being a full-time employee, with benefits and the assumption of some kind of job security. Contractors usually get paid more per hour than other workers, but the distance between a contractor and being back out on the street is not very far at all.

Both consulting and contracting are very common in web design work. Projects often need the strategic vision and high level of expertise generally associated with consultants. And projects often need the short-term boost of throwing in bodies and minds who are competent and easy to move in and out of a project, even if the hourly rate required seems quite high.

Now the terms are often used interchangeably, especially by contractors who call themselves by the more prestigious-sounding term consultant. But, as you enter into or continue your career in web development, keep in mind what the terms really mean, as explained here, and how you yourself prefer to work.

Keeping even with, or ahead of, the Joneses also means using the latest technology. If you work for a company, and keep your sword sharp by experimenting with the latest technology, you may well get the opportunity to do some pretty interesting stuff.

Remember that recruiters and hiring managers for future jobs will read your resume the same way as a Google search engine, looking for how many years of experience you have with whatever hot technology they think will solve their problems — or help their department survive the ax when budget-cutters come along.

This list captures some of the good and bad aspects that are likely to come up when working for a company that's in some business other than web services. Check any specific opportunity you get against this list of potential plusses and minuses.

✔ **Pros:** Stable work, or, at least, stable pay even if work is lacking for a while. Serious responsibility creating and maintaining the web presence for companies with real problems to solve. The opportunity to plan and to integrate your work with serious corporate strategies.

- ✔ **Cons:** Potential for boredom, or manic/depressive work schedules — months of little work followed by weeks of panic as a deadline looms. The most interesting work may go to hired guns from outside, who come and go. Everyone with a "C" at the start of his or her title — CEO (Chief Executive Officer), CFO (Chief Financial Officer), CTO (Chief Technical Officer) — is king.

- ✔ **Salary:** Get your money up front, and a bonus, if you can. Established companies will often pay very well up front for expertise in "name" technologies, but raises will stop as soon as the bloom goes off that particular rose.

- ✔ **Benefits:** Often solid, sometimes amounting to the kind of "golden handcuffs" that make it hard to leave for new opportunities.

- ✔ **Career path:** Cash in on good opportunities with an established company, but only stay as long as the work is interesting, and keeps adding "name" technologies and impressive projects to your resume. Answer those recruiter calls — or make calls of your own to recruiters — when the sun is shining.

Doing web development work for non-web service companies is a mixed bag. It can be great, awful, and everything in between. Manage your career carefully when working for a company, and don't be afraid to leave.

One-man bands

Sometimes you'll get hired to do web development work for a company that isn't a company yet, more a gleam in the eye of one person, or a couple of people. They may have quit their day jobs, or they may still be in them. And they may have a lot of money, or very little.

This kind of work is likely to be performed as a consultant (you bring strategic insight and rare expertise) or a contractor (you're as skilled as a good employee, and willing to work on an hourly basis). It's tough, because one-man bands — really meaning very small, poorly funded efforts — generally want a lot, and can only pay a little.

As in so much else about web work, the trick here is to get a clean, solid definition of the job, and then stick to it as much as possible. (Employers tend to remember that the work wasn't done on time, not that the requirements changed half a dozen times from the start of the project to the end.) Make sure you get paid a chunk up front, and then steadily as you go along, because the strategy, and your assignment, could end at any minute. Find out how much money there is, and make sure to deliver something usable before the money runs out, even if you have to say no to the client on some of his requests.

Surfing the Sullivan curve

Kevin Sullivan was the Human Resources chief for Apple in the years between the first and second Steve Jobs eras — that is, during the early and mid-1990s. He became somewhat famous for a rather cutting analysis of the value of tech workers over time.

Sullivan posited that the hottest employees were those who had several years of experience with the latest and greatest technologies. This meant three or four years, not ten or twenty; hot technologies, by definition, are only hot for a few years.

Sullivan also noted that an employee's salary tends to rise over time, whether she was getting more productive or not.

The Sullivan curve mapped the value of a new college graduate tech employee after she joined Apple. During her first few years out of college, the employee had a lot of new knowledge, but not enough experience to apply it well. However, she was inexpensive to employ.

Then came the golden age — employees who were a few years out of college, with knowledge that was still fresh, and valuable experience. Pay, however, was rising. The job of a tech company was to get the most out of these knowledgeable, experienced employees before the third stage kicked in.

In the third stage, knowledge gets stale, and pay goes up along with years of experience. The benefit of experience doesn't offset the employee's aging knowledge base and increasing pay. Time, Sullivan strongly implied, to get rid of that employee and hire someone fresh out of school.

For you, the trick to beating the Sullivan curve is to keep updating your resume with new and hot technologies — and, sadly, not to let your salary or hourly rate get out in front of your likely value to a company. Think of your salary as a multiple of what your company would pay an entry-level employee straight out of school, and be ready to show how your extra productivity more than offsets the pay disparity.

Working for one-man bands can be very rewarding and a real career-builder and resume-builder too. It produces great networking opportunities as you reach out to people for help, advice, and small contributions of work. (Those opportunities are often paid for by a nice lunch or a drink after work, rather than an actual payment of money.)

Managing the clients' budgets for them is one of the key skills of working for very small companies as clients.

There's a lot to think about when you consider working as an independent contractor — including how things look from the client's point of view. Figure 3-2 shows a web page (`www.sba.gov/blogs/5-things-know-about-hiring-independent-contractors`) with advice from the Small Business Administration about how employers think through the decision as to whether to hire an independent contractor.

Figure 3-2:
The SBA
also tells
companies
what to look
for in hiring
independent
contractors.

Startups

The term *startup* gets used quite broadly because it sounds so cool — and because every project starts up at some point. Here we're referring to a classic, Silicon Valley-type startup.

So that begs the question, what is a Silicon Valley-type startup? Here are a few indicative — not determinative — characteristics:

✔ Founded with a clear idea of the initial product offering; the initial team's job is to get that product to market, even if they have to hire a few hundred people to do it.

✔ Externally financed, or financed by founders who've made money from previous startups, and basically invest in themselves. High-tech company incubators; angels — venture capitalists and other well-off people spending their own money — and venture capitalists spending investor money are the other funding sources.

✔ Founded by a small team that's ready to take on the world, and then beefed up with people (mostly engineers) who get chunks of stock in the company. (One or two founders might have a quarter of the company each; the initial chief marketing officer might get one percent of the stock.)

✔ Run on a tight time schedule to get a product to market and either get-ting bought out (in which case, profits may never appear) or going public (in which case, profits better happen and increase quickly).

✔ Run on a tight value schedule. Investors want to see a ten times or more return on their money in just a few years. You have to contribute strongly to this kind of value increase, or you're just in the way.

There are more ways to describe a classic, Silicon Valley-type startup, but these are enough to give you a feel. So, what does this mean if you're a web developer for a startup company?

First, your resume could end up looking great. Some of the most exciting web development work is associated with startups, even if the company isn't very successful. You should get to work with name technologies and not have to spend a lot of time sitting around waiting for decisions to be remade. In most cases, you won't even have to redo the site — you might think you need to, but no one will have the time or the money.

Second, you could do even better than that. You should get a chunk of stock, and that might well turn out to be worth something. You probably won't get a high salary, though; the stock options and the experience are supposed to make up for that.

Third, there is no better relationship-building opportunity than a startup. The bonds formed in the trenches of a startup — including unsuccessful ones, but more so for the winners — will be a resource for you for your whole career.

Try to serve time in a startup or two early in your career. The experience will be a gift that keeps on giving.

If you decide to create a startup of your own, you'll need lots of advice. The SBA has lots of advice for you, under the category Startup and High Growth Businesses, as shown in Figure 3-3. Check it out at `www.sba.gov/content/startups-high-growth-businesses`.

Small and large companies

"Small" companies can be quite large; there are directories where companies with hundreds of companies can be considered "small." Conversely, "large" companies can act like collections of smaller ones, an amalgamation of regions, language groups, product groups, and lines of business.

On the other hand, you can work at the core of a big enterprise. There is so much money and so much company history in some of these places that you enter a kind of Twilight Zone — "No escape, no place to hide. Here where time and space collide. You have entered the Twilight Zone."

Figure 3-3:
The SBA
will give
you startup
advice
aplenty.

Working in small and large companies is similar in principle. The web development group is a service group. In an established company, there are considered to be three basic types of functions:

- ✔ **Product/services.** You make what the company sells. Whether it's Oreo cookies or high-end consulting services, you are a producer, creating the very thing the company sells.

- ✔ **Sales.** These people close the deal made possible by the producers. They are the miners who bring home the bacon, to mix metaphors.

- ✔ **Everyone else.** You can be director of regulatory compliance, head of technical support, VP of whatever — or head of the web development team. The accountants have one name for you: overhead. In fact, the accountants are overhead too. In a well-run company, there will be people scheming to get rid of you, and replace you with someone cheaper, or outsource your function, or just stop doing it. You are potential roadkill on the corporate superhighway.

No matter what you do in a company, someone will be looking to get rid of you when things are slow, and then hire in specialists when business picks up. Do your best work, but keep your eyes open.

Cultivating corporate culture

The idea of a corporate culture is a beautiful thing. It's just lovely to imagine that the story of a company's founding, the needs of its early customers, the contributions of countless employees, combine to make a whole that is greater than the sum of its parts.

Unfortunately, it's a cold, hard world out there; corporate culture usually doesn't count for that much over time. And, it's a cold, hard world for most web developers too. The work can be fun, but there are few web developers who are corporate lifers. Confronted with a typical corporate situation, your job is to get in, do some interesting and valuable work with cutting-edge tools and technologies, make some money, and get out into a more interesting position. Your job is not to cultivate the corporate culture, or be cultivated as part of it.

So, it's good to understand corporate culture, so you can work productively with others, and better predict the actions and concerns of the people you work with. You might also be called on to reflect the corporate culture in a web property. But don't immerse yourself in it. If you're planning to move on in any event, it's all too easy to waste a lot of time and energy on concerns that will be in your rear-view mirror soon enough.

It is indeed possible to have a long and happy career in a company setting, but if you keep a startup or consultant's attitude, you're actually more likely to last a while than someone who settles too comfortably into corporate life.

As you settle into a company, you spend more and more time learning things that are only useful within the confines of that specific company, and less and less learning new web technologies that will help you be more productive or get your next job. Be very careful about being a "good" corporate employee.

A clock starts ticking the day you go to work for a typical company, steadily depleting your tolerance for corporate procedures and your familiarity with new technologies, interesting people, and the harsh business and technical challenges found in startups and web services companies. Take a little while to get comfortable in a typical corporate job, and then start scheming to make your job more interesting and fun, get a better job within the company, or get out.

Discovering How Not-for-Profits Use Web Developers

Let us start by pointing out that we're making a subtle distinction here. A not-for-profit is any organization that isn't operated like a company for the financial benefit of its shareholders and investors. This includes colleges and universities and government agencies. It also includes the similarly named, but more narrowly defined, nonprofits. A nonprofit has a specific organizational structure that resembles a company, but that is not allowed to make a profit from its activities.

What we want to capture here is the difference between working as a web developer for a for-profit company (whether a web services company, or another type of company) and a not-for-profit. Many not-for-profits have organizational structures very much like companies, and use web developers in the same way.

However, to generalize, a not-for-profit lacks a certain focus and discipline that the need to make a profit imposes on companies of all types. It's a prejudice, but a prejudice with truth in it, that everything moves more slowly in the not-for-profit world. There simply isn't the same fear of quickly losing market share, with the possibility of going out of business, that drives for-profit companies.

What does this mean for web developers planning their careers? Not much that's good. A slow pace, a lack of focus, or a lack of discipline, is slow poison to a web developer of any kind.

There are not-for-profits that work with the latest technologies. In a college or university environment, you might be an early recipient of a new technological breakthrough in some critical web technology. But these situations are the exception rather than the rule.

And there are not-for-profits where you can do good or interesting work. What you want to avoid is getting captured by the gravity of the not-for-profit world. If you're not careful, you can easily end up with skills, knowledge, experience, and connections that will suit you well for moving between one not-for-profit and another, but that don't allow you to move back into the larger, more lucrative, and more exciting for-profit world when you're ready to do that.

Following is a brief summary of the pros and cons of working for a not-for-profit organization. Use it to help chart your course.

- ✔ **Pros:** It feels great to do work you believe in with people who are not always chasing the almighty dollar (or British pounds, or euros, or remnibi). The good feeling of working in organizations with strongly positive purposes may outweigh any negatives that many not-for-profits carry with them.

- ✔ **Cons:** Pay on the low side, demands on the high side. Less awareness of, and less willingness to use, complex technologies. Progress in the use of new technologies can move very slowly, and then just completely stop.

- ✔ **Salary:** Usually low to medium. Not a lot of travel or perks.

🖛 **Benefits:** If you stay for a long time, there may be retirement and other benefits that make this a worthwhile path to consider for your overall lifestyle.

🖛 **Career path:** You can build a worthwhile career in not-for-profits, but consider working out of a web services company, or moving back and forth to the business world, to avoid becoming stuck in not-for-profit world.

Figure 3-4 shows a NASA page promoting the National Grid Computing Forum, one of the cutting-edge technology projects you can find in not-for-profit organizations: www.nasa.gov/centers/ames/news/releases/2001/01_92AR.html.

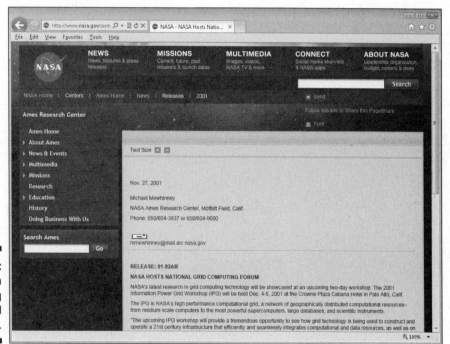

Figure 3-4:
NASA is on the cutting edge of grid computing.

Chapter 4

Seeing Yourself in a Web Development Job

In This Chapter

▶ Understanding why web development matters

▶ Seeing yourself in different kinds of web development jobs

▶ Looking at official statistics and web development job growth

*W*eb development work is one of the fastest-growing and most exciting job categories out there. If you're not in the field, it's a good thing to get into — but not necessarily easy. If you already are in the field, it can be a bit tricky to stay in.

Web development is somewhat amorphous — there are lots of different jobs that qualify, and also lots of jobs with some "web" in them, but that don't really qualify as web development. Why bother to stay in this somewhat messy category? Why not just take interesting jobs as they come up?

The reason is that web development is where the growth is, and where it's going to be for a long time to come. The overall trend of different kinds of human activity moving to the online world is only going to grow, and grow, and grow. That's because the Internet is a flexible, powerful invention, much like the printing press — perhaps more so. See the sidebar, "The history of print," for details.

Understanding How the Web Has Changed the World

With desktop publishing, the power of computers helped drive a new proliferation of form factors and new content in print. But now computers of different kinds are a complete platform of their own, for education, entertainment, shopping, and much more. Increasingly, products of all kinds are created, sold, transmitted, and used mostly or entirely online. Think of songs, movies, books — and, yes, magazines, as well as new forms like blogs. All these media are often mostly or completely digital, from creation through sale to consumption.

The first blogs appeared in the 1990s, along with Napster, the song sharing service — or song stealing service, as some would have it. E-commerce got going in the 1990s too, with Amazon.

Today, screen time competes with — or happens alongside — TV time and radio time. More and more U.S. households, for instance, are "cutting the cord" for cable television, getting all their video via the Internet, with an occasional old DVD thrown in the mix for old times' sake.

E-commerce is on the rise too. In some categories, led by books, about 10 percent of all sales are online, and still growing steadily. No one knows what the eventual, stable share of e-commerce will be versus traditional commerce in different categories. Book sales could go almost entirely online; clothing sales will probably always have a "live" and in-person component.

But that's the point of this little potted history: The changes brought by the online world are just beginning. The web is only roughly 20 years old. It took more than 500 years for the printing revolution to largely run its course.

We can also argue that the Internet will cause bigger changes. That's because it includes not only traditional print products, like e-books, online newspapers, online magazines, and online catalogs, but new capabilities — multimedia and immediate interpersonal interactivity, gaming, and more.

So these bigger changes could, in theory, take more than 500 years to work out. On the other hand, it's said that Internet years are like dog years — that one year on the Internet equals seven in the real world.

Even if that extremely rapid rate of change is fully true, though, that still means it will take 70 years for the full potential of the Internet to be realized. The digital world may also gain additional capabilities during that time, like self-driving cars — giving people more online time — and direct-to-brain interfaces. Those changes will take additional decades to work through.

There's also a great deal of room for expansion in the number of web users. Currently, only about 40 percent of the world's population has Internet access, according to Internet Live Stats. (Visit www.internetlivestats.com/internet-users/ for up-to-date information.)

The *CIA World Factbook* has a comparison of Internet users per country. To access it, visit www.cia.gov/library/publications/the-world-factbook/rankorder/2153rank.html.

The table is shown in Figure 4-1.

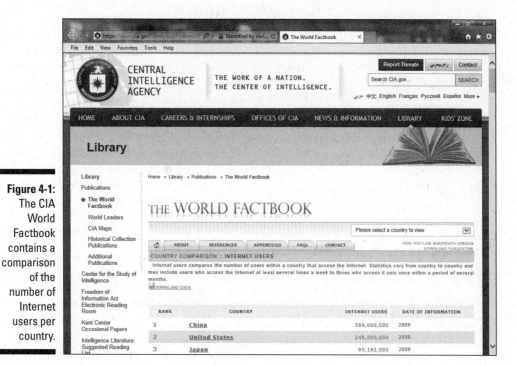

Figure 4-1:
The CIA
World
Factbook
contains a
comparison
of the
number of
Internet
users per
country.

As the number of people with access to the Internet increases, new users will drive demand for new, and different types, of websites.

Much of the growth in Internet use is from people accessing the Internet through smartphones, and there are now more smartphones in use than PCs. That means more and more users will not just use smartphones for some of their Internet use, but for all of it. They will also want information relevant to the places they live, their work, and home lives.

So moving into web development now means more than a lifetime of work, change, and growth. Also, many of the jobs that are added in the web development world will be replacing jobs that will be lost in other areas, such as retailing or print publishing. It's much safer, as well as much more interesting and exciting, to be in the new world instead of the old one.

There isn't anything else out there that has the same long-term potential for growth, change, and interest as web development. This chapter tells you how to get in — and how to stay in, if you're already there, or after you get yourself established through your first web development job or two.

The history of print

It took more than 500 years for the printing press to make most of the changes it was going to make. The first mass-printed book, the Gutenberg Bible, was first made available in 1455. Until then, Bibles were rare, expensive, and very often in Latin. Printing changed this, although not in a totally unlimited way. You may remember the old saying — now out of date — "freedom of the press is guaranteed only to those who own one."

The availability of the Bible to ordinary people made literacy important and led to the rise of Protestantism, religious wars, and much else. Printing was important in the ferment of ideas that led to the American Revolution, both for books and newspapers. And the arrival of cheaper color printing led to the rise of popular magazines in the 19th and 20th centuries — from *Harper's Weekly* and the *Atlantic* to *Time* and *Life* and *Newsweek*.

Catalog shopping, made famous by the Sears, Roebuck catalog in the years around 1900, was the e-commerce of its day, undercutting local merchants in scores of categories.

Finally, computers made a somewhat indirect impact on publishing, with the rise of affordable laser printers and page layout software making desktop publishing a phenomenon in the 1990s. Suddenly, everyone could own his or her own printing press. "Freedom of the press is guaranteed only to those who own one," still, but the capability to own one is nearly universal — just as a new platform is on the rise.

This chapter tells you how to join the rodeo circuit — that is, how to position yourself for an early job in web development. And it tells you how to stay on the rodeo circuit after you've ridden a bucking bronco or two.

Your Journey into a New Frontier

Starting out in web development can mean a huge number of different things. The key is developing content that is primarily delivered online, or working on the technology that delivers content developed by others.

There are three main tracks you can get on to become a web developer. The strongest web development careers, and the greatest success, are most likely to come to those who combine the first two.

Getting into graphic design

Graphic design is simply making web pages look good in a way that also supports them working well for their intended users. Today, people who do strictly defined graphic design work are usually called visual designers, but the overall field they work in is still usually called *graphic design*.

Graphic design combines art, interface design, and interaction design.

Designers mostly create layouts rather than specific, attractive-looking graphics. That's the difference between a designer and an artist.

Also, designers create pages that support user interaction well, but they don't worry too much about optimizing exactly where users click or how they work their way through a multi-step process, like buying a cardigan online. Those roles are the job of the interface designer or the interaction designer.

To get into graphic design, take classes or look for professional opportunities where you create designs using Photoshop. Use these opportunities to start building up your portfolio, as described later in this chapter.

To stay in graphic design and build your career, you need to keep improving your portfolio — both the actual body of work you've done, and its online representation in your personal portfolio (see the section later in this chapter).

Do you have a technical mindset?

There's a simplistic way of thinking about anyone's interaction with technology in a wide range of jobs: there are people who code, and people who don't. But the world of technology is really more complicated than that, and you can use that fact to your advantage.

If you are primarily a designer, it's not hard to learn HTML. It's a very simple code — not really a programming language, in the usual sense. (Programming languages can use logical constructs like if-then-else, or looping through a process several times.)

Learning CSS is not that hard, either. Style sheets are complicated, but they're complicated for everyone. The basic commands are simple, if nerdy, and you can certainly learn to modify existing style sheets to get the job done.

The acid test for most designers is JavaScript. JavaScript actually makes things happen. Many designers have a mental block about using code to accomplish tasks.

Again, borrowing — or *bricolage,* as it's known — is key. Learn to modify existing JavaScripts to get things done.

Also consider that technical help is widely available today. You can create enough HTML, CSS, and even JavaScript to get basic things done — then get help to make them work really well. You may have internal resources at your company, and there are websites such as eLance and oDesk that you can use to hire freelancers to get simple jobs done.

Your bosses don't want to mess with this stuff either, and they'll often be happy to approve minor expenditures to get complex technical tasks completed on time. The trick is that you've learned enough HTML, CSS, and JavaScript to know when you need help — and to manage outside contributors in delivering what you need, at a reasonable cost to the project.

You want to be taking on varied projects — small and large, complex and simple, design-led and content-led. Show that you can do it all. The web is constantly changing, so getting locked into one area where you're an expert can be quite lucrative in the short term — but potentially limiting further down the road.

Starting out as a front-end developer

Front-end developers work with graphic designers to make pages look good. They use three main tools — HTML, CSS, and JavaScript:

- ✔ **HTML:** HTML, or HyperText Markup Language, is the code that tells a web browser what the different elements are on a page. There is an old-school and a theoretically pure approach to using HTML. In the old school, you used HTML to say what something should look like — bold or italic, specific font sizes, and so on. In the theoretically pure approach, you would simply state that something should be emphasized, and not specify that that meant bolding it. (Everyone ended up just bolding and italicizing things anyway.)

- ✔ **CSS:** CSS, or Cascading Style Sheets, are layout instructions that specify pretty exactly how content should look on a page. Text is still allowed to flow as someone resizes a window, for instance, in most cases. But the font size and style, and use of bold or italic text, are precisely specified. Strong use of CSS greatly reduces the amount of work that has to be done in HTML; the way things look is almost completely controlled by CSS, and very little by HTML.

- ✔ **JavaScript:** JavaScript can control both the look of a page and interaction on the page. A simple example is what happens if users type their first name into an entry area that's designed to hold their phone number. JavaScript will be used to look at the characters that are typed in, verify that they're all numbers, parentheses, and dashes, and all placed properly. JavaScript will cause an error message to appear if they're not.

To learn to use these tools, take courses and read books about using HTML and CSS together — that's the best way to learn it these days, because a pure HTML or CSS course won't teach you about how to manage the overlap between the two.

For JavaScript, you'll find many good books that help you learn, and online sites that help you practice. Developing a portfolio site gives you the opportunity to practice using JavaScript on content and functionality that you actually care about.

The secret to success as a front-end developer over time is twofold. First, keep on top of the constant evolution in standards — different versions of HTML, CSS, and JavaScript — and the constant churn and growth in delivery platforms — different browsers and different mobile devices, from phones to phablets to tablets. See the sidebar, "The effect of mobile on front-end development," for details.

The second secret to success is to not only be a front-end developer. Learn enough graphic design to be able to carry out, or at least lead, an entire website project on your own. If you're the graphic designer, learn enough HTML, CSS, and JavaScript to be able to make the pages you design actually work.

To start learning, you can use a bunch of resources that are, of course, mostly online. Codecademy and W3Schools are two of the leaders. For links to these resources and more, visit the Lawrence Berkeley Labs page at `https://commons.lbl.gov/display/pbddocs/Web+Development+ and+Engineering`.

Resources for HTML and CSS are shown in Figure 4-2.

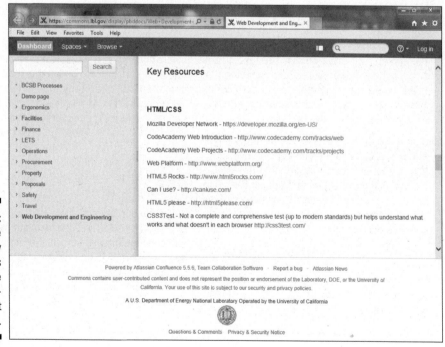

Figure 4-2:
Lawrence Berkeley Labs points to core web development resources.

The effect of mobile on front-end development

The rise and rise of mobile phones and tablets as a tool for content delivery is changing the world of front-end development.

It's critically important that web pages, especially high-functionality ones, work very well on a personal computer screen. People still think of the personal computer as the place to go to when they want to get something important done online. Applying to a university, shopping for a car, finding a product to learn a language with — these are all tasks that benefit from the bigger screen space and finer-tuned control that are only available on a personal computer.

But these days, web pages also have to work very well on mobile devices. There's actually a pretty darn big difference between a tablet and a smartphone here — and there are two kinds of smartphones.

For tablets, the best-known product line is Apple's iPad series. The screen resolution on newer models is comparable to a laptop screen. However, the screen size is smaller, so you have to be careful not to make text too small.

Also, it's hard for the user to position a finger tap as precisely as a mouse click. So interaction has to be simple and oriented toward big buttons and minimal typing. Replacing a typed entry with a complicated pull-down menu does not demonstrate complete clarity with regard to the underlying content.

Further complicating the picture is that people will try to do things on a tablet even when they know the task is more suited to a personal computer. When one of the authors (Smith) had a new iPad with an add-on keyboard and a Windows PC, he would often stick with the iPad even for "real" work or complex personal tasks. The keyboard made it easier, and Smith hated the Windows PC. But he was often trying to perform tasks online that were really better suited to a personal computer.

However, when Smith broke the iPad keyboard and got a MacBook at around the same time, the balance changed. Entering text on the iPad was now harder; the MacBook was much handier and more "instant-on" than its Windows predecessor.

Most tablets support the trifecta of front-end design technologies — HTML, CSS, and JavaScript. However, you should do extensive testing on iPad, and basic testing on a couple of Android tablets, to make sure that pages work as intended.

Smartphones are a widely varied mix. A *phablet*, like Samsung's Galaxy Note smartphones, has a big screen — somewhere between a phone and a tablet, thus the "phablet" moniker. Apple's iPhones have fairly small screens, and their users expect everything to be supersimple. And some users, more so in developing countries, have "feature phones" rather than smartphones; these phones are not very capable, but people still try to accomplish tasks online with them.

You should pick a simpler design target for phones of all kinds and just try to get basic content and functionality across. Consider creating apps for Apple iOS and for Android if you need to deliver more complex functionality. Then, gradually improve the mobile site so its capabilities rival those of the app.

When web designers code, they often aren't coding from scratch. Instead, they're modifying existing code to make it do slightly different things in a new environment. The fancy French term for this is *bricolage* (pronounced like *brick-o-lodge,* but without the "d" sound at the end) — using borrowed materials that you find at hand to create something new. Whatever you call it, learn to borrow and revise as much as you plan and create.

Working as a content developer

Content developers create content for online. That sounds simple, until you ask yourself — what is content?

There are three main kinds of content for online:

- **Words:** Writers for online develop a specialized approach to one of the oldest tasks in the book (ha ha!) — writing in a way that people understand and enjoy. Reading online is physically harder for online users, who are basically staring into a light bulb as they read. So smart content developers use fewer words, lots of headings and bulleted lists, links to complex information, and more pictures. (The saying that a picture is worth a thousand words was never more true than online.)

  Writers for online usually use one or more CMSes — that's Content Management Systems. A CMS lets you enter content once, take it through approvals and publication, and then reuse it in various places. Sometimes, frankly, the mechanics of using the CMS outweigh the need to get useful information online. For instance, many online help systems have content that is so optimized for easy translation that it's almost devoid of actual information and interest. This is the kind of challenge a professional web writer enjoys taking on.

- **Images:** Interesting images are vital for successful communication online, and they're often neglected. Images are often abandoned for display on a smartphone, for instance, so their value to the entire project is therefore diminished — a hefty proportion of the website's users will never see them.

  Also, most web project leaders have a web design background, and they believe that they can gin up a decent, web-ready image when one is needed. So there are many fewer web artists than there are web writers of various types.

But carefully crafted images can do a lot to carry the message of a web page forward — even on a smartphone. Facebook is an example of a web company that has cracked the code for the successful use of images on smartphones — and of advertising to accompany them. If you want to be a web artist, consider making yourself useful as a visual designer first, and then choose projects and job roles that take more and more advantage of your artistic talents.

One important area of growth is infographics — large graphics, often big enough to nearly fill a laptop screen, which convey a great deal of information at a glance. If graphics creation is your stock in trade, knowing how to create infographics is really valuable.

If you don't create graphics yourself, but serve on web development teams, look at the use of infographics online and develop an opinion as to when and how to use them on the sites you work on.

To see how the White House uses infographics, visit `www.whitehouse.gov/share/infographics`.

Figure 4-3 shows the White House's infographics page.

Figure 4-3:
The White House makes its points with infographics.

✔ **Multimedia:** There's a lot of overlap here with web artists, but there's a lot of technology and planning that goes into the successful use of multimedia. One of the authors (Smith) was filmed in an online ad supporting then-Senator Barack Obama in 2008. The ad was carefully filmed against a black screen, with only one person onscreen at a time, and then with only their faces lit. This cut down on the need for compression to handle a full-frame image; most of the background was black, and only a small part of the foreground was moving. The ad appeared very high-quality even with the harsh compression used to render content ready for streaming on YouTube.

To be a successful multimedia content developer, you need a combination of artistic insight and technical savvy that will give amazing results from a very limited budget of time, money, and streaming capacity. You need the ability to meet a strict budget and the ability to create content that can "go viral" and carry a sponsor's message to unexpected corners of the Internet. You also need to constantly update your toolkit with new hardware and software tools and your portfolio with interesting new projects, including a combination of pro bono or volunteer and paid work.

Managing projects

There are a few additional avenues of growth for web developers that are particularly interesting to those on the content side. Content work tends to be stressful and somewhat low-paid compared to front-end development or software development. To solve this, you can either go into management — which we describe in depth in later chapters of this book — or project management.

Project management is a strange beast, a weird combination of general management skills, consulting skills, task-specific skills — most project managers also do "real work" on a project, in some form or another — and the core skills of project management itself.

The best way to learn about, and to learn, the discipline of project management is to become a member of a project management organization

and work toward a certificate. The largest such organization is Project Management International, widely known as PMI, and its core certification is known around the world as PMP, for Project Management Professional.

Adding project management to your toolkit can take your career in entirely new and interesting directions. For one thing, demand for project management professionals is widespread and international. Experienced PMPs can head overseas for a year or two almost at will, gaining valuable experience, high pay, and sometimes even hazardous duty pay while having most of their living expenses paid by the project.

Being a PMP with web development skills puts you in a small and highly desired group. If you need to jump-start and professionalize your career, consider attending a PMI meeting soon.

Looking at the Future of Web Development as a Career

Web development is a unique career. It's a large area of employment, is growing fast, is attached strongly to positive trends in business and society at large, and is very well positioned for future growth.

The U.S. Bureau of Labor Statistics regularly publishes descriptive statistics and projections for web developer roles on its website (see Figure 4-4). This section describes what the BLS says about the profession as of 2012 (government statistics tend to lag a bit), and what it projects for the future as well.

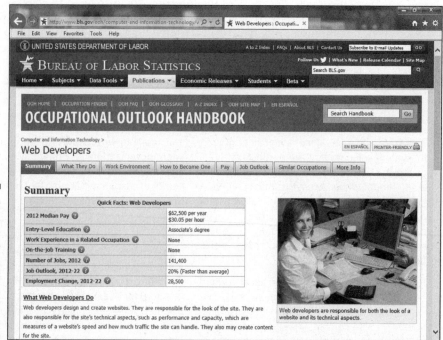

Figure 4-4:
The U.S.
Bureau
of Labor
Statistics
has a useful
page on web
developer
jobs.

You can always find the most recent page at `www.bls.gov/ooh/computer-and-information-technology/web-developers.htm`.

Visit the BLS site regularly to get the latest information about the current situation and prospects for growth in web design and any other area you're interested in.

What web developers do

The BLS gives the following description: "Web developers design and create websites. They are responsible for the look of the site. They are also responsible for the site's technical aspects, such as performance and capacity, which are measures of a website's speed and how much traffic the site can handle. They also may create content for the site."

This is a useful general description, but of course, like any brief description, it misses some key details. The BLS description doesn't disambiguate between visual development, front-end development, and content development. It doesn't highlight the primacy of technical skills in distinguishing an average web development career and most outstanding ones. And it doesn't make clear that graphic design skills are often, largely for historical reasons, a ticket to leadership in web design projects.

Work environment

According to the BLS, "About a quarter of web developers were self-employed in 2012. Non-self-employed developers work primarily in the computer systems design and related services industry."

The statistic about self-employment for web developers being around a quarter is fascinating. That feels right, and is a very high number for any kind of well-paid professional careers that aren't in sports or entertainment. Perhaps all of us in web design and related fields would do well to consider ourselves similar to entertainers, paid to engage an audience for some brief period, collect as big a paycheck as possible, and then get the heck out of Dodge.

The part about developers in regular employment working primarily in the "computer systems design and related services industry" would be accurate enough, except most of the words seem wrong. As the authors of this book, we both believe that a great number of web developers are working in large companies whose primary business is not in technology, but is instead in financial services, sports, entertainment, transportation, and others. It would be interesting for an analyst to take a look at the way BLS classifies job titles and industries to see if it might be undercounting web services positions that aren't in the tech industry and thereby overstating the percentage that are.

How to become a web developer

The BLS describes the educational level needed to become a web developer as follows: "The typical education needed to become a web developer is an associate's degree in web design or related field. Web developers need knowledge of both programming and graphic design."

This is spot on, except for one exception. The part about an associate's degree seems to be understating the case. America really needs a great many more jobs for which an associate's degree — a two-year degree that you can get at a community college — is sufficient, and also jobs that can be obtained through a few months of technical or semi-technical training, as is common in other countries.

However, we think that this description is making a common statistical mistake that can be described as "asserting the central tendency of a bimodal distribution."

A *bimodal distribution* is a range of description or achievement where there are two peaks. A normal distribution is the kind of bell curve we are all used to. That is, there's a peak in the middle and tailing off at both ends.

Figure 4-5 shows a normal bell curve. The figure is from a U.S. Centers for Disease Control (CDC) online course, *Principles of Epidemiology in Public Health Practice, Third Edition: An Introduction to Applied Epidemiology and Biostatistics.*

A bimodal distribution, by contrast, shows two distinct, separate peaks. For instance, a curve of droplet size in clouds, as shown in Figure 4-6, shows two separate peaks, one smaller and the other larger.

So when the BLS asserts that a two-year degree is sufficient for most web jobs, we're reminded that most of the web developers we know have four-year bachelor's degrees from a typical U.S. college — and a smaller number went through technical training, or have no degree at all. It seems to us that the two-year assertion might be a kind of mean between these two groups, but that it doesn't fit very many actual people, compared to the four-year and "no college" groups.

The recommendation, from the BLS and others, that an associate's degree is sufficient for web development jobs might be out of date. To be on the safe side, go for a bachelor's degree.

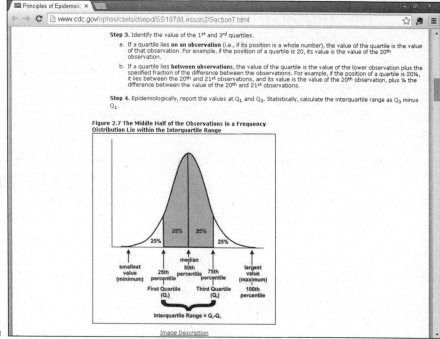

Figure 4-5:
A classic normal distribution, or bell curve, as shown in a CDC course online.

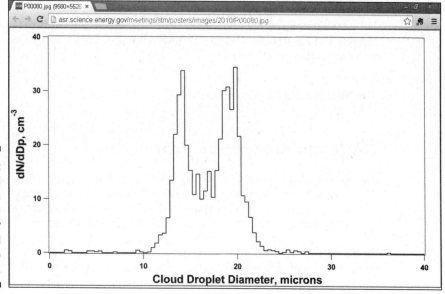

Figure 4-6:
A bimodal distribution is like a dromedary — a camel with two humps.

The importance of mathematics in web design

We assert throughout this book that graphic design skills are most often the entry point for web design jobs — and that technical skills, such as HTML, CSS, and JavaScript coding — are what distinguish the better-paid web developers from others, with those who can "cover the waterfront" for both skillsets being the most desired of all.

Yet mathematical skills are an important underlying element in web design, even for those who are not so technical themselves. Mathematical thinking is clear, crisp, and concise. These characteristics are all desirable in web design. Even if you're an artist or writer, which are roles that do not normally require a math background, having an interest in, affinity for, and ability in mathematics are desirable characteristics.

Not all uses of math for web design require a detailed understanding of advanced mathematics. For instance, design principles such as the golden ratio and the golden rectangle have been used since antiquity, and are still taught in design schools today.

To learn more about how mathematics are used in web design, visit *Smashing* magazine at www.smashingmagazine.com/2010/02/09/applying-mathematics-to-web-design/.

For a fascinating article about how these mathematical principles and others are reflected in nature, visit the NIH website at www.ncbi.nlm.nih.gov/pmc/articles/PMC2988127/.

The NIH article is shown in Figure 4-7.

Web development pay

The median annual salary for web developers is $62,500, according to the BLS. This is significantly less than computer and mathematical occupations overall, which have a median annual salary of $76,270 — a 22 percent increase. But it's far higher than the median for all occupations, which is $34,750.

That's right — a web developer makes 80 percent more than the typical U.S. worker. And web developers with outstanding overall skills, or even just a reasonable amount of technical skill on top of graphic design ability, can easily move up to the $70,000 range, which is double the median for all occupations.

Figure 4-7:
Mathe-
matical
principles
appear in
nature and
web design.

Now these salaries vary quite a bit by experience and expertise and geographic location, as well as by how people work — contract or regular employment, full-time or part-time. Across the U.S., the lowest 10 percent of workers earned less than $33,550 — just about the median for all fields — and the highest 10 percent earned more than $105,200, which is almost exactly triple the median for all occupations.

To get a bead on what these figures might mean for you, you have to look at the area in which you live. Glassdoor (www.glassdoor.com) is a site that has a lot of information about salaries and working conditions for specific companies and in specific regions, as do some job sites such as Monster.com. The point of looking at the national averages is to understand, in a general way, just how well web developers are paid. Use local and company-specific information to get a feel for your particular market before negotiating a starting salary or a raise.

There are very good cost-of-living comparison tools at both Salary.com and Payscale.com:

```
http://swz.salary.com/costoflivingwizard/layoutscripts/
        coll_start.aspx
www.payscale.com/cost-of-living-calculator
```

Working with web developers in person

It might seem odd for a job that's all about cyberspace, but most web developers either work in offices with their clients, which can be internal clients, where everyone works for the same employer, or clients from another company, or meet with them regularly. Skype video calls, full videoconferencing, and online hangouts and chats don't usually replace the need to meet in person.

This reality gives a strong regional flavor to web-related employment. In fact, in some areas, the need to live close to work can come down to a very small number of miles. During boom periods in Silicon Valley, for instance, it can take an hour to get 10 miles on U.S. 101, the main highway connecting San Jose and Palo Alto — the traditional endpoints of Silicon Valley with points north going up to San Francisco, which is getting integrated into the Silicon Valley economy as well.

So a web developer living in San Jose will usually only look for work up to about Palo Alto, and one in San Francisco will try to stay in the city, or at least within the range of the Bay Area Rapid Transit (BART) train network, which does not go down the Peninsula as far as Palo Alto.

A network of shuttle buses with free Wi-Fi cuts distances for employees of some tech companies, and consultants who work flexibly tend to schedule meetings for the middle of the day to avoid traffic that goes until 10 a.m. in the morning and starts at 3:30 p.m. in the afternoon.

Similarly, in New York City, people talk about what subway stops they live and work near to figure out the practicality of different work possibilities. Other world cities and large urban areas are the same. Use information like U.S. national averages as a starting point, but research your local area carefully to learn what you should expect in your area.

Projected growth in web development

The BLS says that web development will grow from 141,400 jobs in the U.S. in 2012 to 169,900 in 2022 — a total of 28,500 jobs, making for a 20 percent increase. This is one of the strongest numerical increases in the U.S. economy, and it's in a professional area that's among the higher-paying as well.

We believe, however, that even this job growth understates the case. While the net growth might indeed turn out to be 20 percent, many web developers move into related positions, whether in technology, non-web or not-strictly-web content development, graphic design, or the arts. It's easier to get into a web development job than most other jobs because of the growth; it's easy to get hired into a non-web development job from within the web development field because the skills involved are well-respected and valued.

The BLS provides an interesting description of web developer job prospects: "Job opportunities for web developers are expected to be good. Those with knowledge of multiple programming languages and digital multimedia tools, such as Flash and Photoshop, will have the best opportunities."

This is a little off in detail — Flash development is, if anything, on its way out — but right on the bigger picture. Combining more technical and programming approaches with graphics, and being up-to-date with the latest and greatest, is the most promising way to build a strong career.

How similar jobs compare

The BLS is kind enough to list some related jobs and their expected salaries. Many of these roles can be sources of the talents needed to become a web developer, or the destination for a web developer who wants to head in a new direction. It's also valuable to see that these roles, while closely related, are not considered part of the web development field.

Table 4-1 shows the roles — all of which require a bachelor's degree — their median salaries, from lowest to highest, and a few notes about how they relate to web development.

Table 4-1	Jobs in Web Development and Their Salaries	
Job Title	*Mean Salary*	*Notes for Web Developers*
Graphic designer	$44,150	A graphic designer not working in the web development area is paid far less — about two-thirds as much as a middle-of-the-road web developer. The added technical ability needed to work on the web pays off.
Web developer	$62,500	This is a mainstream web developer role, an umbrella which includes lower-paying and higher-paying roles.

(continued)

Table 4-1 *(continued)*

Job Title	Mean Salary	Notes for Web Developers
Computer programmer	$74,280	If you're an experienced front-end developer, you'll tend to make somewhat less than a computer programmer because HTML, CSS, and even JavaScript are not considered as technical as "real" programming languages like C or C++. But back-end work, using languages like Python and Ruby, should pay as much or more than mainstream computer programming work.
Database administrator	$77,080	Most websites are database-driven, so this is a logical starting point for website architects and a growth destination for technically minded web developers.
Computer systems analyst	$79,680	Systems analysts are people who decide how systems should work and then contribute to designing them. These high-level skills pay a significant premium.
Software developer	$93,350	The terms "software developer" and "computer programmer" are often used interchangeably, but the software developer is expected to have a systems analyst's view of a project, along with high-level programming skills.
Computer and information systems manager	$120,950	It used to be that becoming a manager was the only way to make a really significant salary in many professions. Today, the top 10 percent of web developers earn more than $105,000, quite similar to a management-level salary without many of the hassles.

Although the BLS is the most widely recognized source for salary information, you might also find interesting additional information from the American Institute for Graphic Arts. Visit `http://designsalaries.aiga.org/#salaries-list/`.

Part II
Core Technologies for Web Development

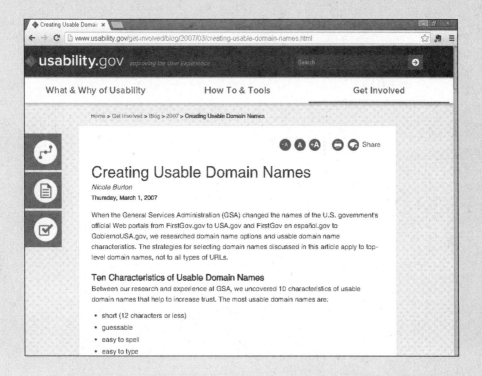

Check out www.dummies.com/extras/gettingawebdevelopmentjob for background on the rocky introduction of CSS to web development.

In this part . . .

- ✔ Choose technologies to build your career
- ✔ Understand how the Internet and web grew
- ✔ Learn how static web pages work
- ✔ See why database-driven web pages are now routine

Chapter 5

Charting Your Path in Web Development

*T*here are a million ways to become a web developer, and all of them are equally valid; "whatever works" is a maxim of web development, and of much else in life.

However, there's a curve connecting the ways in which you might become a web developer to how many good or bad things happen in your web development career. More, and more solid, preparation makes more good things more likely to happen. Less, and less solid, preparation makes good things less likely to happen.

This chapter explains how to chart your path in web development — how to get as many different plus points on your side as possible, and how to steer around the areas where you might have a weakness, or at least not have a strength.

Use this chapter to get yourself started, and then watch and learn in your own career. There are many niches of skill, talent, and expertise in web development. As you add knowledge of such niches to your own background, keep a careful eye on who is well-regarded among your colleagues and who isn't. Watch what the "stars" do and emulate it — in your own, genuine, positive way, not just to tick boxes. You'll watch your impact, and your career, grow as you do.

Distinguishing between Good and Bad Web Development Careers

So what is a "good" web development career versus a "bad" one?

That's actually a hard question to answer. The whole field of web development is constantly changing — the names of the boxes we try to put people into, the size and shape of these boxes, and what it takes to be well-regarded in them don't stay the same for long.

For instance, a few years ago, people might have said, "That web designer who knows all the latest HTML 2.0 tricks, is expert in Internet Explorer and Firefox, and is starting to learn CSS is really on the cutting edge."

Today, to express a similarly positive opinion, people might say, "That visual designer who knows how to replace Flash video with HTML5 video, is expert in design for personal computers, tablets, and smartphones, and just wrote a textbook on CSS template libraries is really on the cutting edge."

In Table 5-1, we list some aspects of what is usually considered a good web development career versus a less satisfying one. Feel free to take issue with our list, and to add your own plus and minus points. In web development, you can design your future just as you design a website — and you can experience the same uncertainty and randomness in how things will really turn out for both as well!

Several of the points that appear in Table 5-1 involve other people, and this is problematic. You can't completely control what other people think or say, no matter how good a job you do. But you are the only one who will benefit from others' good opinion of your work, or suffer from a poor opinion. So play the "meta" game — don't just do good work; sell it to your colleagues and bosses.

And if your colleagues and bosses are too slow, benighted, jealous, or insecure to recognize your good work? Sorry, their problem is your problem. You either need to find ways to get your colleagues and bosses on board with your contributions, or move to a new organization where people will understand and support what you're trying to do.

Table 5-1	Good and Bad Career Points in Web Development
"Good" Career Points	*"Bad" Career Points*
Well-regarded by current colleagues	Poorly regarded by current colleagues
Boss understands and supports your work	Boss doesn't understand your work and doesn't support you

"Good" Career Points	*"Bad" Career Points*
You feel like you get a lot of good work done in a day	You feel like you're not fully productive
You accumulate experience with new technologies as you work	You keep using the same old technologies over and over in your work
You find time to learn and practice with new technologies and tools outside of work	You don't learn and practice with new technologies and tools outside of work
You can show people your accomplishments in public-facing work or summarize it in easy-to-understand numbers	You can't show people your accomplishments in public-facing work or summarize it in easy-to-understand numbers
You achieve internal recognition – meetings, newsletters, congratulatory emails, and other feedback about your contribution	You don't get internal recognition for your contributions
You achieve external recognition — get positive attention or leadership in an external professional group relevant to your work, speak at a meeting or conference, and so on	You don't achieve external recognition
You accumulate both agency and in-house organizational experience as you progress	You feel stuck in a boring job in a non-web development organization — or you feel like you've been on the agency side too long and no longer understand the client's point of view
Your salary increases as you go on	Your salary stays the same or regresses as you go on
You hold jobs for two or three years and then move on, and at least somewhat up, even if the new job is in the same organization	You hold jobs for less than two years, or more than four, without moving either on or up

Exploring Utah's Take on Web Development

The state of Utah has its own take on web development. That state actually administers a course, Web Development 1, that seeks to teach the basics of web development.

The look and feel of the site is very 1990s, and most of the detailed, in-depth content is hosted in PDFs. Most modern websites put important content in web pages and use PDFs only for pieces which are targeted for printed distribution.

As an aside, PDFs are great for reproducing printed pieces and making them available for downloading and printing, but they are awful for hosting important content on your website. It's your job as a web designer to put important information into regular web pages that people can search using Google; that they can forward links to; and so on. Don't take the easy way out and put key site information in PDFs.

The fascinating thing about this course is the fact that it's addressed to high schoolers, grades 10-12, but it covers so much of what you need to know to have a lifelong career as a web developer. Check out the course's home page at www.schools.utah.gov/ate/Skills/it/893.htm, as shown in Figure 5-1, to learn more.

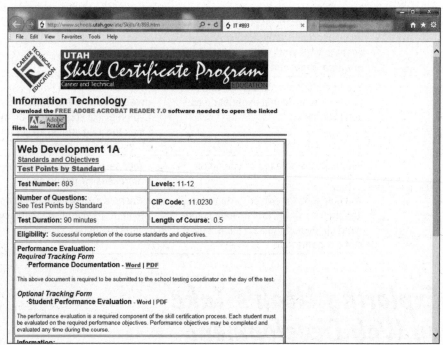

Figure 5-1:
A Web Development I high school course from the state of Utah.

Many sites with key information for web developers were developed in the mid-1990s, when the web was new and people were actively exploring how to get the most out of it. The iconic World Wide Web (W3C) consortium website, which contains all the key information about web standards plus discussion, was developed during this time. Visit `www.w3.org` to go back to the founding days for most of the standards we use all the time in web development.

The Utah course divides web development learning into standards — goals for students to reach — objectives, which are specific sub-goals within the standards; and indicators, or *proof points* that the objectives are being met. The PDF that has this supporting information is shown in Figure 5-2.You can find it at `www.schools.utah.gov/cte/documents/it/standards/` `WebDevelopment.pdf`.

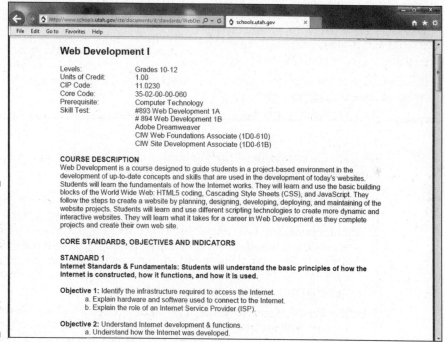

Figure 5-2: The state of Utah site has created standards for web development learning.

If you don't know the information in the Utah curriculum, you should learn it! Much of the information is available on Wikipedia, `www.w3.org`, and through web searches. Other skills described in the curriculum come with a moderate amount of practice, as you'll do on your portfolio site and on web development projects.

How a 1990s website can help you

Don't let the look and feel of a website stop you from taking advantage of the information in it.

As a web development professional, you'll develop a very critical eye for websites. That's because you're looking at your own websites, and the sites of colleagues and even competitors, with that same critical eye. In development, project reviews, and competitive analysis, you'll be looking at your own and others' websites with a view to identifying modern designs, sensible font choices, a balanced use of text, graphics, and multimedia, and more.

However, much of the most interesting information about web design was published when the web was new, in the early 1990s. Or, the information is up-to-date, but it's in a website whose design has not been finalized since the web was new.

For instance, the website for the World Wide Web committee, famously housed at `www.w3.org`, was developed in the 1990s. It contains vital information for any web developer.

Don't let an old page look or site design put you off from finding information you need. Be super-critical of pages that need to be the latest and greatest. But be supportive, as well, of pages that know what they need to do and get it done.

Here are the standards — the top-level goals — for this course, along with a summary of the objectives:

- ✔ **Standard 1, Internet Standards & Fundamentals:** "Students will understand the basic principles of how the Internet is constructed, how it functions, and how it is used." Objectives include knowing how to access the Internet, understanding its history and underlying support structure, how domains and IP addresses work, and the use of protocols such as http, https, ftp, and tcp/ip. Copyright and acceptable use of copyrighted materials are also included.

- ✔ **Standard 2, Fundamentals of HTML5:** "Students will demonstrate creation of 'well formed' web pages." For this standard, students code a basic web page, give files appropriate names and put them in an appropriate structure, use HTML elements and attributes, and use meta tags, image maps, forms, iframes, and HTML editing software.

Some of the tools mentioned in this curriculum, such as meta tags and iframes, are less used today than they were several years ago. However, "old school" web developers will bring them up in conversation, and "old school" websites that you're maintaining or updating will have them, so it's good to know what they are and how they're used.

- ✔ **Standard 3, Cascading Style Sheets (CSS):** "Students will format web pages using CSS." This includes using background, font, and border attributes in a website; using inline, internal, and external styles and style sheets; using selectors; and implementing page layouts.

✔ **Standard 4, Site Planning and Design:** "Students will plan, design, implement, and maintain website(s)." This standard takes tasks up a level, requiring that students analyze the requirements for a project; plan site design and layout; create content for a site; and upload a site to the web and maintain it.

✔ **Standard 5, Advanced Web Concepts:** "Students will explore advanced web concepts." In this course, advanced web concepts include using JavaScript, using newer HTML5 elements, which are widely used today, and understanding how databases, wikis, blogs, forums, and content management systems (CMSes) are used.

✔ **Standard 6, Exploration & Preparation for Careers in Web Development:** "Students will explore careers in web development and prepare a portfolio of projects created." In this section, students identify web development jobs and their responsibilities and create an online portfolio.

There is a whole wide range of things to know for a web development career beyond the topics described here. However, you won't go far wrong by starting with a curriculum like the one described here. After you have the basics, you can branch out into all the new and exciting things that web development has to offer.

The curriculum described here was revised in mid-2013, but it hasn't been brought totally up-to-date. That's okay. Although it drives students crazy, education tends to trail the real world by a few years, which is especially apparent for fast-changing areas such as web design. Also, you really do need to know the old stuff — it's the base for everything new, and will serve you well when maintaining and updating older sites.

Learning Web Development from Lynda.com

Lynda.com is a fantastic training resource for web development, with strong roots in the past, but also relentlessly up-to-date. The topics in the Utah training described in the preceding section are kind of the boilerplate of web design. Lynda.com includes a lot of the spicy stuff, in an easy-to-grasp format.

Lynda.com was founded in 1995, when web development was still quite new. Lynda.com specialized in niche, but important, topics such as using HTML and CSS with different browsers. It grew into a comprehensive site that costs $25 a month for a regular membership that gives you access to all its resources, as of this writing.

Lynda.com offers certification in many topics — a very valuable resource in some instances because it proves you have gone the extra mile to really prepare yourself in a given area. Because Lynda.com is well-known and well-regarded, certifications from this site really mean something to employers and peers. (Even if employers aren't familiar with Lynda.com initially, a little investigation into what the certification means will leave them impressed.)

Many of you reading this book may be new to web development, and need a resource just for vocabulary and basic concepts. Or you may be one of those interesting people who know a lot about one area, such as CSS, but not related areas. In either case (that is, unless you're already pretty well-versed) you need an introduction like the Utah training just to understand the topics well enough to know what to do on a more advanced training site like Lynda.com!

Lynda.com has close to 2,000 training courses and covers all experience levels, with strong instructors and excellent multimedia quality. You can learn everything you need to know about most topics from Lynda.com (www.lynda.com).

There is exactly one topic that is superlatively well-covered by information available on the web, and that's web development. If you are determined, you can learn just about everything you need to know about web development by searching online. But you'll waste a lot of time and take in a lot of useless and out-of-date information and approaches along with the good stuff. So seriously consider using structured resources for much of your learning, such as the Utah course shown here, or Lynda.com, and then using web searches to find specific tips and information in a hurry.

Figure 5-3 shows the web development home page of Lynda.com, which is really the core expertise of the site. Note that the page includes programming using languages such as PHP and MySQL as well as web development standards like HTML and CSS.

Reviewing some of the most popular topics on Lynda.com at this writing gives insights into where the mainstream of web development is today:

- ✔ **HTML Essential Training:** HyperText Markup Language (HTML) is the core of web development, and it's where Lynda.com's popular courses begin.

- ✔ **WordPress Essential Training:** WordPress is a web development environment and content management system (CMS) that began life as a blogging tool. It's very popular, and Lynda.com covers WordPress thoroughly.

- ✔ **JavaScript Essential Training:** JavaScript is the leading scripting language for bringing web pages to life, by a long shot. People often want training in it because they're HTML and CSS jockeys who feel it's a stretch to actually program, even in a simplified language like JavaScript, so this course is quite popular.

✔ **PHP with MySQL Essential Training:** PHP is a "real" programming language and MySQL is a standard for database access. So this course teaches people how to make more capable websites that interact with real data, making the site more powerful.

✔ **Creating a Responsive Web Design:** It's not enough to know how to make things happen; you have to have a feeling for what you might want to do with all that power. This course helps you give users the most functionality with the least strain through your site.

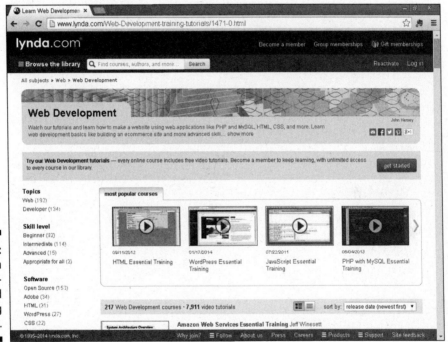

Figure 5-3: Lynda.com is a well-organized training resource.

Chapter 6

Discovering the Technology behind the Internet

*T*he web was originally called the World Wide Web, and that's what the "www" in most web addresses stands for. Today, the web is at a fascinating point in its development.

Because the web was only invented, and initially popularized, in the early 1990s, many people who were active in its initial development and growth are still not only alive, but active professionally, today. The founders are still working, speaking, writing, and generally sharing their expertise and making their opinions heard.

At the same time, the web has been around a couple of decades now. So many waves of new web developers have gotten involved, and the newer people are more and more distant from that early burst of work, energy, enthusiasm, and money. They're also more distant from the core technical knowledge that early web developers had to learn to get anything done, and from the web development lessons that early adopters absorbed.

This chapter introduces the irreducible core of what you need to know about the Internet to have an intelligent conversation with what web developers would call "a technical person." This includes buzzwords and knowledge that most web developers know, so you'll often feel stupid, and sometimes make mistakes — or not be able to get important work done easily — if you don't know it. So study up — and find ways to learn more if you think you need to. Your career will benefit tremendously.

Learning Technical and Cultural Basics

You might wonder why you might need to know technical basics of the Internet and the web to do a web development job. After all, some of the things that web developers worry about today, such as how to make their pages work well on a wide range of mobile devices, are pretty different from what people worried about in the early days, right?

However, you'll find that both technical and cultural basics matter — and that they're strongly interrelated. We tend to think of technical issues as hard, factual, and objective, and cultural knowledge as soft, "squishy," and subjective. However, each type of issue has elements of the other in it, and you need to know them both to be successful in a web development career.

Why technical basics matter

It's important to understand technical basics about the web for several reasons, all of which matter:

- ✔ To do your job better when technical issues affect decisions you're making
- ✔ To participate intelligently in tactical and strategic discussions with other people in your workgroup or on your project
- ✔ To communicate an air of competence and professionalism as you work and socialize with others

This is a case where cultural factors affect technical issues as well. Web development people are proud of the technical competence they develop in their work, and status and pay increase the more technical a job role is considered to be, as well as how technically skilled you're perceived as being within a given job description.

If you don't know your stuff technically, you can be perceived as a *newbie* — someone with little relevant experience — or, the more modern term, a *noob*, which implies someone who is not only new to an area of knowledge, but perhaps not even capable of learning it at all.

Technical basics also matter, of course, in getting the job done. If you accidentally put a photograph with a large file size onto a web page, the page will load slowly. If, on the other hand, you compress the same photograph so it will load faster, but overdo it, the image quality will be poor, and the look and feel of the page will be compromised.

So understanding technical information related to web development as a discipline, as well as issues relating to your specific job, is crucial. This chapter is intended to give you enough basic knowledge to get by, and also enough so you're ready to learn more as the opportunity arises.

You need to have a reference source for when technical discussions go beyond the basics covered in this chapter. Wikipedia gets a lot of criticism, but it's an accessible source of information for almost any Internet, web, or web development topic. And the book *The Internet For Dummies* by John Levine and Margaret Levine (Wiley) is worth reading and referring to. You'll get a strong feel for Internet and web history, basics, technical considerations, and newer topics such as social media.

Why cultural basics matter

There's a unique culture that developed around web development in its early years that continues to this day. Not everyone who does web development is the same, of course, but there is a central tendency around the way people in these roles think and act.

Most people in web development have a few things in common:

✔ **Technically minded:** There's a technical core to web development, and technical understanding and achievement are universally respected within the field. You can rarely go wrong in this arena by becoming more technically skilled.

✔ **Open-minded:** People who took web development jobs early on were people who were ready and willing to try new things — either in their off hours, or during work time when they were really supposed to be doing something else. This desire to always check out the latest new thing continues (and continues to cause trouble some of the time) today.

✔ **Disrespect for authority:** Early web developers created something outside the bounds of conventional authority. There was, though it may seem hard to believe today, little or no money involved, except for time and resources "borrowed" from government, universities, the military, and — gradually — business.

✔ **Disrespect for employers:** There are certainly lousy jobs in web development, with little freedom and low pay. But most web development jobs are relatively well-paid, and people who achieve distinction in a role are usually pretty able to move up or move over to a better job, either within the same organization or (more often) in a different one. So "the boss" doesn't carry as much weight in web development as in other areas.

✔ **Opinionated:** Web development rewards quick thinking and hard work. People who think fast and work hard tend to have a high regard for their own opinion and to be challenging to talk to and work with. In web development, technical skills come first, but if you can mix good technical skills with a reasonable degree of social skills, you can go far.

✔ **Snarky:** *Snark* — a kind of reflexive sarcasm about pretty much everything — is a common feature of web developers' reactions to all kinds of problems and challenges. At its best, it's hilarious, but it can get a bit wearing. Wear your snark lightly away from your web developers.

✔ **Devoted to lifelong learning:** Web developers are constantly exposed to new technologies and new versions of protocols, software, and platforms. They tackle new learning with an inquisitiveness and doggedness that the average person does not have. They are also willing to share their learning freely among their peers to make everyone better at their craft.

A great way to absorb web development culture is to hang out on technically oriented websites that encourage lots of comment, such as reddit. Reddit is so famous for its online exchanges that celebrities and politicians now visit to exchange views and try to influence the very influential reddit audience. Figure 6-1 shows a reddit exchange with Bill Nye, the Science Guy. President Obama has visited reddit as well.

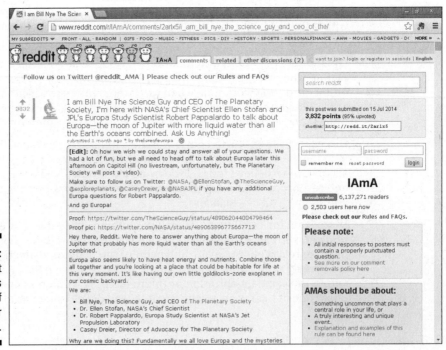

Figure 6-1: Reddit attracts all kinds of visitors for online chats.

The strange case of netiquette

Netiquette is short for "Internet etiquette" — ways of acting online that help you get along with fellow online denizens.

There's something about typing a message as a comment, into an online bulletin board, or onto a website that seems to encourage people to be aggressive, mean, sarcastic, profane, and otherwise socially unacceptable. Netiquette developed as a way to try to make the online world a little kinder and gentler.

Online exchanges can be very harsh, and people can remember them for a long, long time. Be careful with what you say online. You don't want to be truly unkind, and you certainly don't want to do anything career-limiting.

A few netiquette rules that you might keep in mind as you do your work and live your life online:

- **DO NOT TYPE IN ALL CAPS.** Online messages lack normal feedback channels and softeners such as body language, smiles, and so forth. Typing in ALL CAPS just increases the perceived harshness of a message.

- **Don't use profanity.** Everyone can see what you put online. Being profane can be fun and funny in the right place and time, and with the right people. But on the Internet — straddling every place, time zone, and culture — it's always the wrong place and time for some of your audience to see profanity.

- **Don't press Send when you're angry.** When you're upset, type your message in a safe place, such as a word processing or notes program. That way, anything brilliant in it gets recorded. Then wait until you calm down before rereading the message, removing all the ALL CAPS typing and most of the snark, and cut and paste it into the website comment field or email message. Then read it again before you press Send.

In the age of social media, there's a whole new realm of rules and best practices to stay aware of. Be very careful what you put on online sites such as, famously, Facebook. Although web development culture is generally disrespectful of authority and convention, human resources departments at large companies are not. That photograph of you in a crowd of people in various states of undress at Burning Man might get you promoted at Google, but, sadly, it could put you on the "do not hire" list at a wide number of more conservative companies.

Cultural "fit" might seem unimportant, compared to objective qualifications, but both of the authors of this book have worked with many companies that turn down potential employees — often in the later rounds of interviews — because they think there won't be a cultural fit with a potential employee.

How can you make sure not to get frozen out of promising job opportunities because of cultural fit? The answer isn't changing your core beliefs or personal practices to fit what you think a company wants.

Instead, do four things:

- ✔ **Research the company before you apply.** Resources like LinkedIn, Glassdoor, and the company's website can tell you a lot about a company, including what its culture is like. Look at the company's mission statement, vision, and values, or other cultural touchstones — and then see if you can find evidence as to whether they're actually used. (Ideally, they should be reflected in job advertisements.) This will help prepare you for interviews and, if things work out, for working there.

- ✔ **Make sure your grasp of technical basics is solid,** including those described in this book — plus additional information about the areas that you see as being strongest for you. If you're a network engineer, you will want to know a lot about how the Internet developed, and how it works today; if you're a graphic designer, you'll want to understand past experimentation in interface design as well as the range of current practice.

- ✔ **Learn to talk and interact on a friendly basis with everyone.** Web designer cultural traits such as snarkiness, disrespect of authority, and expressing opinions strongly can seem disrespectful or even hostile to people who don't embody these traits themselves. However, it's usually not meant that way. Try to find the point, humor, or meaning of each comment or remark, even if the style or tone in which it's delivered is not to your liking.

- ✔ **Maintain your core beliefs and point of view, and defend them with reason and wit.** Within web development culture, someone who's labeled a phony is not likely to be well-regarded. If you stick to your own point of view and approach, and don't let yourself be baited into arguments over small matters, you'll be respected, even by those who disagree with you.

Figuring Out Binary

Mathematics is the basis of the Internet. All sorts of seemingly abstruse mathematical theory has turned out to have direct application to Internet concerns such as network design, transmission speed, and page load time.

There is one area of mathematics that everyone who works in web development should have a basic understanding of, and that's the use of binary numbers and their translation into base ten — the numbering we're all used to, with digits 0-9 and place values, so 1349 and 9143 mean very different things.

A friend referred to general knowledge of binary numbers and their implications for web development, and computer technology in general, as "the way of the bit." Here's a brief description of binary numbers and how they apply to work in web development.

Electronic circuits are designed to support just two different conditions, or states: on or off. The on state is denoted by the digit 1, and the off state by the digit 0. When each electronic circuit state is described by either a 0 or a 1, that circuit is called a binary digit, or "bit." (It's called a bit to distinguish it from a normal, base ten digit, which can have the values 0-9 in each place.)

The number 0000 means something a little different in binary numbers than in most decimal numbering systems. In daily use, the number 0001 is just a long way of writing 1. But in binary numbers, as used in computing, 0001 means "there are four storage positions, and the first three are in the off position (0); the last one is in the one position (1)."

Binary numbers are related to mainstream digital numbers through a series of coincidences that are used to create terms that are sensible in both approaches. Table 6-1 is a table of the powers of 2 — the values of successively higher place positions in binary digits — the exponential value that the binary numbers represent, the value in base ten, and how some of the numbers are referred to in mainstream parlance.

For convenience, we normally deal with bytes instead of bits. A byte is a binary number with eight positions, such as 10011011. Because a byte has eight positions, it can represent decimal numbers between 0 and 255; or, put another way, it can have 256 different values.

This is convenient because, with 256 different values, you can represent all the letters of the alphabet, conventional digits 0-9, and all the special characters on a typical English-language typewriter keyboard, plus some additional characters, in just one chunk of eight binary digits — one byte.

Table 6-1 shows the values associated with different numbers of bytes. The exact same names apply to bits, but most computing-related discussions deal in bytes.

Table 6-1	**Decimal-Derived Names for Binary Numbers**			
Number of bytes (binary)	**Exponential value**	**Value in base ten**	**Name**	**Comment**
01	$2^{**}0$	1	Byte	
10	$2^{**}1$	2		
100	$2^{**}2$	4		
1000	$2^{**}3$	8		
10000	$2^{**}4$	16		

(continued)

Table 6-1 *(continued)*

Number of bytes (binary)	Exponential value	Value in base ten	Name	Comment
10000000000	2**10	1024	Kilobyte (KB)	Derived from kilo in decimal (10**3)
1....000	2**20	1,048,576	Megabyte (MB)	Derived from mega in decimal (10**6)
1...000	2**30	1,073,741,824	Gigabyte (GB)	Derived from giga in decimal (10**9)
1...000	2**40	1,099, 511,627,776	Terabyte (TB)	Derived from tera in decimal (10**12)
1...000	2**50	1,125,899, 906,842,624	Petabyte (PB)	Derived from peta in decimal (10**15)

The beauty and simplicity of the relationship among increasing binary values and more traditional decimal values is one of the foundations of how the Internet, the web, and all computer technology work, and how they're understood by people like web developers who work with them on a daily basis. If you haven't been exposed to this before, take a little time to study the table and see how the words you use in your daily work are derived from mathematical relationships between the decimal and binary numbering systems.

The web page displayed in Figure 6-2 shows the prefixes for binary multiples described above and also the International System of Units (or SI, the acronym for the French name for these units) names for the same prefixes. SI units are used in science and are therefore influential in technology. The SI unit names have not "crossed over" into general use in the web development world, but you should be aware that they exist, and that you might encounter them at some point in doing your work.

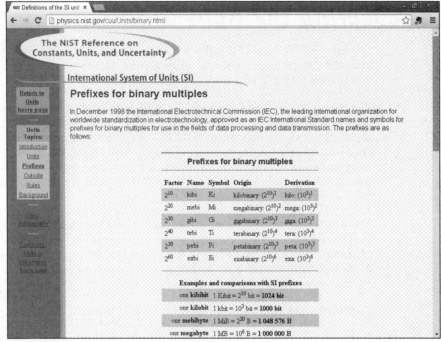

Figure 6-2:
Binary multiples have different names in SI units.

Here is how the different levels of binary/decimal numbers relate to the daily work of web development:

- ✔ **Kilobyte:** Used for file sizes for web pages and digital images. Web page text, code, and image sizes are often managed to total no more than, for instance, 100KB, so the page loads quickly on a variety of different networking connections.

- ✔ **Megabyte:** Uncompressed image files, such as photographs from a digital camera, are typically several megabytes in size. They are cropped (clipped to a smaller image size) and compressed to sizes ranging from a few kilobytes to perhaps 100KB for a relatively high-quality image. File attachments in PDF format are often several megabytes in size.

- ✔ **Gigabyte:** Once considered a very large file size indeed, almost impossible to deal with, a gigabyte of data is not considered as outrageous today. You would certainly warn users before suggesting that they download a file gigabytes in size, but users on fast networks could deal with it.

- ✔ **Terabytes and petabytes:** New computer technology, both hardware and software, that can deal with files of these sizes is currently being actively developed. There is now software that can race through a file petabytes in size and extract key data, summary numbers, or make a decision such as whether to approve a loan application.

Discovering the Keys to Internet Protocol

The Internet Protocol (IP) is the basis for the Internet. Everyone who works in web development can benefit from understanding a few key things about it, and from learning more as specific projects require it.

The basic problem for a networking protocol is moving data from one computer to another across some kind of connection. The Internet Protocol is connectionless, though, meaning that it doesn't handle the details of the connection between the computer. The connections are handled by the Transmission Control Protocol (TCP), and the acronyms TCP/IP and IP are used somewhat interchangeably. When TCP is used, it refers specifically to the connections part of the pair of protocols.

Many networking systems were tried before the Internet was begun, and many more have been discussed or put into use since. There have been competitions, which have sometimes even been referred to as "wars," between these different standards. IP is the current winner, and will probably be the champion for a long time.

There are a few keys to understanding how IP works:

✔ Every device on the Internet is meant to have its own distinctive IP address. (This goal is sometimes simulated rather than fully met, with some devices sharing an IP address or only getting their own IP address temporarily, but the basic idea holds.)

✔ A data file or data stream is divided up into pieces, called packets.

✔ Each packet has information that describes it, the source IP address it began at, and the destination IP address it's meant to go to.

✔ Each packet is launched from the source address onto the Internet separately, and each finds its own route to the destination.

✔ Packets arrive in any order they might, and it's up to the destination computer to re-assemble them into a file or data stream.

✔ The unsynchronized transmission and reception of packets leads to delays — the receiving computer has to get all the packets it needs to complete a file or a burst of streaming, and the receiving computer also has to take the time needed to put the packets in order and save them or stream them.

You can learn a whole lot more about Internet Protocol than this, of course. *The Internet For Dummies* describes it well, and puts it in context with TCP and a bunch of other relevant technical information.

IP is so important, the U.S. Government sees fit to try to explain it to children. The web page shown in Figure 6-3 is a history of the Internet that briefly mentions TCP and IP.

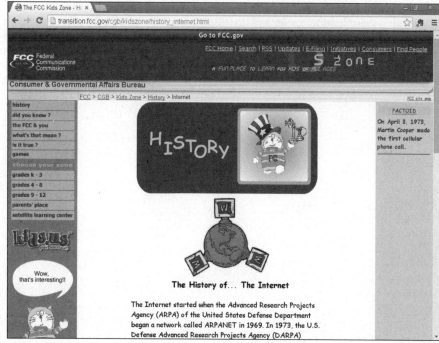

Figure 6-3:
The U.S. Federal Communications Commission thinks the Internet is kids' stuff.

How to make a billion dollars with IP

In trying to explain to friends and family how Silicon Valley works, one of the authors (Smith) describes the get-rich-quick appeal of some technical breakthroughs using IP as an example: If you can find a way to speed up the Internet by 10%, he explains, you'll probably become a billionaire.

People get this example because they have some idea of how pervasive the Internet is, how frustrating delays are, and how valuable it might be to have even a relatively small improvement in Internet transmission speeds.

Similarly, much of the work you do in web development will be about speeding up users' experience of the web. This can include reducing the amount of text or the size of the graphics in a web page, rearranging the elements on a page so the initial part of the page (what the user is looking at initially) loads first, or even putting a snippet of information onto one page so a user doesn't have to click on a link and visit another page to find out what a word or a reference means.

Learn all you can stand to learn about IP and how the Internet works, then think about what you can do to help make it work better for your development team and your users. The gains you make may not be worth a billion dollars, but they could well be worth a lot.

If you want to be taken seriously in discussions with technically literate people, don't refer to "the IP protocol" or "the TCP protocol," because the "P" in both acronyms already stands for "protocol." If you add the word "protocol" afterward, you're basically saying "the Internet Protocol protocol" or "the Transmission Control Protocol protocol." Instead, refer to them both by either their full names or just the acronyms. "I'm having trouble understanding everything I need to know about IP" sounds more literate.

Chapter 7

Introducing Web History

*I*f you're going to be a web developer, you should know two words really well. One of them is *developer,* and there's no big prize for guessing the other one. (Okay, we'll tell you. It's *web.*)

Each of the standards that makes the web what it is today influences what you and others do as a web developer. You also have a lot of choices as to which standards to use to do each part of a given job because there's a lot of overlap in functionality among them.

As mentioned in Chapter 6, having a core of technical knowledge about web development in general is important to communications and productivity across a web development project team. And if you're taking on big parts, or all, of a project yourself, you certainly need to know the basics of every part of the process.

If you know the basics, you can participate actively in a wide range of discussions — and you're ready to build on your knowledge as specific topics come up during the development process. This allows you to participate in more interesting work, get involved with more interesting projects, and find more interesting jobs. (And get more interesting paychecks.)

So use this chapter to get oriented, and to make good decisions in your work and in collaborating with others. Then use the core information we cover here to help you dive deeper as needed.

Discovering How the Internet Started

The Internet has been around for several decades. It was first used for higher education and military connections. Three of the popular early uses, which continue in various forms, were

- ✔ **File transfer:** Just moving files between different computers can be very difficult. File Transfer Protocol (FTP) was a real breakthrough in getting files from one place to another.

- ✔ **Email:** You may be old enough to remember when people on one email system, such as CompuServe email or MCI Mail, were absolutely unable to send email to one another. Internetworking — yes, the Internet — first allowed email to be transferred clumsily between one system and another, and then made email the flexible and capable, if sometimes overwhelming, tool it is today.

- ✔ **Bulletin board systems (BBSes):** Bulletin board systems allowed people to share comments asynchronously (when they felt like it, not at the same time), and for other people to see the comments and add to them.

The Internet is, at the end of the day, a system for transferring files. IP (Internet protocol) breaks files up into packets, which are then reassembled at the receiving end. The power, capability, and flexibility of the Internet and the web, and also many annoying problems, relate to this basic underlying mechanism as to how it all works.

FTP, email (as implemented on the Internet), and Gopher are examples of Internet services. An *Internet service* is simply a specified capability that runs on and depends on the Internet itself. Thinking of the web as just another Internet service is a great way for all of us people in the web development world to stay humble — and to realize that we could start to be made obsolete by some new Internet service development tomorrow.

Before the web, there were file sharing tools called Archie, Veronica, and Jughead — tools for finding files stored at various locations on the Internet. Gopher was a menuing system for listing what was available at a given location.

The web was a great solution to the complexity of these early tools. You didn't need to know how to use them, and you probably barely needed to know what they were. Just remember that these colorful names, and a host of others, graced the early Internet. Take the opportunity to ask an old-school web development hand what those days were like over a cup of coffee sometime.

Figure 7-1 shows a page from the Education Resources Information Center (ERIC) about a document that describes gophers, Veronica, Archie, and Jughead. Look up this document sometime at `http://eric.ed.gov/?q=Gophers%2c+Veronica%2c+Archie%2c+and+Jughead&ft=on&id=ED384536` and use it to get a basic orientation to these early Internet tools.

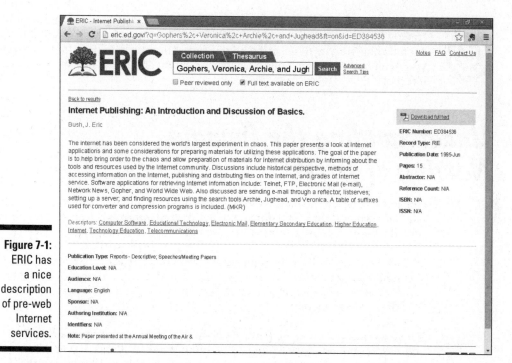

BBSes and netiquette

The need for netiquette (Internet etiquette) started with the tendency of people to be very bold, direct, and rude in email and especially on BBS systems.

Email also seems to encourage intemperate comments, but at least people know who you are, so there's accountability at the end of the day. On BBSes, however, people are usually anonymous.

The combination of text-based messages and anonymity somehow seems to incite people to be rude, profane, and mean. Netiquette developed as an attempt to rein in these harsh tendencies.

Nothing's changed much, though, since netiquette was first popularized in the 1990s. In fact, these problems may have gotten worse. Twitter, which is nothing if not an odd kind of interactive BBS, regularly makes news when public figures send strange, embarrassing, and even harassing or aggressive tweets. Facebook has its share of embarrassments and errors too.

Just keep being careful about everything you share online, and keep enjoying the trials and tribulations of those who aren't.

Schadenfreude (pronounced like "shod-en-froid-a") is a German word meaning "taking pleasure in the discomfort of others." It's a word that you might find useful when you try to describe how it sometimes feels to hear that someone you don't like very much has breached common standards of civility on the Internet.

Understanding the Domain Naming of Parts

One of the keys to the functionality of the Internet and the web is the domain naming system (DNS). The domain name system imposes a set of text names onto data servers that would otherwise only have IP numbers.

DNS also stands for domain name server, which is part of a network of servers that hold domain names. All the computers on the Internet access domain name servers to link a domain name, such as `www.facebook.com`, with the IP address of Facebook's main server.

When you put up a new website, it's hosted on a server with a specific IP address. A domain name is then assigned to that IP address. If you use a web page creation and hosting service such as Weebly or WordPress, that might be part of the domain name: *yoursite*`.weebly.com` or *yoursite*`.wordpress.com`.

Or, you can buy your own domain name, and that is then superimposed on the IP address and any intermediate domain name: `www.`*yoursite*`.com`. The other addresses still work, but people will almost always use `www.`*yoursite*`.com` to reach your site.

Weebly, WordPress, and other similar sites allow you to find an available domain name and buy it from within their service. It's a little more expensive than going to a specialist domain registrar such as GoDaddy, the current market leader, but it's convenient and easy to do.

The magic of DNS, as this example shows, is that it allows all sorts of trickery and chicanery to go on under the surface, while maintaining a consistent and easy-to-remember (for both humans and machines) set of names. For instance, Facebook has innumerable servers; in fact, one of its early competitive advantages was a system for getting more servers online than its competitors could field, at a lower price per server than anyone else.

Yet every time you type `www.facebook.com` into a web browser, the site — customized to your preferences — always comes up. You don't need to worry about which servers have capacity, or how the bytes move across the Internet between Facebook's computers and yours. You just use the same domain name every time, and the site you are requesting appears.

For a web developer, it's worth knowing something about domain names. First of all, a web domain, as opposed to an FTP or other type of domain, is denoted by www — for World Wide Web — at the start of the domain name.

The web is so dominant now that many websites are engineered so that you don't need to type the `www.` — you can just type `facebook.com` and get the same result as if you typed `www.facebook.com`. Not all websites, however, support this. (If you manage a website, make sure yours can be accessed with or without the `www.` prefix.)

The important thing to remember about domain names is that they're processed backwards (except for the presence or absence of `www.` at the start). Here's what we mean. Domain names have several components, which you should know as you pursue your web development career:

- **Top-level domain (TLD):** This is the end of the domain. The most familiar domain names to most users, especially American users, are `.com`, `.org`, and `.edu`. These domain names represent businesses ("com"mercial organizations, nonprofits (nonprofit "org"anizations), and universities ("edu"cational institutions). There are also country codes, such as .ca for Canada — very confusing to Californians, who are used to abbreviating their state name as CA, which is the official United States Postal Service designation for the state. And there are combined TLDs, such as `.co.uk` to represent British ("UK" or "U"nited "K"ingdom) "com"mercial organizations — that is, businesses.

- **Second-level domain:** This is what we think of as the core part of a domain name — the `facebook` in `www.facebook.com`. Popular second-level domains that go with core TLDs, such as `facebook.com` and `savetheseals.org`, are aggressively sought. It can be very hard to find a good, suitable domain name for your company or nonprofit.

- **Additional domain levels:** Technical people like to differentiate sub-sites by using the third-level domain — such as `na.`*`mycompany`*`.com`, `eu.`*`mycompany`*`.com`, and so on for the divisions of a multinational company. This usage is almost completely opaque to regular web users. Consider instead putting the sub-site in the domain name by using a slash, such as *`mycompany`*`.com/na`, *`mycompany`*`.com/eu`, and so on.

If you get involved with choosing a domain name for your organization, you will need to know more than we describe here. However, at least this description gives you the lingo and some key concerns to think about. Dive deeper by doing research online and talking to other web developers if you need to actually do something important in this area, such as coming up with a domain name that will represent a business or nonprofit for years to come.

One good resource for learning more is a web page on the very useful website — no pun intended — `usability.gov`. The `usability.gov` website contains a ton of great information and resources, and the page on usable domain names is worth a great deal just on its own. See Figure 7-2 for a look at the page, then visit here for details: `www.usability.gov/get-involved/blog/2007/03/creating-usable-domain-names.html`.

Visit `usability.gov` for tons of great information about web usability.

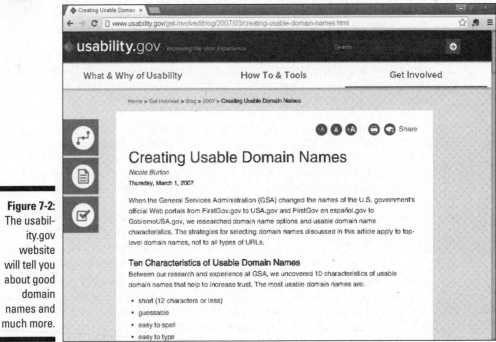

Figure 7-2: The usability.gov website will tell you about good domain names and much more.

The contentious usage of "American"

Knowing how to use words properly in a truly international — even borderless — context is a very important part of being a web developer. One contentious word is *American*.

People born in the USA like to think that "American" refers to them and no one else. But almost all other people in the western hemisphere — that is, those from Mexico and Canada, Central America, and South America — thinks of themselves as American as well.

The negative stereotypes that go with *American* — that is, that people from the U.S. are loud, boisterous, and ignorant of the world beyond their country's borders — are all too nicely supported by those of us who use the word "American" as if it had no possible meaning outside of "Born in the USA," as Bruce Springsteen sang it. Be aware that people from many other countries have at least partial claim to the "American" designation as well.

Discovering How Tim Berners-Lee Invented the Web

The rich range of Internet services that were being so widely used in the '80s encouraged a lot of new users, as well as increased use by existing users. However, usability became an increasing barrier to getting the most from these services. As an early user of pre-web information services, one of this book's authors (Bud Smith) remembers feeling excited by having access to huge amounts of information, but also sometimes feeling lost among the different protocols and options.

Tim Berners-Lee solved this problem, creating a new Internet service for a rather narrow purpose that ended up changing the world.

Berners-Lee worked at CERN, the immense and hugely expensive European physics research facility housed in Switzerland. He wanted to use the Internet to publish early drafts of scientific papers. (It usually takes months for a paper to get peer-reviewed and published, and researchers were left without valuable information that could affect millions of dollars in experiments while they waited.)

For some reason, Berners-Lee focused on creating a very simple solution to his problem. He was already familiar with *hypertext* — the idea of creating links in text so that clicking on a word or phrase could pull up a different document.

And now we have naming of Tim

Non-Brits may not recognize it, but the use of a double-barreled last name, such as Berners-Lee, often indicates an aristocratic heritage among Brits. In the British aristocracy, a merger in marriage between two important families is marked by the creation of a hybrid name.

Berners-Lee is certainly an aristocrat, but of the new kind, rather than the old: an aristocrat by virtue of merit and achievement. He has several awards of merit, including a knighthood from Queen Elizabeth.

There was a huge run-up in the value of website-based companies in the late 1990s, and many companies tried to offer Berners-Lee a chance at riches if he would only join in. He refused several near-certain chances to become a very wealthy man. Instead, he became director of the World Wide Web Consortium (W3C), a hugely influential body in the ongoing development of the web. He continues to find ways to contribute to the growth of the web and the Internet.

But Berners-Lee also had to account for graphics. Graphics are a huge part of a physics paper, and they can range from simple line drawings to highly complicated scatter charts of nucleonic explosions. Berners-Lee included an easy-to-use standard approach to including simple GIF (Graphical Interchange Format) graphics directly in text documents, and a way to link to graphics in other formats, such as JPEG (Joint Photographic Experts Group, a flexible compression standard commonly used for photographs).

This, in the humble opinion of your humble authors, was the secret sauce that really made the web take off. People love images interspersed among words, as the widespread popularity of magazines showed, then and now. (Magazines are still popular today — it's just that many of them are online, in the form of websites!)

Berners-Lee invented the first version of HyperText Markup Language (HTML) and created the first web page, on the brand-new CERN website that he created: `http://info.cern.ch/hypertext/WWW/TheProject.html`.

Figure 7-3 shows the current state of that early web page, which is not saved anywhere in its original form. It was updated every day for years, and some copies of the page in various states have been saved, starting a couple of years after it was first published.

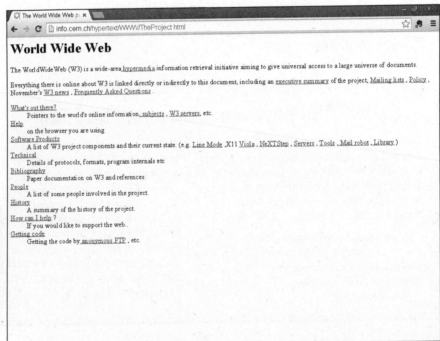

Figure 7-3:
The first web page will remind old-school developers of the early web.

The look and feel of this archetypal web page will remind long-time web developers and web users alike of how the web mostly looked in the early days — like a well-laid-out BBS page with hyperlinks. Widespread use of graphics and attempts to create page layout capabilities required later advances in both technique and the underlying technology, including rapid evolution of HTML and the creation of CSS. We describe the current state of HTML in Chapter 8.

The web evolved quickly. Marc Andreesen invented the first widely used web browser, Netscape Navigator. It became widely popular, and the rest is history.

Chapter 8

Introducing HTML

. . . .

. . . .

The web today is much different than the web before, say, the year 2000 or so. Through the 1990s, as the web emerged, web pages were based on HTML, with limited use of JavaScript. Such web pages are called *static web pages,* and the web of that time is now referred to as the *static web.*

Late in the 1990s, a livelier web came into place, much more responsive to users. Now, when a user visits a web page, the web page is created on the spot through a series of database calls. The ads come from some databases, the header and footer from others, and the main content from others entirely.

All this content is poured into a page layout defined in CSS, with liberal use of JavaScript to make the page lively, dynamic, and responsive. Languages like Python are used for purposes such as interfacing with databases.

This new, livelier web was called Web 2.0 when it appeared, but is better-known today as the dynamic web.

In this chapter, we introduce HTML, the web's core technology — but a technology that is, as we describe here, only part of a suite of technologies in the web pages of today.

Discovering How the Web Became What It Is

In the past, web pages were hand-crafted. Initially, every page was its own beast, hand-coded in HTML. The HTML standard was changing rapidly, and so were the browsers that displayed web pages — mainly Netscape Navigator and Microsoft Internet Explorer, with Firefox and Google's Chrome coming along later.

There were even cultural aspects to your development and web browser choices. If you used a Windows PC and Microsoft tools for development, and the Internet Explorer browser for web surfing, you were a hopeless square. (That's because it was mostly large corporations that were under "account control" by Microsoft that would do such a thing.) Most developers used Macs and Netscape standards and tools. Pages optimized for Netscape Navigator were considered cooler.

In the mid-1990s, style sheets became important. Cascading Style Sheets (CSS) was the standard that was chosen from among several competitors. CSS changed a lot in its early years, as did its implementation in browsers.

The final element of the core troika of early web development technologies is JavaScript. It was originally developed as LiveScript at Netscape, also in the mid-1990s. The name was changed to JavaScript shortly before widespread adoption, even though JavaScript has nothing to do with the Java runtime environment and programming language.

Web pages became quite complex. Each page was a somewhat volatile and hand-crafted mixture of HTML, CSS, and JavaScript. (These three standards are called "the basic building blocks of the web" on the W3C site, `w3c.org`.) Because the functionality of these three technologies can overlap somewhat, every different web page was a new adventure.

Websites today are largely driven by databases. HTML and CSS and JavaScript still matter, of course. But they are used as much to create frameworks for database-generated content as for hand-crafted pages. (And yes, as a web professional today, you very much need to be able to do both.)

This chapter describes the first of these three core technical standards for web pages, HTML. Today's web pages are just as likely to be crafted in DreamWeaver and programmed with PHP as created directly from HTML, CSS, and JavaScript.

But knowing the basics of HTML, and being able to explain them to colleagues who want to know what a web page can and can't do, is vital to an understanding of how the web works. With this knowledge in your hip pocket, you'll be better able to carry out your role as a member of your web development team.

If you already know HTML, review this chapter to make sure you know the basics as well as you think you do, and then use this information to bring colleagues up to speed.

As with other original web technologies and approaches, there is also both a cultural and a credibility aspect to knowing these technologies well. You want to be able to add new HTML, tweak existing CSS, and sling JavaScript with the old hands as well as write clean PHP code with the new.

The W3C website has a course on JavaScript that also relates its use to HTML and CSS, shown in Figure 8-1. For details, visit www.w3.org/community/webed/wiki/Category:Tutorials.

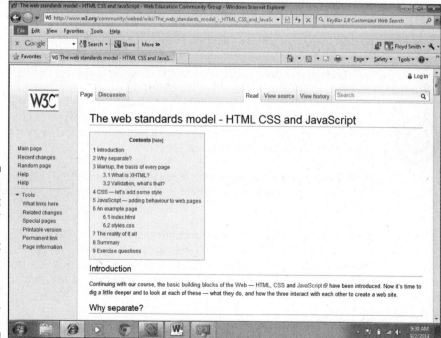

Figure 8-1:
Visit W3C for basics on JavaScript programming and interaction with HTML and CSS.

The HTML tags described in this chapter are representative of what you may use in your own web pages. Showing and describing them gives us the opportunity to comment on some parts of how HTML and CSS work together, for instance. Use a current HTML reference, such as the one at `w3c.org`, for your actual web development work.

Exploring the Creation of HTML

Just about everyone reading this book knows what HTML is. Still, it's worthwhile to describe its creation and evolution because they're still relevant to how the web as a whole, and web pages, are developed today.

The core of HTML is the use of "tags" — little pieces of code — to "mark up," or put formatting or descriptive elements, into text.

Here's an example of simple HTML:

> I like to use `<b>bold</b>` sometimes and `<i>italic</i>` sometimes. And other times I like to add `<a href="w3c.org">links</a>`.

How does this show up? Like so:

> I like to use **bold** sometimes and *italic* sometimes. And other times I like to add <u>links</u>.

The `<a>` and `</a>` tag pair is called the *anchor* tag. Surrounding a piece of text with `<a>` and `</a>` makes the text into a hyperlink. In the anchor tag, you place the URL of the destination of the link.

Now, there has been a battle between two approaches to HTML since the early days. These are basically whether HTML is used for formatting or description.

If you believe HTML is used for formatting, you're very happy with the bold (`<b>`) and italic (`<i>`) tags. However, some web developers preferred to use tags such as `<strong>` and `<em>`, for emphasis. The idea was that it was up to the browser, or other display software, to decide what *strong* and *emphasis* meant.

With the clarity given by hindsight, it's clear that this latter idea is ridiculous – although some people still swear by it. Writers and editors are used to using bold and italics and underlining for certain purposes in print — and they're happy to continue doing that in the online medium. But they weren't ready to stop worrying about whether words were emphasized by bolding, italics, or some other convention.

So HTML continues to be used for formatting. And it will probably be used that way forever.

The following sections describe core elements of HTML. It's worth reviewing them because every web page has to have these elements — even if, in some cases, they're now being implemented more often in CSS or JavaScript rather than HTML.

Even if you don't work directly with HTML, you should familiarize yourself with what it can do. Nearly everyone in the web development field understands the basics of HTML. Don't be the only one on your project team who doesn't.

On the web, you shouldn't use underlining for any purpose except hyperlinks. People are used to clicking on underlined text, and it's just too confusing if you try to do it any other way. (And also, always underline linked text — unless you come up with some other way of signaling "this is a link" that's extremely clear and obvious.)

Discovering Header Elements

The top part of an HTML document is called the header, and is surrounded by the `<head>` and `</head>` tags. The header usually contains mostly header-specific tags, described here. These tags define elements that apply to the page as a whole.

XHTML versus HTML

XHTML is a blend of HTML, which is very widely known and used, and XML, a separate language with much stricter rules for how it's written and interpreted. The blend of HTML and XML is called XHTML, and it's basically HTML written under stricter rules.

In HTML, it doesn't matter if you use uppercase or lowercase; `<h1>` is the same as `<H1>`. You can use the `<p>` tag to indicate a break between paragraphs. And you don't have to put attributes, such as the URL in an anchor tag, in quotes.

In XHTML, you always use lowercase for tags. The paragraph tag is now a pair of tags, `<p>` and `</p>`, that you use to surround each paragraph. And attributes are always enclosed in quotes, such as `<a href="w3c. org">Visit W3C today!</a>`.

Many web teams use XHTML styling as a matter of course, so get used to taking this extra level of care when you write your HTML code. You might also want to change pages to XHTML when you modify them for consistency and predictability across your web pages.

The body of the web page, by contrast, is surrounded by the `<body>` and `</body>` tags. It includes the actual web page content and is where the rest of the tags are used.

Header tags include

✔ `<title>` and `</title>`. The name of the web page. Most browsers show it in the header bar at the top of the page, above the page itself — or in the tab, if you're using tabbed browsers.

✔ `<meta>`. The `<meta>` tag contains general information about the page that's used in various ways. The contents aren't really specified officially, but a few conventions have grown up. You can use the meta tag to specify a description of the site and various keywords that you want search engines to use, but most search engines today don't take much notice of the `<meta>` tag.

✔ `<link>` and `</link>`. This tag is mostly used to link to stylesheets written using CSS.

✔ `<style>`. This is a place to put CSS code that applies to this specific page. If you also link to one or more CSS stylesheets, the CSS code contained in the `<style>` tag will override the CSS code in the stylesheet for use on the current page.

✔ `<script>` and `</script>`. This is where you commonly put all the JavaScript on a page between the `<script>` and `</script>` tags.

Making Use of Core Structural Elements

HTML has several core structural elements. These elements describe the overall layout of a web page.

Search engines vary their algorithms — the rules they use — over time. But a few key elements tend to be used over and over to analyze a web page and what's important in it. The core structural elements of a web page are a big part of this.

Headers are perhaps the most important ongoing element for search engine success. Any web page worth bothering with is going to put core topical keywords in its headers.

The dot-com boom

The early years of the web featured what was widely called the dot-com boom. The *dot-com boom* was a stock market boom that featured a slew of new companies with websites at their core. Because all the highly valued companies used the .com top-level domain, the boom was called the dot-com boom, and the subsequent crash, in 1999-2001, was called the dot-com crash.

The dot-com boom happened because investors believed that there would be very valuable companies coming out of the rise of the Internet, and they were right. However, it was extremely unclear which companies would benefit — and whether the beneficiaries would ultimately be companies that were being traded at the time, companies that had yet to be invented, or companies that had gone into business, but had not yet gone public, and so were not available on the stock market.

During the dot-com boom, companies such as Yahoo! saw their stock prices rise to dizzying heights. In many cases, companies that had yet to make a profit, or even any sales, were worth billions of dollars in stock-market value.

One famous example was pets.com. The idea was that the market for pet food and pet supplies online would be gigantic, and pets.com would be the leader. What ultimately sunk pets. com was that shipping 50-pound bags of dog food to people through the mail just didn't make sense, on a large scale. Although pet store chains today certainly have e-commerce websites, pets.com went under.

The dot-com crash happened in the year 2000. The NASDAQ stock index, which was and is heavy on technology stocks, peaked at over 5,000 in March, 2000 – then crashed, falling to 3,500 a couple of months later, rising again past 4,000, then slumping to a little higher than 1,000 in late 2002.

It turns out that dot-com boom was really a broad technology boom, and that many of the winners only came onto the market later. Many companies disappeared. Others, like Yahoo!, never recovered their previous value. Some others, like Amazon, have gone onto new heights. But the three biggest stock stories since the web was invented included two companies, Facebook and Google, that only went public after the dot-com crash. The third big beneficiary, Apple, which became the world's most valuable company, makes devices that are largely used to access Internet services, but is hardly a dot-com company at all. (Apple does use e-commerce to sell a lot of goods, but the goods are made by Apple itself, and sold in many other ways as well, so the e-commerce part is not the point of the company.)

The problem is that HTML and CSS can be used to create what look like second-level and third-level headers without actually using the HTML `<H2>` and `<H3>` tags to do it. Here are core structural elements of HTML:

✔ `<h1>` and `</h1>` through `<h6>`/`</h6>`. These are HTML headers. A lot of web developers seem to pride themselves on not using HTML header tags. Why? Stop tricking your users and search engines; use search-engine-recognizable header tags in your web page layouts.

✔ `<p>` and `</p>`. This is the HTML paragraph tag. People used to use the `<P>` tag as a way to separate one paragraph (thus the `<P>`) from the next. Or they would use the `<br>`, or "break" tag, which is only supposed to indicate a line break, not a meaningful separation of chunks of text.

✔ `<blockquote>` and `</blockquote>`. This HTML tag pair indicates a block of quoted text. It's a great example of the different types of HTML tags, those that control formatting and those that indicate meaning. This tag pair displays text indented from the left edge of other text.

The HTML header tags, `<H1>` through `<H6>`, impose a specific appearance on the headers on a web page. The appearance is specified by the browser that displays the page. Web developers who want to control the look of headers — which means just about all web developers — for many years created their own header styles. The difficulty is that this undermined search engines that use the header tags, when they're present, to determine what words are more important in a document. However, you can use HTML to specify headers, use CSS to override their appearance, thus customizing the look and feel of your web pages.

Using List Elements

Lists are highly recommended for frequent use on your web pages. They're easy for the reader to scan and quickly pick out key points.

Lists are also good for writers — they make the writer get to the point quickly. This is very important on the web, where people scan pages hurriedly, looking for a key fact or insight, then hurriedly move on.

The main types of lists that you'll use are bulleted lists and numbered lists. Both are great for helping readers pick out key points. Numbered lists work when there are steps or some other process or procedure. Web pages tend to have a lot of bulleted lists, so use numbered lists where you sensibly can.

Here are the most commonly used list elements of HTML:

`<ul>` and `</ul>`: Use these tags to surround an entire unordered (bulleted) list.

`<ol>` and `</ol>`: Use these tags to surround an entire ordered (numbered) list.

`<li>` and `</li>`: Use these tags to surround each item in an unordered (that is, bulleted) or ordered (numbered) list.

You can also create a definition list. A definition list is like a bulleted list, but each bullet item is a definition term — the term that's being defined, usually displayed in bold — followed by the definition itself. The definition list gives you another tool for breaking up your web page, avoiding long flows of paragraph text.

Here are the tags for definition lists:

> `<dl>` and `</dl>`: This is not a tag for putting information on the "down low" (keeping it secret); instead, use these tags to create a definition list.

> `<dt>` and `</dt>`; `<dd>` and `</dd>`: "dd" stands for "definition data." The contents of a definition list include the terms that you'll define (`<dt>`) and the definitions themselves (`<dd>`).

As with header tags, the appearance of lists created using HTML tags is often boring and ugly, and browsers always display them the same way. Many web developers do lists in their own way, not using HTML. However, as with header tags, recommended practice is to use the HTML tags, then override the look and feel of the HTML tags with CSS.

Usability and lists

This book doesn't have room to go into usability much. Web usability is the practice of making web pages easy to use. Usability professionals can be, for example, web page designers with a usability bent; usability professionals who work with all sorts of other team members; and interaction designers, who focus specifically on intense user processes such as completing a purchase on an e-commerce site.

Lists are a great example of the kind of concerns that drive web usability. For your website's users, reading from the screen, as on a web page, is harder than reading a printed magazine or book. That's because the screen is generally low-resolution (although Apple's Retina screens are leading the way in high-resolution screens), and always backlit, rather than lit by reflected light like a magazine or book. Staring at a computer screen has been described as "staring into a light bulb," and it makes your eyes tired.

Because reading from a screen is hard, users get tired doing it. So they remember less information from text they read onscreen than in print. They also tend to rush through onscreen text, just grasping key facts, and scanning it rather than actually reading it.

This is where headers, lists, and other structural elements of a web page can help you. Text in a list tends to be shorter than narrative text in paragraphs. So shorten your text, then put it in a list. That will tend to shorten it further, and make it easier for the user's tired eyes to pick out the key points that they're looking for.

When you've completed a web page, try scanning through it quickly. You should be able to pick out the key points without reading the page closely. If not, make sure the key points are reflected in headers and lists.

One of the hardest tags to remember in HTML, until you get used to it, is the ordered list tag, `<ol>` and `</ol>`. That's because what you're trying to get is a bulleted list, and you would never normally think to call that "unordered" — it actually has an order, top to bottom, and you should put the most important points at the top. (The bottom of a list also tends to get extra attention, so you can put an important point there as well.) These names were given out of the old idea that HTML shouldn't specify formatting (such as "bulleted list"), but should specify meaning ("please, Mr. Browser, do something appropriate with this unordered list"), even though from the beginning everyone's used it for formatting. The tag you use when you want a numbered list is almost as obscure, with `<ol>` and `</ol>` representing the beginning and end of an ordered (numbered) list.

Working with Text Formatting and Image Elements

Text and images are the core elements of nearly all web pages. Only a few HTML attributes were available, in the early days, to affect how they were displayed onscreen, and CSS was not yet invented at that time. So these few tags received a lot of use, and even abuse, as web developers tried very hard to create sophisticated-looking web pages with the crude tools at their disposal.

`<blink>` and hostage-note web pages

HTML is a pretty blunt instrument for making your page look good, but before CSS was introduced and became widely used, it was all a web developer had. Pages looked too much the same, making websites boring. Developers tended to overuse formatting, such as bolding and colored text, in an attempt to give their pages some zing.

The `<blink>/</blink>` tag pair was the most famous example of this effort. Unlike many HTML tags, this one has an easy to remember and descriptive name. It does "just what it says on the tin" — it makes the text that's surrounded by it blink.

Imagine a sweepstakes web page with the words "You may have already won!" in the center, rendered as a clickable link, in a big text size and a bright color, blinking in the center of the page. That's what the `<blink>` tag was invented for.

The `<blink>` tag is not supported in all browsers, so that's one very good reason not to use it. However, it's also so annoying and frustrating to users that you should never use it for that reason as well.

The `<blink>` tag is still something of a standing joke among web developers, and a good thing to know about if you're newer and want to appear (and be) knowledgeable. The `<blink>` tag is also a good reminder not to try too hard to be distinctive or get attention in your web page designs.

The happy move to HMTL5

HTML5 (it's usually written that way, with no space between HTML and 5) is a new, and welcome, addition to the existing body of HTML standards.

HTML5 starts by adding several new tags, such as `<audio>` and `<video>` for multimedia. It also standardizes tags and attributes in an XHTML-friendly manner. And HTML5 includes features for pages that work on mobile phones and other portable devices.

Among the many advantages of HTML5 is that it can easily be used to deliver video in a website without the need for Adobe's Flash tool. Flash doesn't work on mobile devices, and it's often buggy and crash-prone on personal computers too. Moving beyond Flash is a good step for the web.

We won't explain HTML5 in any detail here because it's now the standard that you'll find in any up-to-date HTML book or descriptive website. Just be aware that HTML is today still very widely used and relevant for the future, in no small part because of the changes introduced as part of HTML5. If you want to move to the top of your profession, learning the ins and outs of HTML5, and how to get the most out of it — especially on mobile devices — is very much worthwhile.

Formatting text directly is said to be somewhat against the spirit of HTML, but people care a great deal about how text appears onscreen. HTML was pushed to its limits to create page layout and text formatting, with much difficulty across different browsers, different browser versions, and different types of computers and screen resolutions. Now, browsers are far more standardized, and the same goal is reached more effectively with a combination of simpler HTML code and CSS.

 On its own, HTML doesn't let you specify the placement of an image onscreen; images just go into the flow of text before and after them. This is very much unlike, for instance, magazines, which users and designers alike are accustomed to. HTML and CSS go some way to providing the control which designers want, and users expect, but it takes a lot of skill with these tools to create consistent page designs across platforms.

Here are the main tags that format text directly:

`<b>` and `</b>`. Tags that render the enclosed text bold.

`<i>` and `</i>`. Tag pair that renders enclosed text in italics.

`<font>` and `</font>`. Tag pair that renders enclosed text in a specified font.

`<span>` and `</span>`. Designates enclosed text for formatting commands.

`<a>` and `</a>`. Defines an anchor or hyperlink and formats the enclosed text in a way that designates it as a hyperlink — usually underlined and in blue. The hyperlink is defined by the `href` attribute, as follows: `<a href = "url">`, where "url" is a web page address.

The tags for putting images into a flow of text are

`<img>`. The image tag specifies that an image will be placed in the flow of text before and after the tag. As with the anchor tag, the image location is defined by the `href` attribute.

`<media>`. An early way of specifying a multimedia element, such as a video clip.

Looking at Table Elements

Table tags were originally designed to be used for creating tables within a web page, with rows and columns and a caption describing the table. However, web developers badly wanted their pages to look better, and they didn't have many tools to do it in HTML.

So web developers started making the entire web page a table, and putting text and graphics within the rows and columns. This did give a lot of control. However, it also made web page HTML very complicated and easy to "break," in ways that were hard to find and fix.

Fairly quickly, web developers started using nested tables for page layout — perhaps one table for the top of the page, another for a left-hand column or "rail" with navigation, and a third for the main page content. This went within an overarching table that put the rails, main column, and so forth in place. If you wanted an actual table in the usual sense — a formatted set of rows and columns to organize some information — that just went within all the other tables.

A lot of the energy behind the creation and adoption of CSS was an attempt to get away from all these tables and the problems they created.

Commonly used table tags include `<th>` and `</th>` for a header cell, `<thead>` and `</thead>` for a group of header cells, `<col>` and `</col>` to define a column, and `<colgroup>` and `</colgroup>` to group columns together. `<tr>` and `</tr>` defined rows, and `<td>` and `</td>` defined a single cell in the table. The `<caption>` and `</caption>` tags gave the table's caption — as usual with HTML, formatted and placed according to each web browser's interpretation of the tag, beyond the control of the web developer.

Chapter 9

Understanding CSS and JavaScript

● ●

In This Chapter

▶ Understanding how HTML, CSS, and JavaScript work together

▶ Using CSS for text styling

▶ Using CSS for positioning text and graphics

▶ Designing web pages with WordPress

▶ Using JavaScript in web pages

● ●

The preceding chapter introduced and explained key basics for HTML. Anyone who works in web development needs to know the basics of how HTML works.

In this chapter, we introduce the basics of Cascading Style Sheets (CSS) and JavaScript, which are additional key elements in understanding how web pages are put together. Taken together, this information is crucial for all web developers. But it affects you differently depending on your role.

If you are a novice web developer who will be creating web pages directly, you need to learn this information thoroughly. Good starting resources are the tutorial made available by the World Wide Web Consortium, which you can find at www.w3.org/community/webed/wiki/Category:Tutorials.

If you are an experienced web developer, review this information to gain perspective and clarity on the work you do every day. Consider quickly reviewing the World Wide Web Consortium's tutorials to see if they show you anything new. Then use these pages to help you explain to colleagues and new employees how you work, and how they can best work with you.

HTML, CSS, and JavaScript Together

Originally, web pages were all HTML. HTML font elements, such as `<b>` for bold and `<i>` for italic, controlled the look of text; tables, misused to contain the entire contents of the page (as described in the preceding chapter), controlled layout. But this has been replaced by a combination of HTML, CSS, and JavaScript.

Why use HTML, CSS, and JavaScript together? Well, creating a useful, usable web page is difficult. Using HTML, CSS, and JavaScript together takes that difficult job and divides it into three parts. Each part is handled by the right tool for the job:

- **HTML:** HTML only contains content: text, links, images, and designated names for different blocks of text — from headers to different styles within the flow of text.

- **CSS:** All the styling information, such as font styling descriptions and layout, are controlled by CSS. Because style sheets can be reused, as well as cascaded — with higher-level style sheets overridden, where necessary, by lower-level ones — efficiency and consistency are much enhanced.

- **JavaScript:** Web pages need to behave — that is, to support at least simple interactivity. For instance, if the user enters numeric characters into a country name field, you want this to get quickly flagged — preferably before the user clicks the Submit button. JavaScript is the right tool for this job.

This separation of responsibilities among HTML, CSS, and JavaScript has a bunch of advantages. Among the key pluses are

- **In-memory reuse of CSS files:** If most of your CSS files apply to multiple pages, they get loaded into the browser's working memory the first time they're needed, and then hang around as they're reused by subsequent pages. They only download once per session.

- **Smaller HTML files:** Before a web page can be displayed, the entire HTML file must be downloaded. Putting display specifications in CSS instead of HTML makes the HTML file much smaller. Assuming that the needed CSS is usually already hanging around in memory, the total size of the data that needs to be downloaded for each web page is much reduced.

- **Device compatibility:** You can use different style sheets for different devices. Your same small HTML file can work on a lot of different devices, and only the CSS files that work on a given device get downloaded and used on that device. Bonus: The CSS files for mobile devices will be smaller and simpler, so you're downloading smaller files over the often-dodgy cellular data connections available on mobile devices.

You can find an overview of what you need to know to develop web pages, including solid introductions to HTML, CSS, and JavaScript, at the World Wide Web Consortium site: www.w3.org/community/webed/wiki/Main_Page.

The World Wide Web Consortium has a useful overview of how these pieces work together, although it emphasizes somewhat different points than we do. To see its take on it, visit www.w3.org/community/webed/wiki/The_web_standards_model_-_HTML_CSS_and_JavaScript.

This web page is shown in Figure 9-1.

In addition to all the good reasons for using HTML, CSS, and JavaScript in combination, there's another reason: This combination has become the standard. Learning to work the way most of your colleagues do will save you time, energy, and frustration. That doesn't mean you shouldn't remember some of your old HTML tricks, and you should learn more modern tools, such as PHP, but recognize what the mainstream has been for a long time now, and be ready to work within that framework as needed.

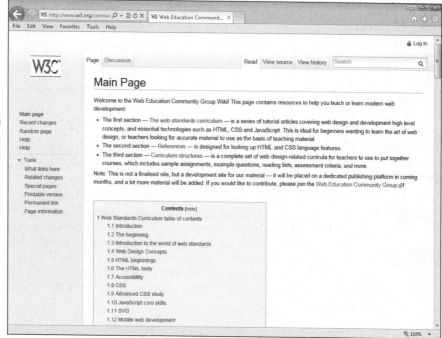

Figure 9-1:
The World Wide Web Consortium site gives an overview of the relationship it suggests you use among HTML, CSS, and JavaScript.

Before you get too far into the weeds, however, it's important to take some time to think about what you're trying to accomplish. Figure 9-2 shows an article called "F-Shaped Pattern for Reading Web Content" from the Nielsen Norman Group. View the article at `www.nngroup.com/articles/f-shaped-pattern-reading-web-content/`.

This article, and others on the Nielsen Norman site, give you some underlying reasons for designing your web pages in ways that will promote usability and usefulness. See the sidebar, "Jakob Nielsen on web design" for some additional perspective.

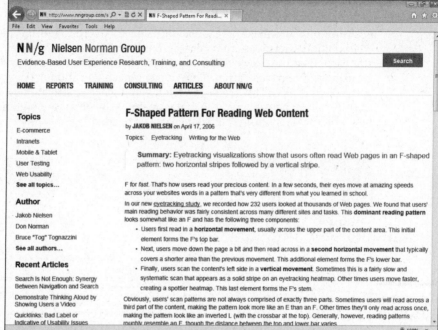

Figure 9-2:
People, as
a group,
read web
pages in a
very specific
way.

WARNING!

No one source on web design is likely to steer you entirely in the right direction. The article referred to here, for instance, doesn't even mention tablets or mobile phones, and these different devices have different needs. Users who consume most of their web pages on one device are also likely to change their expectations about what they see on the others. So it's up to you to read broadly, synthesize input, think, try things out, and own the final result.

Using CSS for Text Styling

As we describe in Chapter 8, HTML was supposed to be somewhat above pedestrian concerns such as how a page actually looked when displayed. Ideally, according to many HTML mavens, you were meant to specify meaning in HTML; the actual display format used to convey that meaning to the user would be decided on by the web browser, such as Microsoft Internet Explorer or Apple's Safari. The display format chosen by the browser would also reflect the specific device in use.

This approach was only really practical when a web page was made up of one long, single flow of text, with no left-hand column for, say, navigation, and no right-hand column for, say, related articles or advertising. As soon as you wanted to go to even a simple two- or three-column format, the original intention of HTML broke down.

CSS, though, actually allows you to use HTML in something like the way that the purists originally intended. Because CSS not only allows you to specify the display format: It actually allows you to address magazine-type concerns such as the look of your text and the layout of a page, sometimes down to the pixel level.

In Chapter 8, we introduce basic HTML. However, when using CSS with HTML, you use HTML differently.

A lot of things which were only added to HTML several years into its development, such as adding a specific font, are taken right back out. Instead, you define the look of common HTML tags in CSS.

Here's an example:

```
body {...
          font-size: 14px;
...}
```

These statements define text within the body of a web page to have a default size of 14 pixels. This works well on most devices. However, you might want to have different style sheets for most devices, which might have different default sizes for body text.

You can also define the look for established HTML tags such as headers and paragraphs. In addition, you can use new names for tags in your HTML file, such as `.editornote`, and then define them in CSS.

`Editornote` is a class, a kind of subset of an established tag such as the paragraph tag. In HTML, you define a paragraph of a given class as follows:

```
<p id="editornote"> ... </p>
```

Then, in CSS, you have to define what `editornote` means, or it will be undefined:

```
p {
.editornote font-weight: bold;
}
```

Here are some other CSS attributes that you can use for text styles:

- ✔ `font-family`: What's normally called the font, such as Courier or Times New Roman.

- ✔ `font-style`: Usually just italic or normal.

- ✔ `font-weight`: Usually just bold or normal.

- ✔ `font-size`: From xx-small through x-small, small, medium, large, x-large, and through to xx-large.

- ✔ `text-align`: Choose left, right, center, or justify.

As Humpty Dumpty said in *Alice in Wonderland,* "Words mean what I want them to mean." When talking about text on the web, be aware that words are used differently in CSS than in normal life. For instance, a font's style would commonly be assumed to include the options italic, bold, and underline; however, in CSS, the `font-style` attribute usually refers only to italicizing, whereas `font-weight` is the attribute for bold.

Figure 9-3 shows an explanation of how to style text with CSS. See this page for details on specific CSS attributes: www.w3.org/community/webed/wiki/Text_styling_with_CSS.

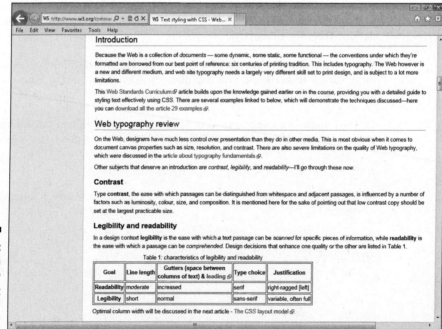

Figure 9-3:
You can learn how to style text with CSS from w3.org.

Jakob Nielsen on web design

One of the best resources for any web developer is Jakob Nielsen's articles on web design, which cover a period of more than 15 years, continuing through this writing.

From very early on, Nielsen addressed basic usability concerns such as the poor resolution of computer screens; the importance of consistency to users; and where users really look when presented with a web page. Nielsen's blog, Alertbox, was famously at the web address www.useit.com for many years.

In recent years, Nielsen teamed up with Don Nelson, once a famous manager at Apple, and Bruce Tognazzini, the founder of Apple's Human Interface Group, to form the Nielsen Norman Group. The site www.nngroup.com now hosts Nielsen's past and current columns.

The site is an intriguing mix of old and new. Check out the Most Popular section under the Articles header. At this writing, the top three articles are "Usability 101: Introduction to Usability, from 2012," "Top 10 Mistakes in Web Design," from 2011, and "How People Read on the Web," from 1997. Despite their varying ages, all these articles — and many others on the site — are still just about required reading today.

However, Nielsen and his colleagues are great scolds, but not always good examples. The www.useit.com site was famously one of the ugliest-looking popular sites on the web for years. Learn from Nielsen and company, but incorporate others' recommendations and your own ideas on best practices as well.

Using CSS for Layout

In the 1990s, as the web grew, web designers became accustomed to using HTML tables for page layout — that is, getting the overall structure of the page right.

For example, a common page layout for the web is a three-column layout, with navigation in a narrow column on the left, the main content or article in a wide column in the middle, and advertising and "related content"-type sections in a narrow column on the right. This kind of layout was implemented as three separate tables within one overarching table that positioned them relative to each other. (People had lively debates about topics such as whether you could do without the overarching table.)

As CSS matured in the late 1990s and early 2000s, it became possible to use it reliably for page layout. To contrast this with the use of HTML tables, such layout is frequently called *tableless layout* for the web.

In 2002, the World Wide Web Consortium published a how-to on "tableless layout," shown in Figure 9-4. This is a good introduction to the topic. Check it out at www.w3.org/2002/03/csslayout-howto.

Figure 9-4:
The World
Wide Web
Consortium
will show
you how to
use CSS for
a web page
layout.

At the time, these layouts only worked with the latest and greatest browser versions because the development of CSS into a tool that could handle the demands of complex web page layouts was a slow and messy process, marked by controversy and some degree of game-playing among major players such as Microsoft and Netscape, which by that time was owned by AOL Time Warner.

Tableless layout and *tableless layout* are good search terms to use if you want to find introductory articles on how to use CSS for page layouts.

Here's a brief overview of some major CSS elements used for page layout:

✔ The `<div>` and `</div>` tag pair mark out an element — a block of text and, potentially, graphics — so it can have specific layout applied to that element directly.

✔ The `<span>` and `</span>` tag pair mark out an area within a paragraph that has specific formatting applied to it, such as italics or a different text color.

✔ Within the `<div>` or `<span>` tag, the display attribute can be set to none to hide content, set to list-item to display an item in a list, and so on.

you always have the option to make JavaScript expertise your main calling card as a web developer.

JavaScript is an interpreted programming language, which means you can write it into an HTML file, and it will be interpreted and executed as the web page loads. (Almost all web browsers contain code, called a *parser,* to execute JavaScript.) You can use various techniques to have some JavaScript only be interpreted and executed after the main page has loaded and some other JavaScript has already executed.

The advantage of JavaScript is that it puts computing power into your actual web page. Usually, if the user is looking at, and responding to, a web page such as a form, you can't do anything with the form's content — such as check it — until the user submits the entire form. JavaScript can shortcut this process, checking content as the user enters it.

JavaScript can control animations in a page or change what appears depending on what the user mouses over. Use it in combination with HTML and CSS. Also in combination with back-end code, JavaScript can check the content of an entry field to make sure it's correct, but you should use back-end code to update a database with the information that's entered.

JavaScript can be put between the `<script>` and `</script>` tags in a web page, or put in a separate JavaScript file that ends with .src, or both. Here's the code to reference an external JavaScript file and to put up an alert if the browser executing the HTML code in the web page can't process JavaScript:

```
<script type="text/javascript" src="yourscript.js">
        alert("If you are seeing this message then this
        browser does not support JavaScript.")
        </script>
```

If you keep JavaScript code in an external file, you can share it among numerous web pages. Browsers cache the file, so it won't need to be downloaded multiple times. And you can more quickly and easily find and fix problems within your JavaScript.

You can also put your JavaScript code into multiple files and load only the ones you need in each of your web pages.

JavaScript is insecure, and anyone who can access a web page can access all the JavaScript code in it. So don't use it for encryption or security because someone will be able to reverse-engineer anything you do simply by looking at your web pages.

JavaScript can change the HTML and CSS contents of your web page. The following JavaScript puts text and a clickable button on a web page:

```
<!DOCTYPE html>
<html>
<body>

<h1>Clickable Button in JavaScript</h1>

<p id="test">JavaScript can change the style of an HTML
        element.</p>

<script>
function testFunction() {
    var x = document.getElementById("test");
    x.style.fontSize = "40px";
    x.style.color = "blue";
}
</script>

<button type="button" onclick="testFunction()">Click
        Here!</button>

</body>
</html>
```

Google completes the web equation

Finding web pages is such a huge element of web use that you should include searchability in all your web development decisions. For instance, you might have a web page with a popular search term used in the middle of the page. Consider moving the term to the top of the page to improve the page's ranking in web searches and spare the user from having to struggle to find the term after they've arrived at your web page.

Search engine optimization (SEO) is becoming a huge part of the process of creating and updating web pages. You want your page to rank high on searches for relevant terms, and this is often a huge challenge. High search-engine rankings on popular terms are so valuable that companies spend millions of dollars trying to improve their position in search.

Because SEO is such a widely practiced art, Google — by far the leader in search — and other search engines, such as Microsoft's Bing,

are constantly changing their algorithms as to what page content will "work" to move pages up or down in the rankings. So if this area is important to you, plan to study hard to learn the basics, and then spend a lot of time keeping up with the latest news as things change.

There are, though, a few basic principles you can safely follow over time. Pick five to seven keywords or phrases that you want to be "findable" on, and use those exact keywords or phrases — not synonyms or variations — repeatedly in your website. Use your keywords in page titles, headers, image captions, the first 50 words of a page, in META tags, and in page URLs, with the keyword set off by dashes.

These tips will be a good foundation for reasonably good search results on their own, and also a good starting point for much more detailed work if you want to get into the dark arts of SEO as a part-time or full-time occupation.

One of the most common uses of JavaScript is for error-checking. You can allow the user to type in a value, and then use JavaScript to parse the value and make sure it make sense. For instance, you can ask users for their phone number, and then make sure that what they enter fits the profile of a valid phone number.

If you need more information about JavaScript, start with the JavaScript tutorials at W3. Here's the introductory one, shown in Figure 9-6: `www.w3.org/community/webed/wiki/Category:Tutorials`.

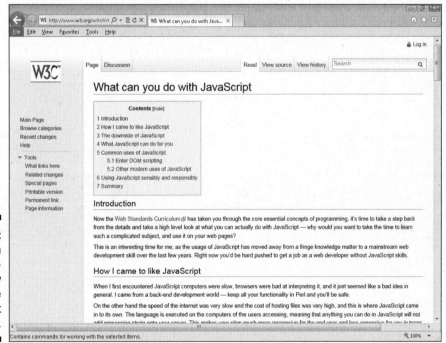

Figure 9-6: You can start learning how to use JavaScript here.

Chapter 10

Tracing the Web Development Life Cycle

. . . .

In This Chapter

▶ How HTML, CSS, and JavaScript work together

▶ Using CSS for text styling

▶ Using CSS for positioning text and graphics

▶ Designing web pages with WordPress

▶ Using JavaScript in web pages

. . . .

*W*eb development has advanced hugely since its initial heyday in the late 1990s. At the time, there was a huge gold rush to stake out space in the online world — and in the minds of web users — for new business ideas. Pets.com, the Mining Company (now About.com), Facebook, oDesk (for freelancers), and AltaVista (once a famous search engine) were all big names, and all of them but Facebook are now defunct or rebranded or merged into some other company.

Now, you can spend an entire career in web development without ever actually starting a new website. A lot of the major players in the online world are already in place, so extending, expanding, improving, and updating existing sites can consume all the efforts of large web teams.

This can be misleading because it's hard to fully understand the reasons that people do what they do on the web if you've never gone through the birth and successful launch of a website — from initial idea, through prototyping and development, to launch and getting more and more users — yourself.

Most web developers regularly work on new features, and new parts of a site, but it's not the same thing as taking on (and downing) the whole enchilada.

Many web developers also work on weblike things, rather than true websites: intranet sites, where the audience is internal; apps, many of which are very weblike (or are even mobile device alternatives for the website that people use on computers — and on mobile devices too); and software that has a weblike, or an actual web interface.

In fact, one of the major reasons for creating and maintaining your own portfolio site, as described in Chapter 16, is just to have the excitement and insight that come from actually bringing your own ideas to life online within a fully developed, and truly new, website.

In this chapter, we describe the web development life cycle, from start to finish. Use the description here to recognize where your projects are in the overall life cycle, and to get a better idea of just what you really need to do to help make them succeed.

Seeing How a Website Gets Started

How does a website get started?

A website gets started to accomplish some goal, or set of goals. Being clear about what you want a website (or any web development project) to accomplish is vital to succeeding, or being able to know whether you're succeeding.

Like other projects that organizations — and individual people — undertake, people often fail to think rigorously about why they create a website. This lack of rigor often causes problems, or even failure, for the entire life of the site.

To gain true clarity when starting a website, or other web development project, ask yourself a radical question: What's going to be different because I did this project?

That is, forget about the project itself. What are the important things that will change? Create a list, and then stack-rank it: Put the most important goals first.

Here's an example of goals for a website project, a stack-ranked list of the things that will change if someone starts a website giving news about solar energy projects — and it's at least somewhat successful:

1. More solar energy projects will get built, so more renewable energy will be used — and less fossil fuel will be burned.

2. Fewer mistakes will be made in building solar energy projects, so they'll be more profitable. Perhaps some injuries or even deaths will be avoided.

3. The founders and the team will be able to make a living doing something they enjoy, so they'll do a good job, there will be less turnover, and the successful business can grow and do more of 1 and 2.

Always stack-rank your list of goals. If making money is your number one goal, that's fine; putting it at the top of the list will help you succeed in your goal.

Note that this is not a list *of what the website will accomplish.* Also notice that it has no details *about the website itself.*

Instead, it's a list of what you're trying to accomplish by creating the website. The website details will be determined by whether they help accomplish the goals.

You should create a list like this for every website project and keep referring to it constantly throughout the project. The clarity you develop as a result will save you endless amounts of time, money, and hassle.

This process usually has some very valuable side effects, including

✔ **Focusing on non-web pieces of a project:** When all you have at hand is a hammer, such as an expert web-development team, everything looks like a nail. Focusing on the effects that you want a site to have helps you figure out if there are things that you need, in addition to the website, to accomplish your goals. (For instance, writing a book might also help better solar projects get built — and you can promote the book on the website.)

✔ **Shooting down useless ideas:** People always want to use the latest and greatest technology in their projects. This can have strong impact — but can also cost a lot of time and money. By having your goals in front of you, you only use the newest tech when it helps you accomplish what you really want to do.

✔ **Keeping the site coherent and focused:** Websites are protean — they can grow and change in a million different directions. By only adding features that contribute to core goals, you help users know just what they can get from your website and keep them coming back for more.

✔ **Keeping meetings short:** When every idea is equally valuable, you can spend endless hours discussing them. When you have clear goals, the most useful ones *for your specific purposes* float to the top.

There's a lot of advice on website design and project management in general that includes advice about focusing. However, we think it's so important that we're devoting this whole section to it — and urging you to keep it at the top of your mind at all times.

Figure 10-1 shows some useful website advice from the U.S. Government's Small Business Administration. Note that "figuring out what you want to do and defining your niche" is right at the top of the list.

You'll often hear references to the "look and feel" or the "functionality" of a website. What are these capabilities, and how do they fit together? We describe these pieces here, to help you better understand how you can play your part.

Figure 10-1:
The U.S. Government's Small Business Administration tells you to stay focused and more.

Google's clear thinking

When Google launched as a search engine, it had a simple goal: to be the world's best search engine. Making money from being the world's best search engine would come along later.

Google's founders and leaders rigorously defined what "world's best" meant in their own minds, and then asked users, over and over, what it meant for them as well.

One key element of "world's best" was speed. They worried about tiny fractions of a second in loading the Google home page, the time it took the user to find the search engine box, and scanning and choosing from among various options. All made a difference in whether users were getting the "best" results from the website.

That's why Google's home page is so simple, with tons of "wasted" white space surrounding the Google logo and the search box in the

middle. The search box has only two options. If you type in a search term, and then press Enter, as most people do, you get the first option: a Google search of the entire web for the best results.

If you type in a search term and then click the button labeled I'm Feeling Lucky, you go straight to the top-ranked result that Google turns up.

The white space is not wasted, of course. It has a positive function, in that it actually helps draw the user's eyes to the Google logo and the search box in the middle. And it has a negative function — everything that isn't in that white space is another example of Google refusing to distract users from their number one purpose in visiting the Google search page.

In more than a decade of existence, the core of the Google home page hasn't changed much, and Google continues to be one of the world's most valuable and best-known companies.

Considering the Look and Feel

The number one cause for website projects getting delayed or even canceled, in our experience, is dissatisfaction from senior executives about the "look and feel" of a website. It's worth understanding this better so that you focus on it at the beginning of a project, when it can still be fixed, rather than suffering over it at the end of a project, when it's too late.

Even when executives see mock-ups early, as they usually do, the look changes in many ways as implementation proceeds. Also, an executive getting asked to approve the launch of a website is facing a much bigger decision than just green-lighting a project at the beginning. They can, and do, hold the nearly final result to a much higher standard.

The look and feel of a website is somewhat ineffable — "incapable of being expressed in words," according to *Merriam-Webster* dictionary — but we're going to try anyway.

HTML and CSS drive the look

In terms of technologies used, HTML and CSS drive the look of a website. Being able to quickly tweak a site design, or a live site, to meet the requirements of a stakeholder or customer is one of the distinguishing capabilities of a web designer. Being expert in HTML and CSS, and how they're used in your organization, enables you to do this.

One of the key goals to pursue across a big website, or across multiple websites run by one organization, is consistency. CSS, in particular, is a big boon for consistency. Say you want to use a different font for top-level headings across your site or sites. In the past, you would have had to tweak every page on the site by hand. Now, just change one or a few style definitions in CSS, and you're done.

Of course, doing your website and template design to support this kind of flexibility is a job in itself — especially when you are working on a database-driven website and the actual pages that are displayed are assembled and served on the fly. If you can master these skills, however, you become a very valuable part of the web team indeed.

You got the look

The look of a website is produced by a number of elements: the colors used, singly and in combination; the layout of major elements of each web page like the header, left and right rails, and footer; the amount of white space; the fonts used and how they work (or don't work) together; and all the other visual elements combined.

Many website demonstrations for senior executives are actually over in a fraction of a second, even if they actually go on for hours. That's because the senior executive doesn't like the look of the website at very first glance. They may or may not know this themselves, and they may or may not tell you directly that it's a problem. But the project, in its current incarnation, is probably doomed if senior executives don't like the look.

This is a huge problem because the look of the site actually ends up determining, and being determined by, a myriad of things about how the site looks and works. There are some combinations of text and graphics, for instance, that just won't fit well on a page together if the central content column is narrow. Articles that seem too long when a large font size and a narrow central column is used may look just fine with a smaller font size or a wider central column.

The person in charge of the website project is usually responsible for the look. That's why graphic designers are so often in charge of these projects, even if other skill areas might seem more important — and why designers who can code well enough to implement their own ideas, or competently lead others in implementing them, are so valuable.

Other team members also have a lot of input into the look of a site, both in the initial design process up front and in the many "small" implementation decisions that end up determining how the planned-for look really appears on the actual site. This tends to make the look better — but also results in widespread disappointment, even shock, if senior executives question or even reject it late in the game.

There are three major things you can do to prevent senior executives from killing your projects, or forcing a painful major revamp, late in the game:

1. **Get senior executives involved in choosing the look up front.** Develop options for their approval and present them. Implement the choice enthusiastically and without major changes, unless you get approval up front for the changes as well.

2. **Keep showing the look to senior executives as the project progresses.** Remind people who will sign off on the project what they've already approved. Get any negative feedback in early, while you can still act on it.

3. **Gather evidence that people exposed to the project like the look.** Ask everyone who tries the website what he thinks of the look. Record the comments. Tweak things where needed. Present the feedback you get to executives as part of project updates, and again in approval meetings late in the game.

Every time you take one of these steps, you make it more likely that the website will have a look that executives like, and you also build trust in your own judgment, openness to criticism, and willingness to adjust. All these factors make it more likely that you'll be able to get your project over the finish line without being ordered to start over — and that you'll be able to recover quickly if you are.

To understand how the goals of a website can be implemented in its look, consider the websites shown in Figure 10-2, the U.S. Department of Defense (or "the Pentagon," which was once called the Department of War); Figure 10-3, the U.S. State Department (as close as the U.S. has to a "Department of Peace"); and Figure 10-4, the U.S. Department of Agriculture (which could be called the "Department of Food").

Figure 10-2:
The
Pentagon
looks like
it's present-
ing just
the facts,
ma'am.

Figure 10-3:
The State
Department
website has
an open
and inviting
layout.

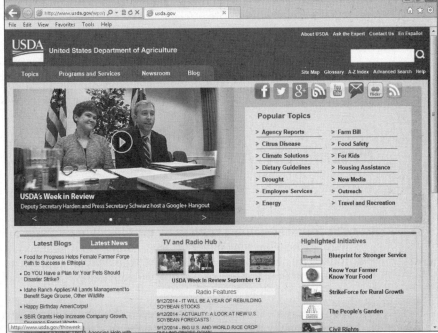

Figure 10-4: The Department of Agriculture website has a friendly look, but with lots of information per square inch.

"I can't believe they just did that"

Perhaps the single biggest tale of woe for web designers is having projects sent back for a redesign late in the game. This often happens based on the gut feel of one or a few executives that they don't like the site they're being shown. It drives project leaders and members crazy because it ignores schedule, cost, project interdependencies, and the hard work, good taste, and good judgment of the people doing the actual work.

Are executives right to do this kind of thing? Well, it's actually their job. They can't let things go outside "the building" — that is, be shown to lots of outsiders — that don't reflect well on their organization. This function of senior executives is sometimes described as being the "brand guardian" or "brand custodian."

Unfortunately, this function is not well-understood and not widely discussed. Conflicts often arise over the extent to which senior executives can and should perform this function. Senior executives often talk about their "gut feel," and the usual thought-but-not-spoken-aloud response of team members is, "You're an idiot."

The late Steve Jobs was famous for implementing strict imperatives on design at Apple. He was also famous for being, not to put too fine a point on it, a jerk, and for behavior toward subordinates that bordered on verbal abuse. Under Jobs, Apple was also widely known for secrecy that was said to border on the paranoid.

So we don't yet have easy ways of discussing design decisions and the thought process that goes into them. Managing this ineffability elegantly is one of the most important skills in leading web project teams.

Each website uses an image clearly relating to its mission. And each has aspects that somewhat fit the public image of the department involved — the Pentagon's is dense and seemingly factual; the State Department's is more open and inviting; the Agriculture Department's is somewhere in-between.

Consider writing down some ideas about how changes to the web design and content for each government department could better reflect its mission and role.

Getting the feel right

The "feel" part of the "look and feel" of a website has a couple of different meanings:

- **The feel of something implied by the look:** When we look at things, we imagine what they might be like to touch, so a certain degree of touch-type feeling goes with looking. A design can look warm, smooth, cool — all descriptions of how the website design might feel if we could somehow touch it.

- **The feelings — emotions — inspired by a visual design:** Design affects us emotionally, although everyone's reaction is different, and the same person's reaction can vary at different times.

- **How it feels to use the website:** The process of moving around and accomplishing tasks on a website can feel smooth and easy, difficult, or in-between.

These different meanings of "feel" explain a few things:

- A website can have a "feel" before you "touch" it by trying to use it.

- The overall "feel" of a website changes as you use it, as you add that kind of "feel" information to the part that you get just from looking at the design.

- Different people can mean completely different things when they talk about the "feel," or the "look and feel," of a website.

Whereas the "look" part of a website is the responsibility of the project head, who usually has a graphic design background, the interactive parts of the "feel" of a website can be the responsibility of several different people. This can include usability people; front-end programmers; interaction designers; and graphic designers.

In a well-run team, everyone gives opinions on everything, but the ongoing responsibility for each aspect of the website is also clear.

Bringing the pieces together, a well-run organization will usually have standards for the look and feel of all its websites, external and internally focused. The standards might be applied loosely for low-use, short-term, and internal websites — which are often cobbled together from existing pieces anyway — but applied more strictly for large, highly visible projects and more novel ones.

Figure 10-5 shows the look and feel standards for the U.S. Environmental Protection Agency (EPA). These standards are such a focus for the EPA that they have a name, One EPA Web. Notice the strong wording used — "complying" and "requirement" for using the standard.

Because big projects often have a wide scope and involve a lot of new work, you may go into the project thinking that there's a lot of room for creativity. However, these big projects also get the attention of gatekeepers: people who believe that organizational standards are very important. (And often the same people who created and maintain those selfsame standards.) So be ready to be creative on new projects, but to respect and improve, rather than replace, your organization's standards as you do so.

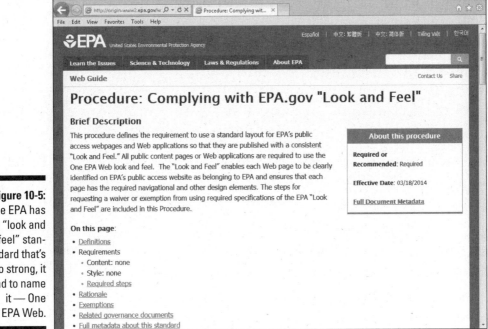

Figure 10-5:
The EPA has a "look and feel" standard that's so strong, it had to name it — One EPA Web.

Chapter 11

Implementing and Shipping a Site

*T*here's a famous phrase in Silicon Valley lore that applies strongly to web development. It's just two words: "Winners ship."

This phrase was quoted in an article about Apple being slow to ship a version of its iOS software which runs iPhones and iPads. The version was iOS 7 and it finally shipped in May 2013, shortly after the passing of Steve Jobs.

The article praised Jon Ivey, head of design at Apple, for cleaning up the look of iOS 7 – but it also said, "Winners ship product, and Apple really can't afford a delay right now."

The phrase "winners ship" came from the old days where the main action in technology was in hardware and packaged software. If you're old enough, you'll remember buying all your software off the shelf, in boxes — and later using early websites like Egghead.com to have boxed software shipped to you.

And that's where "winners ship" came from. You had to stop working on the hardware or software in question, let it go through final QA, fix as many urgent bugs as you could in a day or two, and then it would go to production. Literal production: Machines would manufacture hardware, or copy floppy disks and print packaging for software, and at some point the postal service would come and start delivering packages to customers.

Websites, of course, are ephemeral — nothing but bits. So "shipping" just means letting the public get access to something that you've had online, in a staging site, for days or weeks before the launch date.

But "winners ship" still applies. The greatest website in the world can't really be great if it goes out too late, costing everyone involved money and frustration. You have to think about the ship date from Day 1 of the project to have a snowball's chance in Hades of actually meeting the desired date.

In order for you to do a good job as a web developer, you need to understand the entire life cycle of website development — not just what you do, but what everyone does. This will help you understand others' issues and needs. It will also help you know when it's the right time to introduce a brilliant new idea — and when it's best to just put the blinders on and "get it done."

In this chapter, we describe how the process of "shipping" a website works, and how different job descriptions and roles in web development work together to make it happen.

For clarity, we talk about projects where a new website is being developed. However, most website projects today are updates, rather than "greenfield" new development. These projects still fit within the overall development life cycle, but some parts are shortened because the website already exists. Use this chapter as a model for all kinds of projects.

Phase 1: Grokking User Needs

The science fiction author Robert Heinlein coined the term *grok* in his 1961 science fiction novel, *Stranger in a Strange Land.* The term is used pretty regularly in web development.

To *grok* something means to understand it very deeply and completely — not just intellectually, but emotionally as well. The reason that we talk about grokking user needs in web design is that developers need to be able to predict how the user will react to different designs and different ways of interacting with the site.

To do this properly, developers need to temporarily put themselves completely in the place of the user, which is famously difficult. So a lot of techniques are used to help developers understand user needs.

The best method is to make a developer watch while a user tries to accomplish tasks on the developer's website. The developer is isolated from the user and not allowed to interact with him and her. Developers have been known to cry in frustration while "stupid" users clicked the wrong link, entered wrong information, or failed to read seemingly obvious instructions.

Figure 11-1 shows a web page about remote testing from the `usability.gov` website. In remote testing, you get to watch how someone uses your site without being in the same room with him. This helps you concentrate on what the user is doing and not try to call out to him that he's doing it wrong.

Figure 11-1:
Remote testing is a useful — and relatively inexpensive — way to get useful feedback on your website project.

Short of this, developers need to be good at getting quick feedback from other team members, work colleagues, even friends who are not on the project. They also need to be good at watching themselves as they use websites designed by others, noticing what is and isn't helpful as they move through a site.

In a well-resourced and well-run project, there are several steps where outside input is sought and used. It's much cheaper to get needed feedback early in a project than after the website launches. But many organizations take the more expensive approach.

Understanding user needs is the job of everyone on the project. However, there are usually one or two people on a project who take on the role of "voice of the user." If this is you, consider moving into usability or project management. If you're already the project manager, either develop this skill yourself, or cultivate and encourage people who have it most strongly.

Cognitive dissonance and website success

There's an old saying that "you only get one chance to make a first impression." This is very much true of websites, at every stage of design and development.

When people first meet, they form a strong first impression within just a few seconds — often, before the other person even speaks. The same is true for websites.

Look and feel, as described in the preceding chapter, is a big part of this; so is interaction. And the cues that people use to form their opinions are often not even things they are conscious of.

No matter what your job, learn to see your own work from the user's point of view. Fix things, even if they "work" from a technical point of view, but could be confusing for some or all users. If you can do this consistently, your work will be a source of pleasure to all your colleagues, and to users as well. If you can't, a lot of the things that need to be fixed, during user testing and after a site ships, will end up being on you.

To further help avoid problems, early testing with small numbers of users is critical. If you launch a website and it gets a poor reception, early users form a nearly permanent impression. Bad news travels fast, so people who haven't even used the website get the same bad impression as well.

Early testing keeps any poor reactions to a small group of people who know that the website is in test mode. By improving the site before launch, the initial impression of the first users of the real site becomes positive. Users stay on the site longer, do more with it, buy more stuff (if it's an e-commerce site). They tell others, who then come to the website expecting good things, and a positive cycle develops.

Insist on user testing on your projects. If you don't get it, do informal user testing yourself. Push hard to have the feedback you get implemented as changes to the site. If you do all this, your projects will be much more successful — and so will you.

Phase 2: Developing the Look and Feel

In Chapter 10, we describe the look and feel of a website as "ineffable" — that is, almost impossible to put into words. But words are all we have to tell you about how to design the look and feel of your website, so we'll do our best.

As with user needs, everyone on a project can and should contribute to getting the look and feel right. Your career will take off if the websites you work on have an attractive look and feel and are easy to use; it may well languish if there are problems in these areas. This is true whether these areas are, strictly speaking, your job or not.

Designers are the ones who take the heat directly, or get the credit, for the look and feel of a site. However, everyone on the project benefits when things go well, and looks bad when they don't.

Getting the look and feel right is a challenging process, but here are a few tips and tricks to help:

- ✔ **Pick a target audience.** Identify the most important target audience for your site. Always make sure that the decisions you are making will work for that target audience. Then pick a couple of secondary audiences and consider their needs as well.

- ✔ **Develop personas.** Personas are fictional people you describe in detail, representing imaginary users of your website. Describe several personas in detail. Then figure out what that user will want and need from your website.

- ✔ **Look at sites that are popular with your target audiences.** For each of your target audiences, and each of the personas you create, identify sites that are popular with that group. Then analyze the sites for their look and feel, the functionality they support, and how the functionality is implemented. If you want to do something that doesn't fit these models, be ready to explain why.

- ✔ **Figure out which devices are popular with your target audiences.** Find out how much they use computers versus tablets versus smartphones, and whether they favor apps or websites, when they have a choice. Mac or Windows? iOS or Android? These questions will serve as gateways into your users' circumstances and needs.

- ✔ **Find words to describe your chosen look and feel.** Pick some words that describe what you're trying to achieve – "dense" versus "open", "fun" versus "serious." Then refer back to these word choices when it's time to make design decisions.

- ✔ **Think about apps and real-world tools.** In addition to the website, think about whether your organization will make some or all of the same information and functionality in an app. Also, how do people get the same information, or accomplish the same tasks, if they are proceeding in meat space (the real world), not using a computer or smartphone? How can each type of process be informed by the other?

Figure 11-2 shows U.S. Department of Energy standards for app development. Consider app development when planning your website.

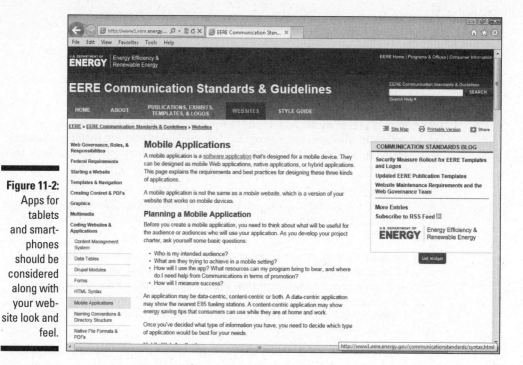

Figure 11-2:
Apps for
tablets
and smart-
phones
should be
considered
along with
your web-
site look and
feel.

Phase 3: Creating Content

Deciding on the content for a website is tough! There are so many things that people think should be on a site. It can be very difficult to decide.

If you're in content development for a site, you should make a point of knowing what's on competing websites and what's on similar websites, which might not compete directly with yours, but which are similar enough in purpose to set expectations in the user's mind.

For instance, new car and used car sites are more similar than different, and a user might easily go back and forth between them in a given session. For instance, new car sites tend to be glitzy and use advanced technologies like 3D look-arounds; used car sites tend to be simple, easily searchable databases and lists. There might be things that each could learn from the other. So look at both kinds when you work on one kind or the other.

No matter what your role on a web project, people will react positively if the "right stuff" is on the site and easy to access, and poorly if they can't find things that they need. So figure out for yourself what should be on the site and push to have it included.

The key is to think of users as coming to your website to accomplish tasks. This is obvious when you think of buying a product or getting a phone number. But getting needed information or entertaining yourself with something funny are also tasks.

So the core content of a website is whatever is needed to allow users to accomplish their desired tasks. This can include how-to information, articles, and more.

There's also a lot of supporting content on a website. This comes in two forms. The first is information that helps users accomplish tasks. The names of navigation links are supporting content of this type.

There is also information that everyone expects to be on a given type of site — such as a list of past press releases, with links, on an organization's main site. The way to get this done is to realize that this is task-oriented information too, provided for certain audiences. For instance, links to press releases are usually provided for journalists first. But they're also interesting to investors, analysts, and even some regular customers.

So meet needs that initially seem to be in the category, "because people expect it" — but think through who's using the information and why. You'll do a better job.

You can think of your website as a Christmas tree. Before you decorate the tree, it's just branches and pine needles. That's the basic structure of your site — navigation, tabs (major areas of the site), and links.

Then you add ornaments. The ornaments are the things users need to accomplish their tasks, and might include an article the user wants to read, a downloadable file, or the capability to buy a product. The ornaments need to be easy to get to by following the basic structure of the tree itself. They also have to be easy to find through search or from parts of the site that they're related to in some way.

An advanced use of content is to develop a content marketing strategy. This means using content, such as blog posts or downloadable reports, to get users to come to your website, and to keep them coming back over and over. Often, content marketers seek to engage customers by asking them to subscribe to an email list, attend an online webinar, or attend a real-world conference or showcase event. That way, when it's time to make a decision — such as, to buy a car, or make a donation to a charity — they buy the car your company makes, or donate to the non-profit organization that you work for.

So think all this through. Different stakeholders will tell you that "of course" you need this or that piece of content on the website. They're probably right, but it's your job to determine why that piece of content needs to be there. You also need to decide which content absolutely has to be there on launch day, and which can wait.

Figure 11-3 shows advice from the Small Business Administration on content marketing. There's much more out there — websites, books, and of course downloadable reports and articles. Consider content marketing as a kind of battery-powered ornament on the Christmas tree of your site that keeps attracting people to interact with it.

Figure 11-3:
The Small
Business
Administra-
tion
educates
people on
content
marketing.

Quick-and-dirty competitive analysis

Competitive analysis is the art and craft of finding out what your competitors are doing in a given area to help inform what you should consider doing.

For instance, say you're doing a shopping website that wants to out-Amazon Amazon.com for, say, sales of warm, fuzzy slippers. You know that your users are likely to be experienced Amazon.com users, that you will have to attract them to your site instead of Amazon, that they're likely to go to Amazon to compare products that

are available and at what prices, and that you'll lose them to Amazon forever if you mess up. You probably want to include a few shoe-oriented or slipper-oriented sites as well.

So how do you do a quick-and-dirty competitive analysis? Easy. Just make a checklist and comparison table of all the relevant features in the competing sites. Don't include really basic stuff like "Has a URL." But you might do quick, informal ratings of how well-known or catchy the site's URL is.

Include items such as assessments of the breadth of product range, the ease of searching, prices (lower or higher than others, on average), and any fun factor in using a site.

Rate these items as dispassionately as you can. For instance, Amazon is very comprehensive, which is a bit scary from a competitive point of view. However, many of its non-book categories are poorly structured and organized. A search for a specialty term such as "mukluks" might turn up slippers, a book, a video, and memorabilia from an obscure Canadian minor-league hockey team.

This isn't actually helpful if you want the kind of slippers that are called "mukluks." This is an area where your site can have an advantage.

Bring all the comparisons together into a single big table. Identify the must-have, nice-to-have, and truly optional features and capabilities your site needs. Discuss your results across the whole team, and with stakeholders as well.

This kind of comparison can save enormous amounts of time and effort, both in doing the right things, and in not doing the wrong things. For instance, if a competitor isn't supporting virtual reality goggle views of mukluks, maybe you don't need it in Version 1.0 either. Or, conversely, maybe it's your star feature. Competitive analysis makes you think about these things carefully, and forces you to make choices up front — which saves time and effort during the project.

Phase 4: Developing Functionality

Website functionality will drive you nuts. Developing functionality is really important, and really hard.

Website functionality is, strictly speaking, the concern of project management and software developers first, and everyone else second. However, it's dramatically obvious when functionality on a website doesn't work well, and a real pleasure when it does.

As a software developer, try to get stuff working well before you declare yourself done. Consider asking friends or family to poke at it as you go along. They can ask "obvious" questions that you might have missed, and that will make your work better. Then your project colleagues, and ultimately your end users, will really appreciate that the functionality you create works the way they expect it to, right from the start.

Same for project managers — work closely with developers and get stuff working well before you inflict it on other colleagues and internal testers, let alone real users.

Everyone on the team should pitch in. "If you see something, say something." It's not always fun to tell people that their stuff just doesn't work, or even just that it can use improvement, but it's a vital role on any web development team.

What does "website functionality" even mean? It's probably clearest in the case of an e-commerce site. Amazon.com's One-Click buying is a clear example of website functionality. So much so that Amazon claims patent protection for this important feature.

But there are all sorts of things you might like on your website. Forms so users can ask for information easily. The capability to search the site, or articles, or bug reports. Pop-up windows with brief help information or definitions of terms. And on and on.

Each piece of web functionality that you want added to your site is usually a project of its own. For some reason, there's an immense temptation to put off starting on web functionality until late in a web development project. On a three-month project, people wait until six weeks before launch — or four weeks before launch — to start on a six-week project to add functionality.

This is, of course, is mildly insane. It's very rare indeed that your six-week project really only takes six weeks. Functionality is often able to be worked on separately from other aspects of the website, such as regular update cycles. So as soon as you determine that a piece of functionality is the next most important thing to add to your website, start working on it. Don't stop until you're done.

Web functionality is usually implemented by engineers — some combination of front-end engineers for the user-facing part, back-end engineers to interface with databases and other existing systems, and perhaps also plain old software engineers (not web-specific) to handle complicated functionality. But project managers, designers, usability people, and just about the entire development team should also be involved.

Figure 11-4 shows an online article about the FBI adding new functionality to its online stolen art database. Better website functionality can make a big difference in all sorts of important things. Take it seriously, and your career will blossom.

Manage website functionality changes separately from changes in navigation, content, and design. Website functionality projects are real software development projects, with all the headaches which that implies. (Including the famous dictum, of Mythical Man-Month fame, which says that half of all software projects fail.)

If you haven't read *The Mythical Man-Month* by Frederick P. Brooks (Addison-Wesley, 1995), stop what you're doing and read it right now. It's called "the classic book on the human aspects of software engineering" for a reason. Then go read *The Soul of a New Machine* by Tracy Kidder (Little, Brown & Co., 1981). It's the ultimate story of a technology development project, including the famous "death march" that often occurs in the weeks and months before a product (or website) ship date. After you read each of these books, take a day or two off and think about what you've read. You'll be better at everything you do in technology for the rest of your career as a result. And you'll have something very valuable to talk about with other cognoscenti.

More features, fewer bugs, on time: Choose two

One of the most educational experiences one of us (Smith) ever had was product-managing the release of part of Apple's QuickTime suite of software back in the 1990s. MacWorld Expo was coming up, and the new software had to be ready.

There is a famous saying about product development in Silicon Valley that goes something like this: For product development, you absolutely need three things: All the features you specify; a small, acceptable, and minimal number of bugs; and to meet your ship date. But even if you're really lucky, and you have a great team, and you do everything right, at the very most you'll get two of those three things.

A week before MacWorld, our testing manager told me a stark truth: We either had to pull a feature, or delay shipping until after MacWorld. (Notice that he didn't offer the option of shipping with an unacceptable number of bugs.)

I went over the problem with him carefully, but he was right. We pulled a feature. Unfortunately, this was the main user-visible feature for this release; the remaining "features" were bug fixes and architectural improvements for the future, plus better documentation. Important, but hardly earthshaking.

Luckily, though, we did have partnerships to announce (and the "hidden" features that remained in the release were important to those partners). So we went ahead with the MacWorld launch. It went very well indeed. And we added the missing functionality soon after launch.

But keep this maxim in mind when you are working on a website project: more features; fewer bugs; meeting the ship date. Pick two.

Phase 5: Creating the Test Site

A test website is a thing of beauty. If you are on a website project where you create a test site, test it with users, and incorporate the feedback, you're probably on a well-run project.

In all too many web projects, the test site part ends up getting skipped — or never put in the schedule in the first place. The live site at the end of the project ends up serving as the test site. The public gets to use a crappy site, and fixes only happen after many people get a bad impression of your organization from the under-tested website's problems and the resulting bad publicity.

So, as you rise into project management — or just get a reputation as a tetchy and demanding team member — part of your to-do list is to see that test sites get created; get tested by real users; and that the feedback gets incorporated into the site on this development cycle, not the next one.

This is not easy, given the pressures involved. But it's also the mark of professionals.

No matter what your role on the team, take test sites seriously. Of course they're not "live." But a test site is your best chance to help make sure the live site shines from the minute people start using it. Pay attention and contribute strongly.

One of the things that you can test in the test-site phase is the accessibility of your site — how usable it is to people with various kinds of disabilities, such as vision impairment or blindness.

You may not be able to make your site fully accessible overnight. But if you can improve accessibility with each release, you'll soon have an unusually accessible website.

Figure 11-5 shows a useful initial list of website testing tools. To access this list, visit `www.w3.org/WAI/ER/tools/complete`.

Accessibility might seem arcane if you don't personally know any disabled web users, or if deadline pressure is making you buggy. But accessibility is not only valuable in its own right, and it's not just required by law in many jurisdictions. It's also the best way to make your site more usable for everyone. Pay attention to accessibility and usability together, and the websites you develop will become remarkably easy to use.

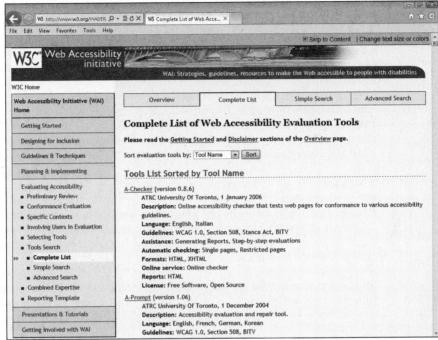

Figure 11-5:
Accessibility
testing tools
help you
get accessi-
bility — and
usability —
right.

Why don't people always do test sites?

It takes considerable discipline to plan, implement, deploy, and respond to feedback on a test site. Here's why: People want updates to websites (as well as other technology products) quickly. Say an executive asks for a feature. You tell her that it's going to take three months to get it.

To the executive, this sounds ridiculous. But you know better. Every time you open up the website for change, you need, say, a month for planning at the beginning, and then you do the work, and then you need, perhaps, another month for review and testing at the end. So, if you tell the executive it will take three months for a new feature, you have one month of precious implementation time in the middle.

And this is where the need to have a test site becomes a desire, a wish, or even a fantasy. It might take a couple of weeks, or more, to bring the test site up, get feedback, and implement changes that users suggest. Now you're telling that same executive that it will be four months to implement that new feature, if everyone involved is lucky — five or six months if not.

Many organizations don't have the guts for this. Some do. The ones that do separate feature development onto a separate track. Feature development is ongoing; features that are ready get integrated into the site the next time the website development window is open.

Complicated, right? But that's why top-notch web developers get paid the big bucks. Conversely, if you want to make the big bucks, learn to handle this kind of complexity. And learn to stand up to demanding executives.

Phase 6: Launching the Site

Launch time for a new or updated website is so worrisome — and so exciting. All of us in web development live for it, even if we have a hard time admitting it.

The development team is usually exhausted by this point and just wanting the *#&@&@# thing to get out the door. And everyone internally is bored with the new features, the new look, and the new functionality, which she may have been hearing about for a year by now.

That's why it's good, for every role on the team, to "muck in," as the Brits put it, at site launch time. Try to take a fresh look at the site. Check that links work. Proofread stuff. Try to break it. Then, when you do, tell your colleagues, in a positive manner. There are always going to be problems with a new site; fixing them fast, before many people see them, is something the best people do as a habit.

Still, you can only take so much of a fresh look yourself. You need some new blood to help with launch — or for the existing "blood" to find a way to get a new attitude. Here are a few tips for a successful site launch:

✔ **Look at the new site from a user's point of view.** What are the top three cool things about the site? Just before you launch, identify these winners. Tweak them; improve them; make sure they "do what it says on the tin." The top few new features are likely to get a huge amount of attention, and everything else is likely to get very little.

✔ **Look at the new site from an internal point of view.** What are the top three things you were trying to do with this launch? (Hint: They're unlikely to be exactly the same as the top three user-visible features mentioned in the preceding bullet point.) Identify these goals. Improve the implementation where you can; fix problems where you must. And if the implementation has fallen short of the original goals, be ready to explain why.

✔ **Find the top three bugs or problems.** Find the worst three things about the site. Fix what you can. Be ready to explain what you must.

✔ **Compare to a couple of top competitors.** Look at a couple of competing sites. (Not necessarily direct business competitors, but sites that your site will be compared to.) What's better on your site than the competition? Worse? Be ready to answer this, and to describe plans for improvement where needed.

✔ **Run it by your "worst enemies."** Show the nearly live site to your toughest critics internally. Find out what they think. Fix any problems you can immediately, and make a longer-term plan to address any problems that you can't fix on this go-around.

✔ **Publicize as much as you can.** There's usually a limit to how much publicity you should do for a website launch or relaunch. But within that limit, get the word out. If some new feature is likely to get attention — such as the FBI's newly improved capability to track stolen artworks — get the word out in advance.

✔ **Keep a list for next time.** It's amazingly easy to forget all the good ideas you had at the end of the last round of changes to your website. Especially keep track of executive comments. These people run your company; getting their pet bugaboos fixed is valuable all around.

Figure 11-6 shows a press release for a new website update from the city of Boulder, Colorado. View the press release at `https://bouldercolorado.gov/newsroom/july-29-2013-city-of-boulder-launches-new-website`.

Figure 11-6: The City of Boulder doesn't get right to the point in its press release.

Unfortunately, the first paragraph of the press release is way too internally focused. It cites a "new layout and design" and "several features" that make the site easier. The first paragraph should include at least one specific feature that people will notice and like about the new site.

Sadly, some people in your organization may resist calling out one or two key new features in a website relaunch. They don't want to prejudice users in favor of just one thing, or fail to acknowledge everyone's hard work on the redesign. Unfortunately, unlike the kids in Garrison Keilor's Lake Wobegon, not every feature in a website redesign can be above average. Pick one or two key features to hook the public into checking out the whole thing.

The first paragraph of the Boulder press release also gives the date of the last new site design; sorry, but no one cares, at least not enough to put that in the first paragraph.

As web designers, we know that people scan content, and often only notice one or two key points on the very top of a web page. You should apply this insight and expertise to your press releases and other communications as well as to your websites.

Part III
Getting Your Education

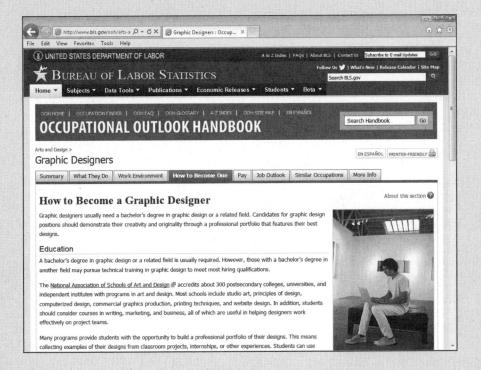

Check out www.dummies.com/extras/gettingawebdevelopmentjob for details on the move from tables to CSS in web development.

In this part . . .

- ✔ Find out what your educational options are
- ✔ Learn what's "required" for a web development job
- ✔ Check out value-added educational options

Chapter 12

Getting an Education for Web Development

• •

• •

*T*his chapter describes some of the higher education programs that you can pursue if you want a career in web development, either before you get started or after your career is underway. One key lesson: Don't stop learning just because you've started working.

A successful career in web development is all about what art critic Robert Hughes called, in his book of the same name, "the shock of the new." Web development careers exist because new advances are being made. The people who work at the cutting edge of these changes need to be learning continually in order to stay at the forefront of their professions.

Learning takes many different forms, but formal education is usually a vital part of the mix. If you think of your educational advancement being divided into study on your own, on-the-job training, and formal education, only the last one is easily measured and substantiated.

So don't ever stop learning, any and every way you can. But include as much formal education as you reasonably can in your mix. A bachelor's degree is becoming an entry-level qualification for most people in most web development jobs. Courses completed, certification programs completed, and advanced degrees are valuable ornaments on the tree of knowledge that you build as you pursue your career.

Understanding the Value of Undergraduate Degrees

Most web design jobs require some combination of education and experience. This is tough! The traditional route for good-paying jobs in the U.S., and many other countries, is to finish high school; get a four-year degree at a college university; and then get hired into an entry-level job in your chosen field, a job that requires (or just about requires) a college degree.

The U.S. Bureau of Labor Statistics, also known as the BLS, uses this approach to web design as a career, as shown in Figure 12-1. Its *Occupational Outlook Handbook* summarizes pay and typical education for a graphic designer, which is an expert — but non-technical — role when found on a web development team. The BLS considers a bachelor's degree as entry-level education for graphic designers and also for more technical roles.

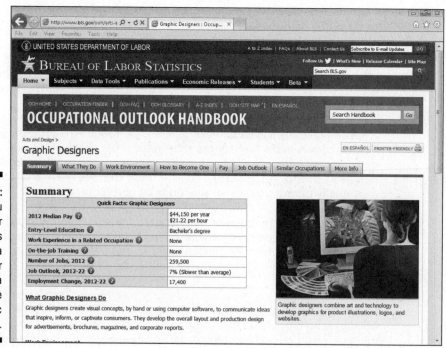

Figure 12-1:
The Bureau of Labor Statistics treats a four-year degree as a prerequisite for graphic design.

Balancing real-world experience and education

The world of web development is full of stories of people who have totally inappropriate educations for web development roles, often including little or no higher education at all.

One of the authors (Smith) is an example of this trend. He first started working in technology as a data-entry clerk for a cable television company. He did not have a college degree at the time, only about two years' worth of classes completed at the University of California, San Diego, a legendarily tough computer science school.

After the data entry job, he became a database programmer, computer book author, and technical publications manager. His skills grew, but his formal education didn't. Finally, he rose to the level of competitive analyst and marketing manager at Apple Computer, all without a degree.

However, he sensed that his luck was about to run out. He went to an extension program at the University of San Francisco while still working for Apple. He was able to complete his Bachelor of Arts (BA) degree in information systems management in about two additional years, going to school and studying at night.

And it was just in time. The dot-com boom was starting, and these new companies were mostly hiring younger people — almost all with freshly minted college degrees. Smith would have been frozen out if he didn't have his BA.

He then moved to the U.K. for several years; he got a work visa through the United Kingdom's Highly Skilled Migrant program, which awarded him points for, among other things, his BA. Also, the British job market is much more oriented to degrees, formal certification programs, and years of experience than the much more meritocratic Silicon Valley environment. That BA degree was absolutely indispensable, both to get him into the country, and to get him employed once he was there.

In fact, the BA didn't feel like enough. Now in his forties, Smith entered a graduate program at the London School of Economics. He finished with a Master of Sciences (MSc) in Information Systems two years later. And the new degree proved a huge help in subsequent roles with HSBC in London, and then with Kyocera, Visa, and others after his return to Silicon Valley.

This is just one person's story, but many others in web development can tell similar tales. The ratcheting back and forth between jobs and degrees is common among many people in web development and related fields.

In web design, however, treating a four-year degree as a first step can have a big drawback. To a greater degree than in other kinds of jobs, hiring managers want experience even from new graduates. Having a four-year degree but no actual work experience can put you in a very challenging situation as far as getting that first job.

You may want to consider going to a two-year college, getting a two-year degree, and then getting some work experience. (It may not pay much, but it will help a lot in getting a solid initial career-track position.) Then get a four-year degree that leverages both your two-year degree as well as what you've learned while working.

Is it who you know?

There's an old saying, "It's not what you know, it's who you know." This saying has a lot of truth, and it applies in every field, not just web design.

Most people in web design know people who don't have college degrees and have moved from job to job on the strength of their work experience, personal recommendations, and their portfolio. However, for most of us, the majority of our colleagues do have a bachelor's degree (also called a four-year degree).

When you don't have a degree of some kind, you're more dependent on connections and recent experience with specific technologies. And you could get frozen out when close

connections move to a new gig and can't bring you along because of degree requirements at their new employer.

Connections are great, but they're only so powerful. We recommend that you start out your career with a bachelor's degree if possible. During your degree program, build up your portfolio, and try to find a way to get work experience. If not, at least get an Associate of Arts (A.A.) or Associate of Sciences (A.S.) degree (also called a two-year degree), start getting some work experience, and find a way to move up to a four-year degree as soon as you can.

This is a complicated and somewhat non-traditional path, but it allows you to interleave paying for college and making some money, and is probably a surer path to a good job than just going through a four-year program without working. Consider all your options as you make your educational decisions.

Getting a Two-Year Degree First

As mentioned earlier, experience is just as important as education in getting a web development job.

So, to a greater degree than in many fields, web developers sometimes get a two-year degree — an A.A. (Associate of Arts) or A.S. (Associate of Science) degree. This can be from a community college or a technical school. Then they go to work.

An A.A. is more often awarded for an arts-centered or design-centered course of study. Using Photoshop, for instance, can be very technical, but it's used for art and design, so you'll see more Photoshop in a program that offers an A.A. degree. If your program teaches JavaScript, intermixed with some more traditional programming languages — even on top of design work — it's more likely to award an A.S. degree.

Associate degrees are usually only awarded at community colleges and technical schools. (Some smart four-year schools are starting to offer them too, giving their students a lot more options.)

These colleges are usually far less expensive in terms of tuition, fees, and even book costs than four-year schools. Many community college students continue to live with their parents while working at least part-time outside of school, further stretching their education dollar.

For those reasons, going to a two-year college (without incurring much debt), getting some work experience, and then finishing at a four-year school as a transfer student from the community college has a lot of advantages.

In a two-year degree program, you'll learn how to use software such as Photoshop (for graphics) and Dreamweaver (for web page and website design), plus take additional classes in topics such as typography, color, layout, and design.

If you have work experience, you might find this boring. However, as each of the authors experienced, there's value in hearing something that you mostly already know being taught in a structured, organized way. If you can keep paying attention through the boring bits, you'll learn new things about what you're doing — and about how people react to the information that you already know. These insights can be valuable, although they're sure to feel hard-won after sitting in a class that only has tidbits of new information for you.

Avoid interrupting or correcting the teacher, for the most part, even if you disagree or know more than the teacher does. She has an approach or technique that has worked for previous students. Interrupting her is likely to throw the teacher off her game and confuse your fellow students.

Seattle Central College has a strong two-year web design program, shown in Figure 12-2. The program includes a lot of programming and technical aspects and awards an A.S. (Associate of Science) degree, more highly prized than an A.A. (Associate of Arts). You can see the description for yourself at www.seattlecentral.edu/programs/webdesign/.

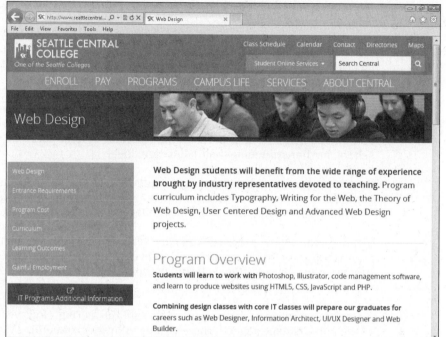

Figure 12-2:
Seattle
Central
College has
a strong,
technically
focused
web design
program.

The technical pay gap

More technically oriented jobs in web development tend to pay more. They also tend to demand more education. Or, put another way, the less education you have, the harder it is to get higher-paying, more technically oriented jobs.

Say your education is in a non-technical area, such as graphic design. We would argue that such an education still helps in getting more technically oriented jobs. You're given more credit for your expertise in the area your degree is in (ka-ching!), and you're assumed to be more credible by adding technical depth due to additional study and work experience (ka-ching! again).

There's a good brief summary of web design jobs on the About.com website. To see it, visit `http://webdesign.about.com/od/jobs/a/web_design_jobs_2016_outlook.htm`.

This summary says that web designers tend to earn about $50,000 a year and web developers about $70,000. These salaries are much higher in highly competitive job markets, such as Silicon Valley, and a bit lower in some quieter spots, but the differential still feels about right to us for many mainstream positions. For highly skilled web developers in competitive job markets, though, salaries can go through the roof — much more so than for web designers.

So yes, you can get a web development job without a four-year degree, and yes, you can get a web development job without being technical. But either of these additional qualifications, let alone both, will add to your employability and your earning power. So try to build yourself up to be a powerhouse — in education, experience, and technical depth.

Getting a Four-Year Degree

There are two different paths to a four-year degree. One is with previous experience, and the other is without experience.

In brief, it's tough to manage your life while you get some schooling (but not a four-year degree), get some work experience, and then get your degree — but it's a less expensive path, and you're learning while you earn (and vice versa). If you go straight for the four-year degree, you need to either get work experience through internships, develop a killer portfolio, or be stellar, either in your prestigious degree program or in your accomplishments within the program.

Getting a four-year degree with experience

If you already have experience in web design, getting a four-year degree is usually a great idea. Why?

You won't waste your time and money in school. Because you have some work experience, you know what you want to study. You know that you're interested in the degree program, you're good at the type of work involved, and that there are career opportunities for you post-graduation. Also, with experience and a four-year degree, it's very easy to get — or keep — a job.

Figure 12-3 shows the BLS page describing education for a graphic designer. It emphasizes four-year programs, but is a good starting point for all graphic designers doing web work.

There is one problem with getting a four-year degree with experience. Having this degree (no pun intended) of education, plus experience, should be enough to get you a hefty salary. However, you might be held back by your old salary.

If you're continuing with the same employer, this can be a big problem. Your current employer will want to pay you your former salary, plus some kind of bump — say, 10%, or $5,000 or so. This is nice, but may not be appropriate compared to new hires who have the education and experience that you now have as well. The usual cure for being underpaid at one employer is to move to a new employer. But even that might not immediately solve the problem.

Moving up educationally can still create a problem with a new employer. They will already have a salary range for the position. But if your former salary (fitting for someone with a two-year degree, or no degree) was lower, they'll want to discount from the salary range, or stay at the low end of it, with the idea that you're still getting a pretty good raise.

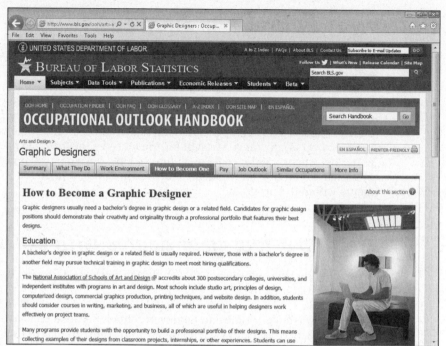

Figure 12-3:
BLS gives
you a good
brief guide
to graphic
design
certification.

The only cure for this is for you to figure out an appropriate salary figure, ask for that salary, and then stick to your guns. Be willing to walk away rather than come in with a salary that isn't worthy of you. Usually, given the demand for highly educated and experienced web designers, the employer will test you a bit, and then cave. If not, look for a different employer that will treat you appropriately.

The U.S. Department of State's human resources people have some good advice for any professional negotiating a salary, shown in Figure 12-4. To check it out in depth, visit `www.state.gov/m/dghr/flo/c21638.htm`.

In the big picture, salary problems are, in a way, nice problems to have. As an experienced web designer with a new four-year degree, you're likely to be a hot property. Work it.

Getting a four-year degree with no experience

The most common route into web development work is to get a four-year degree, and then get a job. If you don't manage to get some experience on the way to your degree, however, this can be risky.

Figure 12-4:
The State
Department
tells you
how to
get more
money.

If you don't yet have web design experience, and you get a four-year degree, you may have trouble finding a job. You can find yourself over-educated for entry-level positions and too inexperienced for higher-level positions. You might be willing to work around these barriers, say by taking a lower salary temporarily, but employers might not be.

There are only a few situations where we can recommend going straight for a four-year degree in web development, without getting solid experience along the way:

✔ **Your program is technical, full stop.** If you're studying to become a web software developer, or a software developer with a web bent, you'll be fine. Software developers are expected to have four-year degrees and can find appropriate entry-level positions straight out of school.

✔ **Your graphically oriented program has a big technical component.** If you can find a four-year program that includes solid web design work, plus technical depth in CSS and HTML, plus JavaScript, plus Python, plus database access, you're likely to be evaluated more as a technical pro than "just" a designer — and to find an employer who will give you a start.

✔ **Your program is really, really prestigious.** The very best programs are strong enough that many employers will take on their graduates without experience because they assume that these graduates will learn quickly.

✔ *You* **are really, really prestigious.** What we mean here is that even if your program is good rather than great, employers always want the best. If you can find ways to stand out in your program, you should be fully employable, even if some of your colleagues in your program aren't.

✔ **You find ways to get experience.** Paid or unpaid summer internships, side jobs, and volunteer design work all make a big difference. It's hard to find the time while studying, but worthwhile. Get solid experience on the side, and get it into your portfolio (see Chapter 16).

✔ **Your program has an excellent success record for jobs.** Along with all the preceding factors, you're going to do well if your program has a strong record of getting its graduates into jobs. Ask about this and make sure you like the answer before you enroll in a four-year program.

The Sullivan Curve

One of the most famous theories in technology and education goes by the name the Sullivan Curve. The Sullivan Curve is named for Kevin Sullivan, an early head of HR at Apple.

The Sullivan Curve holds that newly graduated technical people are very valuable. They add to their value as they get a few years of work experience. However, their salaries also increase steadily.

According to Sullivan, after a few years, the employee's value levels off. There are new developments in the field that these employees aren't thoroughly grounded in; their on-the-job training and self-education are likely to be hit and miss. New university graduates will have learned these new developments thoroughly — and, remember, they get paid less.

The problem for the longer-term employees is that they're moving up in their careers and expecting more money, just when their education is losing some of its relevance. According to Sullivan, experience doesn't fully make up for this. For most technical people, Sullivan favored getting rid of them after ten years or so.

Harsh, isn't it? Don't let this story discourage you; plenty of experienced web development people do very well indeed. But do let this story remind you to keep your education up-to-date and your skills sharp.

If you want to avoid being Sullivaned, as we might call it, stay current. Professional associations, Meetup groups, developer conferences, tech blogs, and other ways of visibly interacting keep your skills sharp and your profile high. This kind of interaction also makes you more ready to do well if and when you do take the time for more formal education.

Chapter 13

Exploring Certificate Programs and Advanced Degrees

In This Chapter

▶ Building your own program

▶ Continuing your education

▶ Learning from Stanford's example

▶ Getting an advanced degree

*W*eb development is constantly changing. Although it's true that formal community college, college, and university degrees are very valuable, as described in Chapter 12, they're not entirely necessary, and they're not always sufficient.

Degrees are not entirely necessary because web developers are in such high demand, and because the work that you do can be "self-evidencing." That is, public-facing websites that you've helped create or modify, your portfolio site, and colleagues' recommendations can add up to a powerful argument for your value on a web development team, almost regardless of formal education level.

However, as we mentioned previously, we do recommend getting a college degree. It's very easy for the people who shuffle papers in the hiring area of a company to only put resumes in the "yes" pile if they list a college degree. Even for relatively savvy hiring managers, a person with a degree is going to stand out over someone without one, all other things being equal. So you stand a better chance of getting the job you want, at the salary you want, with a degree or two in hand.

One difference between web development and a lot of other relatively good-paying office jobs is that a two-year degree, called an *associate degree* — an associate of arts (A.A.) or associate of sciences (A.S.), which is more technical — is sometimes sufficient for web development careers, at least for getting started.

However, over time, you're likely to be regarded as more technically capable, to get hired more easily and more often, and to be paid better, if you move up to a four-year degree — a B.A. (Bachelor of Arts) or B.S. (Bachelor of Sciences).

But the fact that a degree is necessary, or almost necessary, is one thing. Why might a degree, even a four-year degree, not be sufficient?

Because web development is constantly changing. New tools, new programming languages, and new ways of working are constantly coming to the fore.

There are many ways to learn these new tools. Trial-and-error on your own; articles with tips and tricks; online courses; and live, in-person courses are the major approaches. You can also find a degree or certificate program that wraps a bunch of pieces together, although some parts may be uninteresting or repetitive for you.

One argument in favor of structured courses is that they make you take the time for learning. That is, you might be able to learn something yourself in a few days of trying things — but as long as you're at work, you don't get the time to do that. So instead, by signing up for a course, you're taken out of the daily hubbub and allowed to focus on learning.

There are trade-offs, as well, in online and in-person learning. In general, online learning is more flexible. If you can whiz through a relatively familiar topic, online learning might be the best bet. But in-person courses get more of your attention and focus, simply because you're physically present. You also may have better opportunities to ask questions and to network with others, both about learning the material and future job possibilities.

With all this in mind, do seek out structured opportunities to learn. Find out which approaches work best for you. Use the things you learn on the job and also in projects for your portfolio (see Chapter 16). By using what you've learned, it sticks much better than if you only ever use the new skills in a learning environment.

Building Your Own University Program

Many colleges and universities allow for a lot of flexibility in their degree programs. Others offer the additional option of specialized majors that are expressly designed to let you do almost whatever you want.

When you go looking for a job, it's easier if you have a recognized name for your studies, such as computer science. If you want to take a cluster of courses in a particular area, such as database design, you might be able to find a major that has that area in its name; otherwise, you can simply tell potential employers that you had an "emphasis in" the area that you focused on.

You can also put together double majors or interdisciplinary programs. If the healthcare area fascinates you, you can do a combined program of some sort in healthcare, biology, or physiology, along with computer science courses.

Web design jobs are constantly changing, and web design touches just about every area of business, government, and the non-profit world. So combined degrees can be very useful ways into a particular area that interests you.

You can also pursue areas that you might not use directly. A minor in literature or philosophy might help you pursue your own intellectual interests without distracting from your major. Even a double major or interdisciplinary program featuring a non-technical major is unlikely to hurt you much: It shows that you have a broad range of interests, are independent, and have "learned how to learn." (And, as a practical matter, a break from highly intense computer science courses during your college time might be a good thing indeed.)

According to the U.S. Bureau of Labor Statistics, management jobs in computer science usually require a bachelor's degree, and the same is true for web development. So if you want to be a manager, and you don't yet have your bachelor's degree, figure out how to get one. What specific courses you take on the way to your degree is probably not all that important, as long as each of the courses help you increase your skills in some way.

Figure 13-1 shows the educational requirements for manager's jobs in computer science, as part of the overall occupational outlook for this area. To see this page, visit `www.bls.gov/ooh/management/computer-and-information-systems-managers.htm#tab-4`.

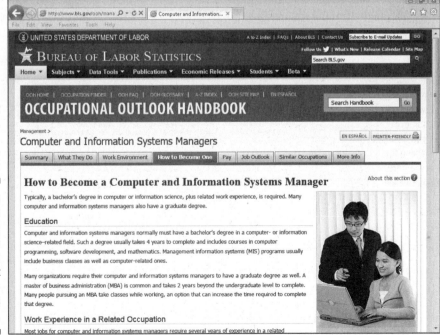

Figure 13-1:
The BLS sees a bachelor's degree as a requirement for manager's jobs in tech.

Finally, you can ask about auditing courses that interest you. Auditing means sitting in a class, and potentially even taking the exams, without getting university credit. Many professors welcome auditors, as they are often working professionals who lend a nice balance to the bright, but inexperienced, young things who fill most of the seats in their courses. It's a great way to learn, to meet people, and to consider your options for further education.

Wonder what kind of requirement's a major university's computer science program has? Stanford is probably the leading school in the world for computer science, and it's famous for birthing start-ups, with Google being only the most spectacular of many examples, so we use it for examples here. Figure 13-2 shows the home page for the Bachelor of Science degree in Computer Science at Stanford.

Figure 13-2: Stanford's course requirements are a set of marching orders for some, but an à la carte menu for others.

Mathematical core courses are outlined in Table 13-1.

Table 13-1	Mathematics (26 Units Minimum)	
Course Number	*Course Name*	*Units*
CS 103	Mathematical Foundations of Computing	5
CS 109	Introduction to Probability for Computer Scientists	5
Math 41 and Math 42	Calculus and Calculus	10
Two electives	N/A	4

Stanford's core curriculum in science is shown in Table 13-2.

Table 13-2	Science (11 Units Minimum)	
Course Number	*Course Name*	*Units*
Physics 41	Mechanics	4
Physics 43	Electricity and Magnetism	4
Elective	N/A	3

For the core courses in technology in society, you simply choose your own course from a wide range listed in the catalog.

The requirements in engineering fundamentals are outlined in Table 13-3.

Table 13-3	Engineering Fundamentals (13 Units Minimum)	
Course Number	*Course Name*	*Units*
CS 106B or CS 106X	Programming Abstractions or Programming Abstractions (Accelerated)*	5
Engr 40 or Engr 40A or 40M	Introductory Electronics or Programming Abstractions (Accelerated)*	5
	Fundamentals Elective (may not be 70A, B, or X)	3-5

Table 13-4 outlines Stanford's requirements for writing.

Table 13-4	Writing in the Major (13 Units Minimum)	
Course Number	*Course Name*	*Units*
CS 181W or CS 191W or CS 194W or CS 210B or CS 294W	Computers, Ethics, and Public Policy	5
	Writing Intensive Senior Project	
	Software Project	
	Software Project Experience with Corporate Partners	
	Writing Intensive Research Project in Computer Science	

The computer science core requirements are covered in Table 13-5.

Table 13-5	Computer Science Core (15 Units)	
Course Number	*Course Name*	*Units*
CS 107	Computer Organization and Systems	5
CS 110	Principles of Computer Systems	5
CS 161	Design and Analysis of Algorithms	5

Note the presence in the Stanford Engineering course requirements of CS 106X, Programming Abstractions (Accelerated), in case plain old CS 106B, Programming Abstractions, isn't, perhaps, abstract enough for you.

If you do pursue a double major or interdisciplinary program, what you're doing is likely to be more or less unique. Use your portfolio (see Chapter 16) to create projects that use a wide range of your skills and learning.

You should also consider courses that increase "soft skills," such as skills in communications and project management. Look for courses where you have to do project work in a team and present the results. Also, some schools offer project management courses that are very career-focused. In some cases, at the end of the class, you can sit for a project management certification, such as the first-level Project Management Professional (PMP) certificate.

Technologists are famously irreverent, and looking at Stanford's core curriculum for computer science is a good test as to whether you have the "irreverent" gene. To some people, a list like this one instantly raises the question, "How am I going to do all that?" These people instantly go into planning mode.

Rice lays down the law for Stanford prospects

The presence in the Stanford curriculum of tough courses like CS 106X, Programming Abstractions (Accelerated), brings to mind a famous anecdote about Stanford. Some years ago, Condoleeza Rice was provost of Stanford; she later became secretary of state for George W. Bush. While she was provost, Rice was asked if a high school student wanting to get into Stanford should take a regular course, with a good chance of getting an A, or an honors version of the same course, where she was more likely to get a B. She replied that solid prospective students for Stanford would generally take the honors version of the course and still get an A.

Looks like a duck

Sometimes you have a school or work project that would be perfect for your portfolio, but you can't use it in a public-facing website for various reasons. For school, you might have collaborators who don't want you to use their work on your site; at work, you might have commercially sensitive information or customer information in a project that your employer doesn't want to share.

In this case, the most efficient thing to do is to create a "looks like" project for your portfolio site. Create a project with a slightly different user interface, which leaves out specific intellectual property from collaborators and excludes any personal or customer information. But make sure that the portfolio project includes the core functionality of the actual project it's reflecting; you might even be able to add more functionality to the portfolio project than was in the original.

As an alternative to excluding collaborators' work, ask them what part of their work they're willing to let you include. Often, the answer is "quite a bit," especially if you give them credit.

Creating a "looks like" project is a very useful work around for the common problem of not being able to show your most interesting past work to prospective employers. If you do it soon after the original project, or in parallel with it, it's not much additional work, and having it under your complete control gives you the opportunity to make it look and work exactly the way you want it to. Heck, the project on your portfolio site might even end up looking better, and being more interesting, than the academic or commercial project that it's modeled on.

If you have the "irreverent" gene, though, the first thing you might think is, "Well, about half of that looks interesting. The other half, not so much." And you start picking and choosing interesting and not-interesting courses. You'll start flipping through the Stanford course catalog, looking everywhere for other courses that might go into a major of your own design. If that's your reaction, you have the irreverent gene — and a turbulent, but quite possibly highly successful, career in front of you.

Picking and choosing

Negotiation is a valuable skill in life — and not necessarily one that web developers are good at. We come from a world of right and wrong; code compiles, or it doesn't. A specific HTML tag or attribute works in the latest version of Internet Explorer, or it doesn't. But education is a people business, and things are not so black and white. Treat a course catalog like a menu in a Chinese restaurant, picking and choosing what you want. Then negotiate for how much you can actually get from what you want. Remember, higher education is a business, and ultimately — even in higher education — the customer is king.

Pursuing Continuing Education

Continuing education is an odd part of the education industry. (If you think of it as an industry, you'll do a better job of making smart decisions about consuming what it offers.)

From your point of view, as the consumer, continuing education can be a time and money sink, taking a lot from you without giving you much in return. On the other hand, it can be a very powerful force in opening up new pathways for your future.

It takes a lot of forethought, creativity, and hard work to make continuing education pay off for you. But it can pay off very well indeed, whether in new knowledge, professional achievement, personal satisfaction, or a combination of those.

Figure 13-3 shows the home page for a web design certificate program offered in North Carolina. It's a fairly complete 13-course program, with the technical side represented by a JavaScript course called JavaScript for the Non-Programmer. Check it out at www.oshr.nc.gov/psp/webdesigncert.html.

Should you take online courses?

This is an easy one. Take in-person courses when you can. You tend to learn more, the networking is better, and more prestigious programs have more of their courses and degree programs available in-person than online. Then take online courses to fill gaps, to pick up a new technology quickly when you don't have time for an in-person course, and to make up for living someplace that isn't convenient to the type of courses you want to take. Should you do an all-online course? If you can't find time, energy, money, or geographic convenience for an in-person course, sure. It's probably going to be less prestigious, but easier and less expensive to complete, and it's still likely to be worthwhile.

Figure 13-3:
This web design program covers the basics and then some.

Investigating the strange case of Stanford Continuing Studies

Stanford's Continuing Studies department is a great example of the pressures faced by major university continuing education programs — and of the rewards possible for students, despite the pressures.

If you look at the website for Continuing Studies at Stanford, you won't find a single computer science (CS) course. CS is the crown jewel of Stanford's curriculum, both in terms of its academic reputation and its revenue base; Stanford isn't going to let people get the rewards of CS courses by, as it were, coming in the side door.

Figure 13-4 shows the website for Continuing Studies at Stanford. Check it out at `http://continuingstudies.stanford.edu/courses/courses-by-department`.

Especially note the online courses, which you can take from anywhere in the world. Then check out the offerings at colleges and universities in your area, as well as ones you've attended previously.

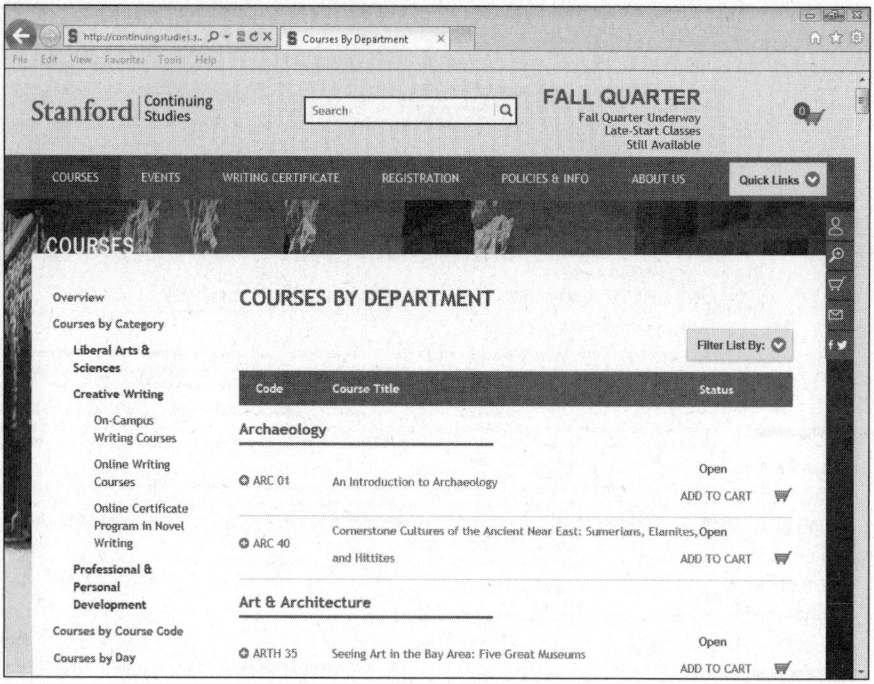

Figure 13-4:
Stanford
Continuing
Studies lists
most of its
web devel-
opment-
related
courses
under
Technology.

But look through the listings carefully, and you find hidden gems. On Stanford's site under Online Professional and Personal Development, you'll find Tame Data to Drive Big Insight: An Online Course. If you click through to the description, you'll find that this is a course in the area of big data, which is one of the hottest areas in technology, and directly relevant to web development.

In that same heading is another course, Beginning Programming (PHP): An Online Course. PHP is a very popular language for web development, and it also has a big data aspect to it.

Finally, under Technology is a treasure trove of web development-related courses, including website design, WordPress, and JavaScript. The courses mentioned previously as appearing under Online Professional and Personal Development appear here too.

When you take courses as a regular Stanford student, a lot of nice things suddenly appear on your resume. But you can get a lot of cool technology names, plus the Stanford name, on that resume really quickly and easily through continuing studies courses.

To MOOC or not to MOOC

A big new thing is Massive Open Online Courses, or MOOCs. The idea is to take popular courses and make them available online for free.

Stanford is a big participant in MOOCs, with several of if its computer science and programming-related courses available. You may even be able to get a certificate of completion for a small fee, but be aware that this option is changing fast across MOOCs as we write this.

At this writing, you can't get college credit for MOOCs. They're great for learning, for trying courses to see what you like and can handle,

and for preparing for regular college work. This is all really valuable. But until MOOCs offer credit, you can't use them toward a degree.

Do take MOOCs, work hard, learn the topic, and put the experience on your resume, though. Be ready to answer questions about what you did and what you learned during a job interview. (The fact that you're talking about Stanford and you in the same sentence can only help, unless of course you already have a degree from there.) This is a new alternative that you can get some mileage out of if you put the effort in.

How Smith got Stanford on his resume

One of the authors (Smith) was able to add Stanford to his resume in a fun and worthwhile way. Smith took two web design courses at Stanford — a school everyone has heard of — after graduating from the University of San Francisco, a school far fewer people have heard of, particularly in computer science. The

courses put the word *Stanford* on his resume, as well as adding credibility to his burgeoning web-related work experience. Ten years later, Smith graduated from a master's degree program at the London School of Economics, further strengthening both his knowledge and his resume.

Tips for continuing education

Continuing education is, by its nature, highly flexible, and everyone's educational background and work situation varies. So we can't give hard and fast rules as to how to work the continuing education game.

Entrance requirements for continuing education programs, as well as for graduate school, are often surprisingly low, and can often be negotiated. They want to take your money! So consider yourself empowered to get into, or talk your way into, any program you're interested in. Take a "no" to mean "not today." Ask the admissions office what you can do to turn a "no" into a "yes."

Here are a few tips, though, that will help many people in many different situations:

- ✔ **Choose big-name schools:** Where possible, use continuing education to get the name of an impressive school onto your resume. If you already have impressive schools, this doesn't help much, but if you can take a single course at Harvard to add luster to your community college–heavy education, do it.

- ✔ **Consider taking certificate programs first:** Getting a certificate, or some other recognition of completing a program of some sort, can be similar in its impact to a degree. A certificate program can also serve as the first part of a full Master's degree program. Look at certificate programs and see if any of them make sense for you.

- ✔ **Go small or go big:** For resume purposes, either take one or two courses to add a bit of luster to your resume, or complete a program of some sort. Four or more random courses don't help your resume much more than one or two do.

- ✔ **Pick big-name technologies:** Take a course in the latest hot technology and put that course, and perhaps one other, on your resume. You probably will just clutter things up by listing more courses than that.

- ✔ **Build toward a degree:** Some continuing education courses can be used toward an advanced degree. Others can't be counted directly, but are about as good as the regular course. Choose those if you can.

- ✔ **Mind your connections:** Taking classes toward a certificate is a fantastic networking exercise, one that can easily lead to new jobs. Do well in your courses, speak up in class at least a bit, and make a point of getting to know your fellow students. Try to hire talented students into your company as well as looking for a new career yourself.

- ✔ **Quality over quantity:** Spread your courses out over time and do well in each one. This is not so much important for your academic record as it is for networking and for effectively being able to use your new knowledge in your career.

- ✔ **Watch out for executive education:** High-priced courses and programs, often called "executive education" or something similar, are designed to be paid for by your company — not by you directly. You can drain your checking account in a big hurry if you pay for such courses yourself. (They can still be pricey even if you pay for half of them yourself, as some companies require. You can negotiate this with your employer as well as with educational institutions.)

- ✔ **Remember that continuing education is not magic:** If you don't get along well with colleagues, are having trouble completing assignments on time, and so on, adding continuing education courses won't fix it. Ideally, you can do a good job, get along well with colleagues, and take continuing education courses as a plus.

You're perfectly free to take many continuing education courses as you'd like for your own growth and development. But you'll only want to put one or two courses, or one or two certificates, on your resume. Beyond that, additional courses won't build your credentials much.

When in doubt, talk to friends and colleagues about their experience with continuing education. Try to include friends who've done hiring, or ask around on LinkedIn. The education industry can take a lot of your money without giving you very much direct benefit, so caveat emptor.

Many of the advantages of an advanced degree also apply to a bachelor's degree, and vice versa. Read both this section, about bachelor's degrees, and the next section, about advanced degrees, to get a well-rounded idea of the advantages of all kinds of higher education in web development jobs.

Getting an Advanced Degree

In a field where hiring is driven by your portfolio and your connections, and where the need for a bachelor's degree is controversial, what about advanced degrees? Isn't an advanced degree completely unnecessary?

There are three kinds of advanced degrees for most web developers to consider:

- **Master's degrees:** Master's degrees come in two types: an MA, or Masters of Arts, and an MSc, or Masters of Sciences. An MSc degree is more technical and likely to bring somewhat greater financial rewards. Either distinguishes you from people with a bachelor's degree or less.

- **Doctorates:** A doctorate only comes in one type, the PhD, or Doctor of Philosophy. Most people who get a PhD get an MA or MSc on the way to the PhD. A doctorate strongly distinguishes you and positions you to be a senior manager or thought leader in your field.

- **MBAs:** Many technology company leaders have engineering degrees at the bachelor's level and an MBA (a master's of business administration degree) on top of that.

If we had to answer the question, "Do I need an advanced degree?" with a simple yes or no, the answer, for many web developers, would indeed be no. You can have a long, successful, and lucrative career in web development without an advanced degree. And there's a good case to be made that working longer hours or taking on a side project could well be more lucrative over time than taking courses.

Is it tough to get into an advanced degree program?

It's always tough to get into advanced degree programs, except when it isn't. And it often isn't. The requirements stated in college course catalogs are often intimidating, but university departments often have a lot of discretion in individual cases, like yours. There are also advanced degree programs that are specifically designed for people with work experience; keep an eye open for those.

Universities like to fill their programs, and if an incoming class isn't full, they can be quite flexible. (Especially when they're trying to launch a new, specialized program that's a bit different from what they've had before.) Universities also like to add working professionals to programs full of smart, but unseasoned, younger students. Figure out what you want to do and ask. If a given program says no, ask where there might be openings — in other programs at the same university, or at other universities. You're likely to get good, and useful, advice.

However, a longer answer would cite some advantages of advanced degrees that are hard to get any other way:

- ✔ **Personal satisfaction:** It feels good to master complex material and to get recognized for doing so, with a lot of hard work and some personal sacrifice required to get there. Pieces of paper do mean something when they're granted by credible institutions and recognize years of hard work. It feels good, forever, to have achieved everything represented by an advanced degree. It feels even better when you're able to use your knowledge in a meaningful way at work.

- ✔ **Prestige:** People have at least some understanding of what goes into getting an advanced degree, and that can translate into a certain degree of respect, an advantage when applying for new positions, and the ability to teach others in a university setting if you choose to do so. We don't suggest pursuing an advanced degree with prestige as the main reason, but don't be afraid to enjoy it a bit once you get there.

- ✔ **Pay:** Studies reliably show that more education results in a higher lifetime income. One can easily see this happening within web development, where it's easier for your resume to float to the top of the pile, easier to land that speaking engagement, and easier to get that raise you've been pushing for when you have an advanced degree.

✔ **Structured knowledge:** Sure, you can learn how to do PHP programming out of a book, or using a stand-alone online course. The cool thing about degree programs is a combination of the information in them and the structure in which the information is delivered. This meta-information is valuable to deep understanding of the material itself, and for learning something about the institutions that deliver information in this particular way. Learning about the institutions helps you understand the value of what they have to offer, so you can make better decisions about which teammates to seek out, and whom to hire when you're the one making the decisions.

✔ **Truly incredible networking opportunities:** If you want to start your own company someday, for instance, there's a very good chance you can find your cofounder in a degree program, or through one. Advanced degree programs are good ways to find your next job — or your next new colleague at your current job — as well. The teaching, speaking, and alumni activity opportunities that come with your degree are all networking opportunities as well.

Different advantages of an advanced degree matter more or less to different people. The key is that, in web development, unlike in other careers, an advanced degree is not always an unadulterated plus. Pursue one for your own reasons, and don't pursue it if you don't think you'll enjoy it.

Because technology-oriented people tend to be irreverent and disrespectful of authority and tradition, it isn't helpful to put on an air of superiority if you're pursuing, or achieve, an advanced degree. Tech people respect competence. So think of your degree as something you achieved while learning things that you really wanted to know, both for the sake of knowledge itself and to be able to do more cool things at work. And don't expect anyone to give you anything — a job, respect, even winning an argument — as a result. Instead, use the skills you learned in getting the degree to get what you want.

Is It tough to afford graduate degrees?

Private universities can be very expensive, and executive programs even more so. However, your work is highly likely to pay half of your tuition and book costs, student loans are available for the rest, and you're quite likely to make back whatever you invest in a few years from a higher salary. Finally, in-state tuition for public universities is often quite reasonable. So yes, it's expensive to get an advanced degree. It's a big investment of time and money — but you can usually figure out ways to reduce the amount that you pay yourself and to get a good return on your investment.

LSE? Yeah, you know me

One of the authors (Smith) is a late bloomer educationally, but a successful one. Smith left the University of California at San Diego a couple of years into a computer science degree program to work. He got his Bachelor of Arts in information systems management from a program at the University of San Francisco at age 30 while working for Apple Computer. Nearly 20 years later, while living and working in London, he was accepted to the London School of Economics (called "the LSE" by graduates, staff, and professors) for a new program in information systems. He received his MSc (an MSc, rather than an MA, because of three tough statistics courses) and graduated at age 50. The new degree helped him get hired by global banking giant HSBC, Visa, and others.

Chapter 14

Knowing Web Graphics Tools

In This Chapter

▶ Discovering key tools for web graphics

▶ Exploring Photoshop and GIMP

▶ Getting to know Illustrator and CorelDRAW

▶ Becoming familiar with InDesign, QuarkXPress, and others

*W*eb development tools are a vital part of any career in the field. It's far easier to get work done using tools that you already have experience with. Your expertise in making a given tool "sing" can sometimes get you a job. Your skill with a specific tool can even seem more important than the skill you have in the actual discipline that you're using the tool for!

A major hurdle to getting a web development job is often whether you have experience, and just how much experience, with one or more tools that are the standard in a given workplace.

This can lead to a major "chicken and egg" problem that's a version of the age-old work-related quandary: You can't get a job if you don't have experience, but you can't get experience if you don't have a job.

With tools, you can't get a job using a tool if you don't yet have experience using that tool, but you can't get experience using a tool unless you have a job using it.

In this chapter, we start by describing how to get experience using a tool, and then give brief descriptions of some of the major graphics tools used in web development. In Chapter 15, we tackle website development tools and content management systems.

The lists of tools and their descriptions will help you decide how to target your learning efforts.

Getting Experience with Web Dev Tools

Here's a quandary: You need experience using a tool to get a job, but the main way you get experience using tools is via on-the-job training. Tied to the problem of getting experience using a tool is how to get access to the tool itself. Many web development tools are very expensive, such as up to $1,000 for a major tool like Adobe Photoshop.

We discuss the major ways in which you get experience using tools and how, within each of these different approaches, the issue of getting access to the tool itself is usually handled.

College and university programs

College and university programs are great ways to learn how to use the major tools in a given web development discipline. You can even get for-credit courses in using major tools like Photoshop or InDesign.

It's kind of wonderful and annoying, all at the same time, to take a course in how to use a tool. It's wonderful because you can really give the tool some focused time, learning all the tips and tricks. It's annoying because courses are usually taught to the less experienced and slower-to-learn people in a classroom setting. If you already have some experience with a tool, or are just quick to pick things up, waiting for the class to get around to teaching you something new can feel like watching paint dry.

If you're really not getting much out of a course, you'll have to move on. But when in doubt, hang in there. The information in a course is valuable, but so is the structure it's delivered in. You see how professionals communicate information so that other people can absorb it better, and how each new concept depends on previous ones. You can use this approach in working with colleagues. The contacts you make when taking a course are also worthwhile, especially if you're "head of the class" and can help other people out.

Try to spend a good chunk of your time on tool-related courses. Each tool you learn can make a difference in the job world later.

Another great feature of college and university courses concerning software tools is that they normally offer free or very low-cost access to tools that, out in the real world, are quite expensive. Employer policies vary, but most web design professionals like to have personal licenses for the tools they use the most. Colleges and university offerings often include access to key tools not only while you're in college, but a way to "graduate" to continued low-cost licensing afterward. Check into this carefully.

Many key web design tools are becoming available on a monthly licensing basis. The licenses, although they can add up to a fee that's expensive over time, allow you to get through periods when you're between roles — such as after you leave school, but before you start work — without having to consider spending thousands of dollars for new permanent licenses for key tools.

Online courses and self-study

There are now a plethora of online courses available for major software tools, and you can use a book — or online resources that you stitch together — to develop your own miniature curriculum as well. This approach can end up being somewhere between the structure and networking potential of a college or university course (see preceding section) and the more haphazard approach that most of us take to on-the-job training (OJT; see the following section).

The difference between self-study and OJT is that self-study is time that you consciously set aside to delve into the workings of a software tool, without being driven by needing a particular trick or technique for the work immediately in front of you. Being able to spend a few hours in this more exploratory and reflective learning mode every so often, for each of the tools you use, is extremely valuable. It also makes you more productive and increases your feeling of satisfaction with your work.

If you know a certain genre of software, you can pick up a different program in the same genre pretty easily through online courses and self-study. For instance, if you know Photoshop, learning the freeware alternative GIMP is not that hard. Quickly learning the key points of one new tool by using your knowledge of an existing tool of the same type is often a good technique to use to get up to speed before a job interview or the first day on a new job, but learning your first program of a given type requires more effort and commitment, such as an in-person course.

Using self-study is also great when you are trying to learn about a tool — that is, exploring whether it's something you want to add to your personal toolkit. You'll often want to do this kind of exploration before committing to either purchasing a tool yourself or — perhaps just as big a commitment of your personal resources — getting your corporate IT department to approve it for purchase.

Figure 14-1 shows a list of online learning resources for CalJOBS, an employment website for California. You can start checking out the CalJobs site at `www.caljobs.ca.gov`.

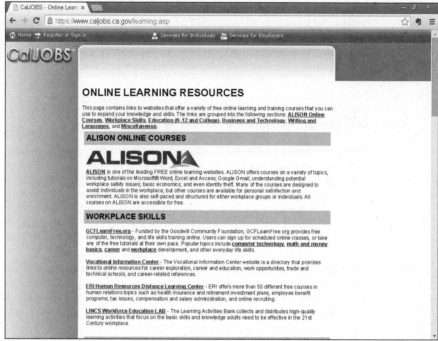

Figure 14-1:
CalJOBS
gives you a
list of online
learning
resources
to help you
get a job in
California.

The licensing situation for online courses and self-study is often poor. Many tools give you a free month, for instance, of using a tool before you buy it. That's helpful, but it leaves you rushing to do your experimentation or use it before the month is up. And you might then have a difficult decision to make as to whether to buy the software or give up on it.

Having monthly licenses available, as more and more web design software does, certainly helps. But there's no ideal solution for getting new tools into your personal toolkit.

On-the-job training

Many of us learn to use key tools by messing around with them in the process of doing our work. This is usually accompanied by occasional questions directed at colleagues, extensive use of the Help system for the software in question, perusing of YouTube videos on the topic, reading of books on the topic, and extensive searches of online bulletin boards used by people experienced with the software.

On-the-job training (OJT) is a great way to learn things, and it's the default method for a lot of software education. However, because you're picking things up as you go along, you don't know what you don't know. There can be entire approaches to using a tool, or key tips and tricks, that you simply never run into if OJT is all you have.

We suggest augmenting OJT with an online course or a book. Either will give you the outsider's perspective and collected folklore needed to take your use of the tool to the next level.

Because OJT happens in a work environment, the licensing situation is usually pretty good as well. Major tools should be covered by site licenses such that everyone who needs to use a tool has it, and everyone is on the same version.

Figure 14-2 shows a list of on-the-job training and apprenticeship programs for the U.S. Department of Veterans Affairs, widely known as the VA. You can find the list at `www.benefits.va.gov/gibill/onthejob_apprenticeship.asp`.

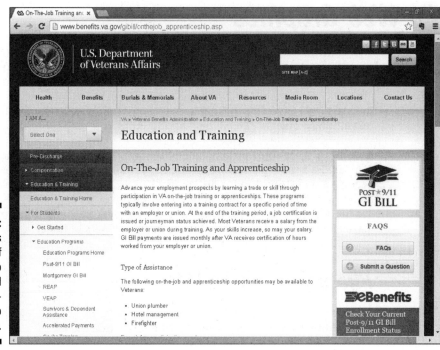

Figure 14-2:
The VA has a list of on-the-job training and apprenticeship resources.

Corporate IT often tries to save money by limiting licenses tightly, not upgrading to a new version of software, and so on. There is also often limited internal support for tools beyond the core office productivity suite. It often comes down to the company saving a few thousand dollars while people who are, as a group, making millions of dollars a year in salary are slowed down or stopped in their work. Coordinate with other web development professionals in your workplace to call attention to inadequate licensing and support policies, and get them fixed — or consider moving to an organization that can make these basic necessities available to you gracefully.

What is often challenging at work is getting the tools that you use at work, especially the latest versions, onto your own personally owned computer that you might prefer to use for some work at your job, as well as for side jobs outside the main workplace. Try to get support for licensing that lets you use all the tools that you can bring to bear, including your own personal computer(s), to do the work that's in front of you.

Getting to Know Key Tools for Web Graphics

There are scores of popular tools for web design and hundreds of less-popular ones. In fact, the range of tools available is basically endless, as people will write their own tools, tweak open-source programs, create libraries of templates and samples, and take other steps that can make the learning curve for working in a new environment into something more resembling a cliff.

In order to bring some order to the chaos, we're going to use Adobe's Creative Suite as the organizing spine for much of this discussion. Adobe has tried to become a one-stop shop for design of all kinds and web design in particular. By using their software catalog as a starting point, we can help give you the insight needed to steer your own way through the maze — and through the maze of jobs at workplaces that favor particular sets of tools.

Photoshop and GIMP

Photoshop is the granddaddy of all web design tools. It's the leading raster image-editing software program. Er, what does that mean?

Raster means that, to Photoshop, an image is a collection of pixels. Each pixel can be entirely unrelated to all the pixels surrounding it. Photographs are inherently well-suited to manipulation with raster image-editing software.

Suite news from Adobe

Part of the advantage that Adobe has cultivated in building up its Creative Suite of collected design tools is the advantage that Adobe offers software buyers of having a one-stop shop for core tools. As Microsoft did when it created Microsoft Office, Adobe can offer bundle pricing, unified upgrade cycles, unified technical support, and so on. Adobe saves money by sharing a lot of its internal functions, such as marketing, sales, and support, across many tools, yet can charge a premium price for mainstays such as Photoshop.

Adobe has moved to a monthly pricing model for its core applications. This is a great boon for freelancers, both full-time and part-time. It prevents previously agonizing situations, such as working in an older version of Photoshop because you didn't want to spend the money (and, perhaps, invest the training time) for moving to a new version. With monthly subscriptions, you do have to move to new versions right away — but so does everyone else who's using the subscription model. You have to invest the time to get trained, but you know you won't be odd person out. (Nor will you be likely to have to work with other people who are.)

At this writing, individual options include $9.99 per month (with a year's subscription) for Photoshop; $19.99 for any major Creative Suite application, plus a portfolio website and cloud storage; and $49.99 a month for Photoshop, Illustrator, and other applications, plus the portfolio website and cloud storage. There is also a special, with this last offer on sale for $29.99 per month.

The one-year commitment is a real hassle if you're between jobs or otherwise expecting to get paid-for access to the apps in the near future. However, the yearly option is still much less of an expense up-front than buying one or more applications as new software.

To illustrate this, imagine a photo of a man with short hair. Then imagine that you wanted to make him look bald. If the man's hair, for instance, were an object, you could select it and remove it. But it isn't, and you can't.

Core Photoshop functionality allows you to edit each and every pixel of the photograph to replace pixels that portray hair with pixels that portray either background or skin. Lots of shortcuts built into Photoshop allow you to more easily select the pixels you want to get rid of and to smooth the existing background, for instance, into the areas where the hair sticking up from the head has been removed. But you're still working on pixels. Editing images with Photoshop is often slow and exacting work.

Photoshop is a beast. The program itself comes with scores of additional tools. You can buy add-ins and plug-ins and extensions. It really is the core of a suite.

Photoshop is the number-one tool for all kinds of design professionals, including nearly all web designers. Photoshop is an excellent tool for mocking up example pages for a website. (And yes, ironically, in doing this work, you're using a lot of vector-type tools.)

After the page is actually created in HTML and CSS, you can grab parts of your page mock-ups created in Photoshop and use them as images within the page.

Don't try to do web design work without learning at least the basics of Photoshop. The product's name is even a verb; when you want to make an image look better, or to make it deceptive, you "Photoshop it." Take the time and effort to learn how to Photoshop it.

Neither of the authors of this book, much to our embarrassment, has ever learned Photoshop past the beginner stage. We are each expert in a number of tools, and competent in others, but — past the very beginning stages — Photoshop has baffled us.

Although other tools can be learned casually, Photoshop is challenging, and most potential heavy users need various kinds of training. If you're a potential Photoshop user, or already using the tool, set aside time for training and improvement.

If you're interviewing potential candidates for a web design job, drill down on Photoshop experience. If Photoshop is a key tool for a given job you're hiring for, don't be afraid to test for competency before hiring someone. And if you're the candidate, be ready to be challenged on the details of your Photoshop expertise.

There's also a huge marketplace around Photoshop for training and support.

And, finally, there's Photoshop Elements. It has a great deal of the functionality of Photoshop, but costs less than $100. It's a great way to learn, to get through spells where you don't have a current Photoshop license, and to introduce others to the Photoshop world.

Open-source tools are very popular in government agencies, where "free" is a popular price tag, and where there are resources to provide training and support that might otherwise be lacking for free tools.

GIMP is an open-source alternative to Photoshop. It's free! One great thing to do when you have a gap between jobs is to learn GIMP. Learning GIMP gives you a tool that you may be able to use for freelance jobs rather than buying a Photoshop license, it increases your overall expertise, it helps you get jobs where GIMP is an alternative (Photoshop is still almost always the standard), and it gives you an alternative once you do get a job.

Figure 14-3 shows the training page for GIMP on the state of Nevada's website: `http://it.nv.gov/uploadedFiles/ITnvgov/Content/Sections/Application_Development/Web/Procedures/GIMP-ResizeImages.pdf`.

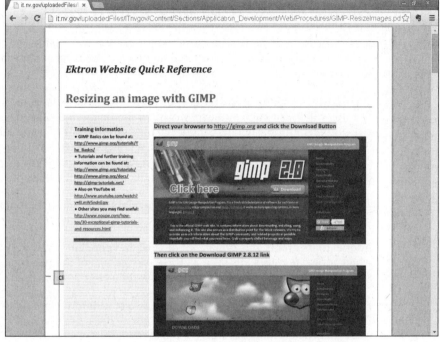

Figure 14-3:
You can get GIMP training resources from the state of Nevada.

GIMP does not directly support Pantone colors. Pantone is a color standard that makes colors reproducible across different media. GIMP also lacks the training and support options of Photoshop. However, it's a solid enough alternative that its popularity continues to grow.

Building expertise on tools

One way to make a name for yourself and to stand out in your work is to become an acknowledged expert on a tool, or some aspect of a tool. Develop a lot of expertise and then create a blog, write articles, give talks, and respond to inquiries from the trade press. This will contribute greatly to your employability and your salary.

To do this successfully, you have to look for a good opportunity that suits you. For instance, there are already many experts on Photoshop who have written books, led training sessions, and so on.

However, because GIMP is newer and free, there's more room for people to become acknowledged experts. For instance, you could create a blog focused on GIMP use by students or freelancers.

If you find a tool that you really enjoy, consider taking on an expert's role of this kind.

Adobe Illustrator and CorelDraw

Illustrator is the most-used tool for vector graphics — that is, graphics where each part of the image is considered an object. The biggest alternative is CorelDraw.

Technically speaking, in raster graphics, the image is, at bottom, a collection of color values for each and every pixel in the image. The image has a specific size and resolution, such as 1280 x 800 for a screenshot of a typical laptop. In vector graphics, the image is, at bottom, a collection of objects such as lines, circles, fill colors, and fill textures. The image can be displayed or printed at any size or resolution, without affecting the underlying image.

The two leading tools for vector-based graphics are Adobe Illustrator and CorelDraw. Illustrator is the leader, more expensive, and more widely used.

Adobe, to its credit, has done a lot of work to keep Illustrator easy to use while adding features. It's seen as the easier to use of the two tools, and at the same time the more functional, which is not an easy combination to achieve.

Figure 14-4 shows the use of Illustrator as a standard format on the National Parks Service's website: www.nps.gov/hfc/carto/map-symbols.cfm. Note that the editable versions of files are in Illustrator format. (The PDF versions, the other alternative, are not editable.)

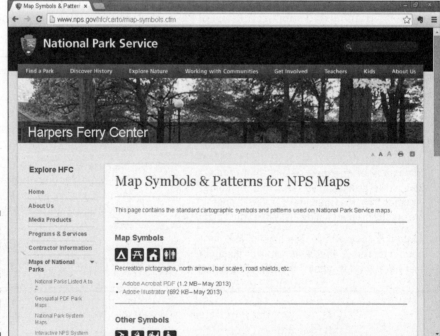

Figure 14-4: The National Park Service uses Illustrator as a standard format.

CorelDraw is the tool that a lot of people started on because it's less expensive than Illustrator, and was for a long time considered easier to use as well. CorelDraw has added a feature called *lenses* to handle opacity and related requirements, which is considered to be difficult to use.

CorelDraw also faces the issue that always bedevils less-used software, which is that most clients and major design houses want files in Adobe Illustrator format. Although CorelDraw can save in Illustrator format, there are always potential problems, such as the user forgetting to save the file in the non-native format or encountering conversion problems with the files.

Many web designers use both a raster graphics program (such as Adobe Photoshop or GIMP) and a vector graphics program (such as Adobe Illustrator or CorelDraw). There are real ease of use, support, and updating advantages to using the two Adobe programs together, which of course is Adobe's intent in building its product lineup the way that it has.

Although it's useful to know both programs, you can probably get through most of a career using just Adobe Illustrator. If you already use Illustrator, consider investing time and energy to get better at Illustrator and/or Photoshop. If you already use CorelDraw, consider looking for ways to add Illustrator to your toolkit.

Adobe InDesign and Quark Xpress

Page layout for the web is a fraught and highly contentious topic. There are two main reasons for this:

- ✔ Web pages are displayed on such a wide range of layout that the promise inherent in trying any kind of complicated page design can be more unhelpful than helpful.

- ✔ Browsers are so inconsistent that the displayed results for any kind of sophisticated page design are more likely to promote multiple rounds of debugging than further creativity and substantive improvement.

Adobe's history in this area is also complicated, and in a way not completely helpful to users. A small company called Aldus had a program that was very popular in the early years of web development called PageMaker. Adobe bought the program, continued upgrading it for several years, and then killed it in favor of InDesign.

Quark Xpress might be the strongest competitor to any of Adobe's Big Three — Photoshop, Illustrator, and InDesign. InDesign has gradually become a good program, after years of being, well, non-essential. But to many, Quark, as it's called, is the Photoshop of web page design; powerful, capable, interesting, fun to use, and well-supported by formal and informal training materials.

Figure 14-5 is a page that hosts U.S. government brochures designed in Quark Xpress: www.ahrq.gov/research/publications/pubcomguide/stayhealthy-specs.html.

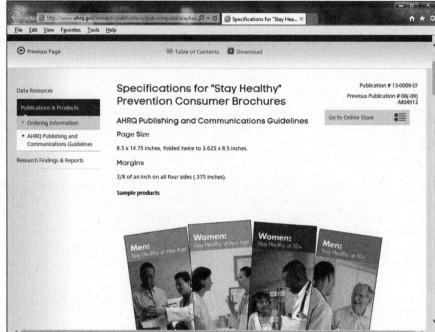

Figure 14-5:
The U.S. Federal Agency for Healthcare Research and Quality specifies layouts for brochures in Quark Xpress.

Unlike raster or vector illustration tools — that is, unlike Photoshop or Illustrator — when it comes to page design, you can't reasonably hope to coast through your career using only the Adobe tools. If web page design is a prominent part of your career, you may well have to learn both InDesign and Quark. And, unlike the situation with the other two categories, neither InDesign nor Quark is particularly affordable, easy to use, or fast-performing.

Unfortunately, you probably just have to develop expertise on one of these programs early in your career, and be ready to add the other one later.

Investigating Additional Adobe Tools and Others

Adobe has a few other category leaders, or at least strong contenders, to be aware of:

✔ **Lightroom:** Lightroom is basically a replacement for the Macintosh Finder or Windows Explorer for graphics files, and is well-regarded on both Mac and Windows.

✔ **Premiere Pro:** Premiere is the leading video-editing tool. There's a light version, called Premiere Elements, for under $100, just like with Photoshop.

✔ **AfterEffects:** Great for special effects for video, for creating titles and credits, and adding motion graphics.

There are also some key non-Adobe tools that are leaders in their categories that you'll need to know:

✔ **Avid Pro:** The "high-priced spread" for sound editing.

✔ **ProTools:** The most widely used sound editing package; often taught in schools.

✔ **Blender:** A powerful open-source animation tool. Did we mention it's free?

✔ **Final Cut:** Powerful video editing software.

There is a huge range of alternatives, add-ons, and extensions to the tools described in this chapter. However, knowing the tools described here will give you a skeleton of the major categories of web design tools and a starting point for discussion and learning in every category.

Part IV
Charting Your Career Path

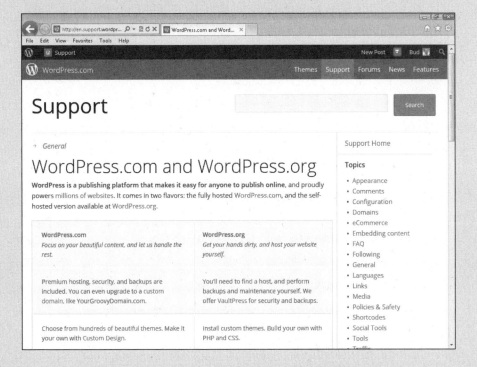

In this part . . .

- ✔ Find a web development job
- ✔ Create your portfolio site
- ✔ Land the job and do it well

Chapter 15

Using Dreamweaver and WordPress for Your Sites

. . . .

In This Chapter

▶ Understanding why Dreamweaver is king

▶ Using downloadable WordPress software

▶ Creating your site at WordPress.com

. . . .

*W*eb development has, in some important ways, settled down.

The core technologies for most website development today are the latest versions of the same set that people have used since about the year 2000: HTML (today, HTML5), CSS, and JavaScript. Also, web browsers on personal computers are getting more and more similar in how they display web pages, so you don't have to worry nearly as much about what your pages will look like on various browsers. Today, you don't have to learn a lot that's new about core technologies to do the basic work of creating websites.

This makes it much easier on the people creating web development tools. More and more of your work can be done directly in a tool, without much, if any, hand-tweaking.

Adobe Dreamweaver is the tool of choice for mainstream professional web developers. It is, arguably, the most complete tool on the market. Dreamweaver is also expensive, costing hundreds of dollars a year. On the upside, it allows you to position text and graphics precisely, to create pages that work across mobile and desktop platforms relatively easily, and much more.

WordPress is the tool of choice for many other web developers, including bloggers who don't think of themselves as web developers at all. WordPress is also used by real pros who specialize, more or less exclusively, in WordPress development. By some estimates, roughly half the sites being published today are WordPress products. WordPress is free or very inexpensive to use and isn't really designed for precise visual control, nor for knowing exactly what you're going to get as your site is viewed across mobile and desktop platforms.

These two tools are very different, but they cover the majority of site development work undertaken today. As a web development professional, it's worth understanding both. Then you can choose the right tool for the job, or choose a job where you get to use the tool you prefer.

Discovering the Biggest Trends in Websites Today

Today, websites are more and more database-driven, assembled on the fly, with content provided by calls to various databases. This change prioritizes two things.

The first new reality caused by database-driven web pages is that page design is more about creating a container for content than it is about fine-tuning the page's look to the last pixel. You put buckets on the page and expect them to only fully come to life as you pour content into them.

Amazon is a great example of this. Most of the content on the page is at least semi-customized and updated on an ongoing basis. As a designer, you're creating page designs and sample pages; it's impossible to predict, let alone control, exactly what each and every user will see.

The second new reality brought about by database-driven web pages is that it's increasingly considered a web designer's job to know a fair amount about interfacing to various databases. Knowing how to do some work in Python and SQL, the two standards for accessing databases, can be a huge help. Even just knowing enough to tweak existing code — similarly to the way a lot of web designers work in JavaScript — is a big advantage. We don't cover this topic in this book, because it's too extensive, but knowing some Python and SQL is important for many web designers.

The other big trend that affects page design is that the range of screen sizes and types of devices that your web page will ultimately appear on is now both hugely extensive and ever-changing. The "mobile" category stretches from small-screen smartphones, through iPads with high-resolution Retina displays, to laptops, to main displays and external monitors that can hold 20 or 30 smartphone screens' worth of text and graphics.

The range in screen sizes means more than it used to, as well, because more and more web access comes from mobile usage. So the days when you could put a special version, representing only a fractional part of your "real" website, on mobile phones are long gone.

The differences in screen sizes are so great that you have to include or exclude entire parts of a page design depending on how large the screens involved are. So part of your design process might be to have two or three different "suites" of screens — perhaps smartphone, tablet, and laptop display and up. But even this decision, though it might simplify specific design problems, is a big deal, requiring thought, attention, care, and maintenance of standards definitions, plus periodic review.

Taken together, the increase in database-driven web pages and the proliferation of target screen sizes means that web design tools are all the more important. There's just not much percentage in hand-tweaking the HTML, CSS, and JavaScript for individual web pages. Instead, your page designs have to be both highly flexible and pretty darn bulletproof.

With these changes, the role of web design tools is growing steadily. In this chapter, we discuss the two biggest web design tools: Dreamweaver and WordPress. There are many others, but these are the two beasts that will do the most to give you flexibility in your career if you know them — and that may impose challenges for your career if you don't.

Choosing Adobe Dreamweaver

A review in *PC Magazine* sums it up: "As an advanced website editor, Dreamweaver has no serious completion . . . for building up-to-date multiplatform websites."

Dreamweaver has a graphical user interface that supports nearly all HTML5 and CSS features, reducing the need for hand-coding. However, although Dreamweaver offers a lot of cool features that are implemented in JavaScript, you can still do a lot more if you tweak the JavaScript that Dreamweaver generates and write new JavaScript code of your own.

There are a great many Dreamweaver resources available, including free tutorials. Figure 15-1 shows a free tutorial available from the Utah schools. The website that provides the tutorial is very basic — not a strong example of what you can do with Dreamweaver — but the information is useful, and the site provides sample graphics and other resources.

To access the tutorial, visit www.schools.utah.gov/ate/marketing/ curriculum/ecommerce/course1/sitedevel/linkcolors_dw4.htm.

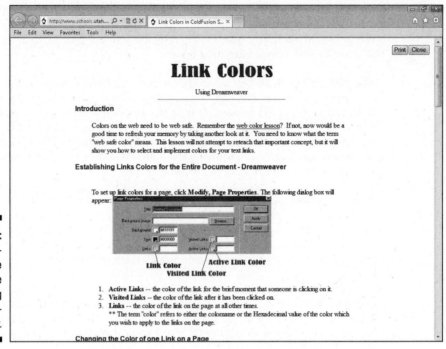

Figure 15-1:
Utah pro-
vides free
online
training
for Dream-
weaver.

Dreamweaver started life as the flagship product of a company called Macromedia, but was acquired by Adobe in 2005. In the decade since, Adobe has improved the product greatly and integrated it with other Adobe tools.

The most current version, as of this writing, is called Dreamweaver Creative Cloud. It's only available as a subscription service, although you can buy older versions of Dreamweaver from many sources.

Figure 15-2 shows a table of Dreamweaver versions. This is useful information to have in case an organization that you're thinking of joining still uses an older version of Dreamweaver.

Pros of Dreamweaver

Take a look at some of the major features that make Dreamweaver the tool of choice for web development — features you'll have to match if you want to use a different tool, or if you hand-code your website:

  ✔ **Fluid-grid page layouts:** Fluid-grid page layouts automatically resize to fit different screen sizes, without the need for you to hand-code CSS to support the changes.

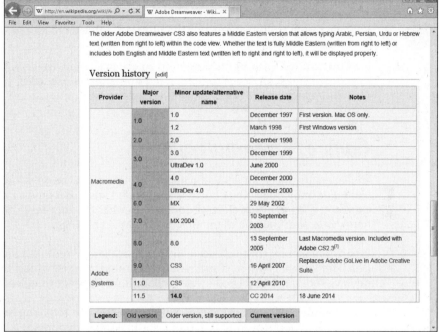

The older Adobe Dreamweaver CS3 also features a Middle Eastern version that allows typing Arabic, Persian, Urdu or Hebrew text (written from right to left) within the code view. Whether the text is fully Middle Eastern (written from right to left) or includes both English and Middle Eastern text (written left to right and right to left), it will be displayed properly.

Version history [edit]

Provider	Major version	Minor update/alternative name	Release date	Notes
Macromedia	1.0	1.0	December 1997	First version. Mac OS only.
		1.2	March 1998	First Windows version
	2.0	2.0	December 1998	
	3.0	3.0	December 1999	
		UltraDev 1.0	June 2000	
	4.0	4.0	December 2000	
		UltraDev 4.0	December 2000	
	6.0	MX	29 May 2002	
	7.0	MX 2004	10 September 2003	
	8.0	8.0	13 September 2005	Last Macromedia version. Included with Adobe CS2.3[7]
Adobe Systems	9.0	CS3	16 April 2007	Replaces Adobe GoLive in Adobe Creative Suite
	11.0	CS5	12 April 2010	
	11.5	**14.0**	CC 2014	18 June 2014

Legend: | Old version | Older version, still supported | **Current version**

Figure 15-2:
Dreamweaver
has a rich
history of
ownership
and
versions.

✔ **Interactive CSS design:** Dreamweaver allows you to drag and drop complex features like shadows and curved corners, which causes the appropriate CSS code to be inserted into your page.

✔ **Interactive JavaScript-supported features:** You can use UI widgets to create pop-up dialogs, menus, and other UI features. These widgets cause the appropriate JavaScript code to be inserted into your page.

✔ **Interactive multimedia support:** You can insert a multimedia element into your page and specify whether it will be supported by HTML5 or Flash. Even though it's provided by Adobe, which has good reason to push its own Flash format on people, Dreamweaver has full support for HTML5 as well.

✔ **Template management:** Dreamweaver makes it easy to create templates, and includes the capability to make areas of the template editable or uneditable — just the kind of control you need for a complex, database-driven website.

✔ **Flexible previewing:** It takes just a few clicks to see a live preview of multimedia content or your page layout.

✔ **Browser support:** Dreamweaver features, such as fetching data from a database, work in all modern browsers.

Microsoft's offering that competes with Dreamweaver, Expression Web, supports a crucial feature for most modern sites — pages that fetch data from a database — only in Microsoft Internet Explorer, which is just unacceptable.

✔ **Integration with Photoshop, and so on:** In Dreamweaver, you just double-click an image to open it in Photoshop — assuming you paid for Photoshop as well as Dreamweaver, of course!

Cons of Dreamweaver

Dreamweaver has a lot going for it. For one thing, it's the only tool in its class. For individuals, the choice is simple and stark: Become a Dreamweaver expert, try to get other, cheaper tools to do what Dreamweaver does, or hand-code your pages and templates in HTML5 and CSS.

When considering these choices, look at the "Using WordPress Software" section later in this chapter. WordPress software is the most widely used inexpensive tool out there. Dreamweaver does have some downsides, however:

✔ **Complexity:** Dreamweaver is a very complicated tool. You have many ways to perform most functions. For instance, if you want a live preview, you can preview just multimedia; the whole page; or actually publish to an intranet or the web, and see what things will really look like. Other tools give you simpler options.

✔ **Cost:** Dreamweaver can cost nearly $1,000 as a stand-alone tool, or add a big chunk to your Adobe software subscription. Either way, the cost of Dreamweaver is a big issue, especially when compared to all the freeware tools out there that support writing HTML5 and CSS directly.

✔ **Keeping up:** After you adopt Dreamweaver, you're locked into an ongoing cycle of upgrades, learning new features, deploying the features, and (if you wish) giving feedback. You become a "Dreamweaver person" rather than just a web design expert.

It's all about columns

Dreamweaver creates grids of vertical columns for your work. Pages targeted for phones use four columns; for tablets, eight columns; and for desktop displays, twelve columns. This provides a strong visual metaphor to support the range of screen sizes you'll be dealing with, although no such approach can fully match the complexity and trade-offs of working on pages that will appear on widely disparate screen sizes.

Dreamweaver gives you a really good start, however. Consider using Dreamweaver as your starting point for multi-platform web publishing.

Resizing your page layout will only get you so far; you want to add different content areas for the larger screens and drop them for the smallest ones. Having content areas appear conditionally is confusing. Consider using two or three different page layouts to cover the full range of screen sizes.

Using WordPress Software

So, as described earlier, Dreamweaver is the leader in its market — multi-platform web publishing. Are there real alternatives?

There definitely are, and the leading alternative is WordPress software. WordPress, in this form, is downloadable software that you can install and modify.

WordPress software is open-source, so you can change just about anything in it that you want to. And you don't have to do the work yourself; there's a lively community with lots of expertise out there.

With WordPress, there's only a small core team of paid professionals who are responsible for updating and releasing the core software. (Often in annoyingly small releases that are prone to lacking focus and direction.) The rest of the work is done by the WordPress community. Much of the work is done for love, although of course many in the community make their living doing WordPress-based work for clients as well.

WordPress has many different page looks referred to as *themes*. Each theme is a combination of HTML and CSS. WordPress themes are "deep" — they're highly capable, and you can modify them really extensively using CSS as well as HTML.

You can modify them or add JavaScript as needed to add the functionality that you want.

By using WordPress software, you inherit a great deal of functionality and expertise at low cost. However, there are a few issues that limit the use of WordPress software among website developers:

- ✔ **Sameness:** WordPress pages famously have a certain look and feel that seems to persist across themes. It can feel challenging to find or develop a WordPress-based site that doesn't feel like you've seen and used it somewhere before.

- ✔ **Blog focus:** WordPress was originally developed as blogging software, and the blogging focus continues today. Most business sites de-emphasize blogs or don't support them at all. (In fact, many business sites are written from scratch, but have blogs associated with them that are WordPress-based.)

✔ **Complexity:** WordPress software has developed in layers of inspiration and change over more than a decade. This often means there are new capabilities layered on top of old ones in a confusing and occasionally brittle manner.

✔ **Performance:** Written and changed over many years, WordPress software can run slowly, and the CSS and HTML maintained by the WordPress community are often "thicker" than they need to be. Making changes, debugging, or enhancing performance can be wearying tasks.

✔ **Maintainability:** After you modify WordPress software, you have a Hobson's choice each time a new release of the core software comes out, or there are improvements to a theme you're using: Do you take the new release and add your modifications to it again, or do you take things from the new release and add them to your modified WordPress software? The tendency in the community is to take the new release and modify it as needed.

✔ **Control:** Web development professionals and organizations that have one or more websites are used to doing their own thing, on their own schedule. (And to redoing sites every few years for freshness and functionality.) Being subject to someone else's development schedule and release calendar can feel strange and frustrating.

We refer here, many times over, to *WordPress software*. This is software you can download to your own system, tweak, and then use to host your own websites, or even whole networks of websites. Confusingly, there's an easier-to-use, but less flexible, WordPress–based alternative, WordPress.com, described in the next section. (The naming of these alternatives by the company that controls the core of WordPress, Automaticc, has never been very helpful.) Most expert website creators will want to use WordPress software, rather than WordPress.com, for most of their projects.

There are thousands and thousands of jobs relating to WordPress software development. Though some developers look down their nose a bit at WordPress, because you don't have the same degree of control as with tools like Dreamweaver, lots of great work gets done in WordPress, and it's a rich source of jobs.

You can get a comparison of WordPress software and WordPress.com at `www.wordpress.com`. It's useful, but it soft-pedals the restrictions on using WordPress.com described in the next section. To see the comparison (See Figure 15-3), visit `http://en.support.wordpress.com/com-vs-org/`.

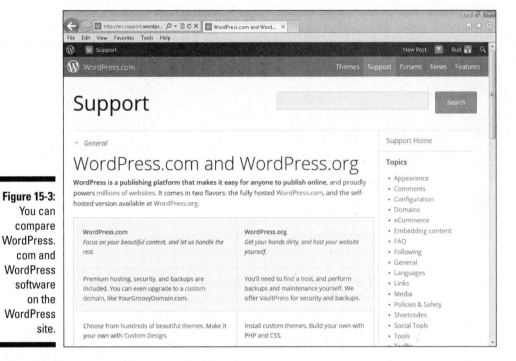

Figure 15-3:
You can
compare
WordPress.
com and
WordPress
software
on the
WordPress
site.

Using WordPress.com

One of the quickest and least expensive ways to put up a surprisingly capable website is to use WordPress.com to develop and host your site.

WordPress.com gives you a wide choice of themes and add-ons. You can have a good-looking, highly functional site up in a day. If you have content handy, it can be quite impressive.

The site includes hosting at no cost for a small site, and at reasonable cost for a larger one. WordPress.com also makes it easy to find and register a custom domain name, although you have to pay an annual fee for the name.

Because WordPress.com is such a useful tool for getting a site up fast, many web development pros use it when they need to do a website for friends and family, or colleagues who are doing personal projects.

However, WordPress.com is much less capable and flexible than WordPress software. You have a much more limited choice of themes and add-ons. You can pay for the right to customize the CSS in the theme for your website at a small monthly charge, but you can't modify the software itself.

WordPress.com also has the same concerns as WordPress software, but to a greater extent. For instance, the tendency of sites to look the same is stronger. With a wide, but still limited, choice of themes and add-ons, it's hard to create a site that feels very different from a thousand other sites out there.

E-commerce and advertising are not allowed on WordPress.com websites. This is fine for many sites that either have a personal focus, or represent a business online. But if you need these capabilities from the get-go, you need to use WordPress software, or some other approach.

WordPress.com sites often show advertising to users — not your advertising, but Automaticc's. You don't get to see the advertising because it's not shown to anyone with a WordPress account. You can pay a small fee per month to have the advertising removed.

If you do need advertising options, WordPress will tell you what you can do; see Figure 15-4 for details. Google AdSense, the most popular advertising option, is not allowed on WordPress.com sites. To see the full set of options and restrictions, visit `http://en.support.wordpress.com/advertising/`.

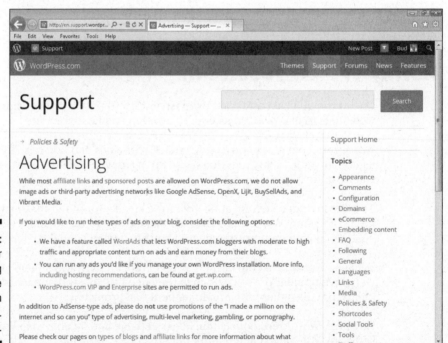

Figure 15-4: Your advertising options are limited on WordPress. com sites.

You can get a comparison of WordPress software and WordPress.com on the WordPress.com website. It's useful, but it soft-pedals the restrictions on using WordPress.com described below. To see the comparison, visit `http://en.support.wordpress.com/com-vs-org/`.

If you need to add these capabilities later, you'll have to move your domain name and site content to a new host. There are people who specialize in doing this, but it's not completely easy or free.

With all these limitations, why does anyone use WordPress.com? It's very easy and very inexpensive. In particular, as a web developer, it's the easiest way for you to help friends who need a site without tying them or you into a lot of hassle and expense going forward.

It's not that hard to get a WordPress.com–type experience from one of the many WordPress developers out there. They'll host the software for you and add the capabilities you need. You can search online or ask friends and colleagues for their experience.

Chapter 16

Building a Competitive Portfolio Site

....

In This Chapter

▶ Checking out Sarah Rudder's graphics-led portfolio site

▶ Looking at Matt Rudder's coding-led portfolio site

▶ Creating your own portfolio site

▶ Discovering how creative people get work on the strength of their portfolios

....

*Y*ou've probably seen an artist or art student carrying a portfolio. The word means two different things at the same time. The first is an over-size container that holds the works in one place. A typical dimension for this meaning of the word *portfolio* — for the extra-large binder that holds the pieces in it — is 14" x 18", but some are larger.

The second meaning of the word *portfolio* is all of the designs or artwork you've created that you want to show other people (that is, for the pieces of paper in the portfolio). The pieces of paper can include drawn or painted art-works, sketches, cels from animation, and blueprints. The portfolio might or might not contain typed or even handwritten descriptions of the pieces that it contains.

For our purposes, we're going to use the word *portfolio* in yet another way: as an online representation of the breadth and depth of your work. We'll call the printed-out pieces that you've seen artists carry around a *print portfolio*. (If you're a designer, you may have one of these yourself.)

But our focus in this chapter is on something that has largely replaced the printed portfolio for many developers: the online portfolio site. The site is a container in which you can show off your best work.

Many artists, art students, and designers put a great deal of work into curating their print portfolio. They keep it under lock and key when they're not using it, and go to great lengths to protect it if they're taking it with them somewhere and rain threatens. And when they create a piece that they're especially happy with, they'll set it aside and say, "That one goes in the portfolio."

It's the same thing with your online portfolio site. It should contain your best work and, at the same time, be representative of the breadth of what you've done.

In this chapter, we show you what a strong but not too complicated portfolio site looks like.

Introducing Sarah Rudder's Portfolio Site

Sarah Rudder is a young visual designer of the first water, as the Brits say — meaning, she's at the top of her game. She has a wide range of abilities, combining visual design and coding skills and a lot of relevant experience.

Sarah's background and experience are an excellent example of how a web developer can start with skills into design and grow into an all-around web-development badass, all before turning 30.

Sarah's career so far

Sarah's career and the online presence she's developed based on it are good examples for anyone with a design-based career in web development to look at and emulate in his or her own career path.

Sarah was an honors student at California State University, Fresno, graduating in 2008. She studied mass communication and journalism.

While still at CSU Fresno, Sarah worked as an assistant to a photographer, helping with both photography and marketing. Her work included photo editing, the use of filters, and touch-up — basic skills for a designer.

Also while still in school, Sarah worked as a production assistant at the local city magazine, *Fresno*. She did graphic design and page layout, with lots of work in the Adobe suite of design tools, using Photoshop, Illustrator, and InDesign.

After graduation, Sarah worked as a graphic designer for Logos Bible Software in Bellingham, Washington, for more than four years. She helped create a new brand identity for that company, and she implemented it in site content, email marketing pieces, web-based ads in Flash (remember, this was way back in 2010), and even in videos she helped produce.

Sarah was also developer relations coordinator for the company. She worked in PHP, AJAX, and the Big Three of modern web development — HTML5, CSS3, and JavaScript.

Sarah then returned to the Bay Area, where she took contract positions and worked as a freelancer for two and a half years.

Recently, Sarah took a position as a web developer for Asana, a company that makes communication tools for teams to use. Its slogan is "Teamwork without email." Web development is crucial to the product itself, not just to the company's website that describes what it makes and how to buy it.

You can see Sarah's LinkedIn site in Figure 16-1. You can also visit it yourself at www.linkedin.com/in/sarahrudder.

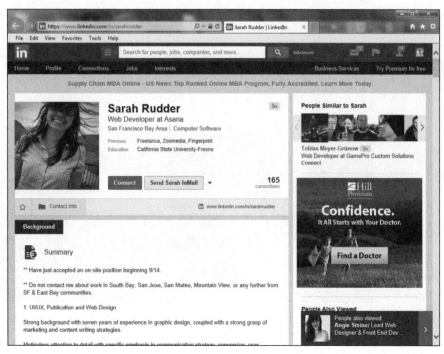

Figure 16-1:
Sarah's
LinkedIn
page
shows a
burgeoning
web devel-
opment
career.

Sarah's LinkedIn page is a good example of how to handle periods of contracting and freelancing in your portfolio. She gave each of the longer contracts (between 6 and 12 months) a brief, separate entry in her online resume, and then combined smaller jobs into a period of contracting about a year and a half long. For these smaller jobs, she just listed the client names, without any detail about what she did for each.

Sarah's portfolio site, above the fold

Check out Sarah's portfolio site as an example of a good portfolio site. We include a few screenshots to illustrate our points. If you can, however, you should also check out Sarah's site yourself. It's at www.sarahrudder.com. You can see the home page in Figure 16-2. Sarah has chosen to put everything on a single page.

Single-page websites have become popular as a way to quickly get across a focused idea or set of information, without inflicting the complexities of creating and maintaining navigation between pages on the site's owner, nor inflicting the complexities of finding things located at different spots on the website on users. The user just has to scroll up and down, and everything in the single-page website is revealed.

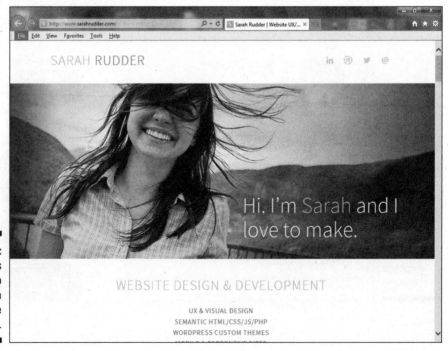

Figure 16-2:
Sarah's portfolio site packs a lot into one page.

Using a single-page website doesn't excuse you from the need to do web design, though. Like any good web developer, Sarah knows that a well-designed site makes a visual statement when you first see it.

This means that the home page of the site — which is the whole site, in this case — and, in particular, the area above the fold — are extraordinarily important in setting expectations for the site as a whole.

Of course, people look at the web on all sorts of devices these days. But generally, *above the fold* refers to content in the top 350 to 400 pixels of a web page.

Take a look at what Sarah has put above the fold on her portfolio site:

- **Her name:** Her name, in all caps. The upper-left corner of a web page is where the user's eyes go first and return to again and again. So that's where you should put your brand — or, in this case, your name.

- **Links:** Sarah's page contains icons that link to her LinkedIn page, Dribble — a site that hosts designers' images — Twitter, and an email link. Including these links helps Sarah keep her portfolio page simple because users have other places to go for additional information.

- **Photo:** Sarah has a fun, sassy photo across the top of her page — much like the big photos that Facebook has added to its pages. Note also that the photo, while friendly, obscures enough of Sarah's features that you wouldn't recognize her in public from it.

- **Statement:** It's good to have some brief statement summing up what you're offering. Sarah's career is varied enough that this is not easy. So she says, "Hi. I'm Sarah and I love to make." This covers all her many different skills and is also a subtle reference to *maker* culture, associated with Burning Man, 3D printing, and other cool stuff.

- **Descriptive header:** This initial header describes what Sarah does, at a high level: "Website Design & Development." People looking at the page, and perhaps hoping to get help with a project, can easily make an initial decision as to whether to keep looking.

- **List of key skills:** Sarah then lists her key areas — basically, things that someone might want to hire her for: UX and visual design; semantic HTML, CSS, JavaScript, and PHP; custom themes for WordPress; mobile and responsive sites; wireframing and prototyping; and content strategy. There are probably some other things here that Sarah could have added. A list like this is usually not just the kind of work that you've done in the past, but also the kind of work that you'd like to do in the future.

The part of Sarah's home page that's above the fold conveys many powerful messages, and even offers a fair amount of functionality, with just a few words, icons, and a single large image. Visitors can definitely figure out immediately if they want to scroll down and learn more, or go somewhere else — and that's one of the key things that any web developer tries to accomplish with her page.

The rest of Sarah's page — and site

We can describe the rest of Sarah's home page, and the entire site, at the same time because the entire site is only one page. Figure 16-3 shows another screenshot of the home page, from farther down on the page. However, the entire home page is about a dozen screens deep. To scroll down through all of it yourself, go to www.sarahrudder.com.

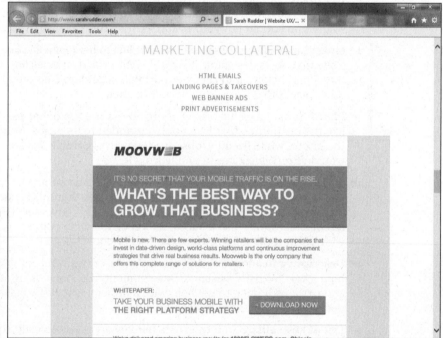

Figure 16-3:
The Sarah Rudder site packs a lot of information into one page.

Here's what you'll find on the rest of the page:

- ✔ **Cepheid site:** This is a medical products site, and the Sarah Rudder websites shows both an extended screenshot and an iPhone screenshot of the site (cleverly overlaid onto a picture of an iPhone).

- ✔ **Natera site:** Also shown are three pages from the site for Natera, a genetics testing company.

- ✔ **HTML, CSS, WordPress, & .Net subheader:** This is followed by thumbnails for Faithlife Bible, Faithlife Women, and Vyrso, a site for Christian-themed ebooks.

- ✔ **Marketing Collateral major header:** The specific skills listed under this header are HTML emails, landing pages and takeovers; web banner ads; and print advertisements. Following this is an HTML email with a lot of content, carefully laid out. Again, potential clients can quickly see whether Sarah has the skills they need.

- ✔ **Further headers for email design and code and CONTENT DESIGN:** These areas provide additional depth on the remainder of the skills that Sarah is promoting on her portfolio site.

- ✔ **THE STORY SO FAR major header:** In just seven paragraphs, Sarah tells a few pieces of her life story, along with a brief description of her philosophy for web development.

These pages clearly show Sarah's graphic design expertise because they're full of information, but feel light and open. They also use color and photographs effectively.

By providing so many examples, Sarah also helps those who want a designer with expertise in a certain kind of content. Someone creating a medical-oriented site, for instance, would see lots of examples from that field here: someone creating a sports-oriented site, not so much. Sarah doesn't make any broad claims about what she is or isn't good at; she lets her work speak for itself.

Sarah's work leaves a strong overall impression: If you had a medium-sized web project to do, you'd certainly feel assured by both of these projects that Sarah was someone who could lead the project or, if you already had a lead in mind, be a big contributor to it.

You also get the impression, because of the extent of the examples provided, that Sarah might be a good person to bring on board if you needed something similar to her previous work done quickly, yet with polish.

Showing an entire home page on your site implies that you were the lead person for creating, or extensively revising, that site. If not, make it clear on your page what your role actually was. If you played a supporting role in creating a site, go ahead and show it on your portfolio site, but provide an explanation: "Provided UX services on a team of 12 that created the Vickenlooper website," for example.

The power of links

One of the weird things about the web is that it is truly just a collection of individual web pages. The only reason we call a collection of pages a website is because they share a main domain name, look and feel, and navigational structure.

When these conventions are broken — for instance, when a link that looks like part of a navigational structure pops up an email message instead — it can be quite disturbing.

The Sarah Rudder site shows how you can make a small site — even a single-page site — feel much bigger by using links cleverly.

The very first link that the site provides, the first link in the small collection of links in the upper-right corner of the site, is to LinkedIn. Now lots of people link to their LinkedIn page in emails or on personal websites. But this link is different. When a portfolio site and LinkedIn are connected, each provides vital support to the other.

Your LinkedIn profile gives vital background information about the who, what, when, where, and why of the work shown in your portfolio. Your portfolio illustrates how you actually carried out the assignments alluded to in your online resume.

The Dribble link also extends Sarah's portfolio site. It gives her a way to highlight specific works and comments others have made on them.

Minimalism is a big part of what good design means on the web. (And in consumer products; compare an early iPhone to a then-current BlackBerry, with its built-in keyboard. All of Apple's products have minimalism in their gene pool.) It's certainly possible to take minimalism too far; the recent trend toward single-page sites, for instance, is probably being overdone. But the Sarah Rudder site uses minimalism, plus links, effectively.

Always look on the bright side of life

We think Sarah makes a subtle mistake on her portfolio site. She uses a light bright orange for some text — for her first name, and for the headers on her site. When this orange is against a dark background, it's easy to read. But when it's against a light background, as it is in two places on the home page and above the fold, it's hard to read. Our guess is that Sarah designed this on a conventional monitor, which is usually up to the job of showing deep, rich colors.

On our systems, the orange-on-white text shows up fine on a conventional monitor, tolerably well on a MacBook screen and an iPhone — and not very well at all on a Windows laptop.

Windows laptops are made by different manufacturers and vary widely in their color range, how well they maintain their initial color range over time, and in other aspects as well. Always consider a very wide range of potential target machines when making design choices, especially important ones like text contrast with its background color. And test your results on a wide range of machines.

"Above the fold" in the news

The phrase *above the fold* comes from the newspaper world. (This might seem obvious to people over 40, but to younger people, perhaps not so much.) The fold is the strong physical horizontal fold that results when you fold a newspaper in half.

When people pick up a newspaper, they naturally scan the top half of the front page to see what's important. They then unfold the newspaper, which reveals the bottom half of the front page, and then open it, exposing more and more content.

A smaller version of the same phenomenon occurs for the internal sections of a newspaper — the sports section, local section, and so on. Above the fold matters.

If you're a writer, and you get a story on the front page, you definitely want your story to have *play above the fold*. That makes it one of about half a dozen things that the newspaper's editors have seen fit to highlight that day.

Photographers also want their front-page photos above the fold, especially in the "hero" spot, a few columns wide, and taking up perhaps as much as a quarter of the space on the top half of the front page.

You have to unfold a newspaper to open it, so *above the fold* means less for internal pages. But it's still a thing; people notice content above the fold more than content below it.

Keep physical dynamics like these in mind as you do web development. The user's attention is a precious thing; keeping concepts like *above the fold* and *below the fold* in mind will help you make better use of it.

Introducing Matt Rudder's Portfolio Site

There's a funny line on Sarah Rudder's portfolio site about working with teams of developers: "I got along so well with the developers that I married one."

The words "I married one" are a link, and they go to the site of Sarah's husband, Matt Rudder. Matt's portfolio site is shown in Figure 16-4. You can also visit it at `mattrudder.com`.

Matt's a software developer, so, unlike his wife Sarah, Matt can't just show graphics that he created and let the site visitor figure out that he created them. Instead, he shows product logos and describes his contribution to each project.

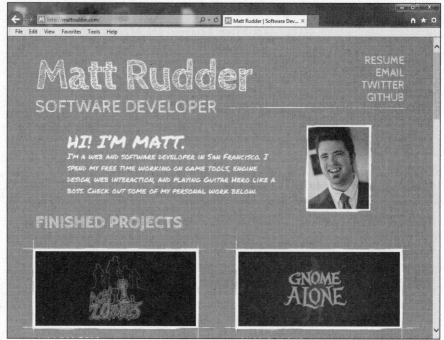

Figure 16-4:
Matt
Rudder's site
uses a multi-
page layout
and gives a
description
for each
project.

Here are some highlights of Matt's site:

✔ **Finished Projects, In Progress, and Research:** Matt divides his projects up into three groups, showing that he's capable of a wide range of work.

✔ **GitHub links:** GitHub is the most popular online repository for code. Matt provides links to all his projects.

✔ **Resume link:** Matt provides a link to his resume, in PDF format. (Matt is also on LinkedIn.)

Note that Matt's site is attractive, interesting, and not very wordy. Yet it's full of relevant technical terms for web development work, including C++, Direct3D, ActionScript, JavaScript, HTML5, and much more. Someone holding a job requisition in his hands could quickly see whether Matt had at least some of the specific skills needed for the position he was trying to fill.

Matt's resume is shown in Figure 16-5. You can access it at `mattrudder.com/media/Matt-Rudder-Resume.pdf`.

You can compare Matt's PDF resume to his LinkedIn page, shown in Figure 16-6. See his LinkedIn page at `www.linkedin.com/in/mattrudder`.

Figure 16-5: Matt Rudder's resume is chock-full of the names of software tools he uses for development.

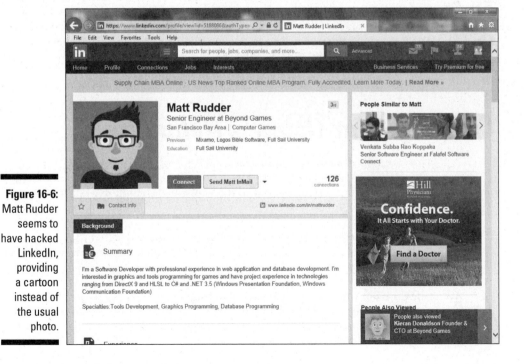

Figure 16-6: Matt Rudder seems to have hacked LinkedIn, providing a cartoon instead of the usual photo.

Matt's resume is full of technical terms, even more so than the home page of his portfolio. It includes a link to his GitHub repository and uses an innovative format to list key technologies and programming languages down the left side of the resume.

Matt follows an older model, which many people still follow today, of fitting his entire resume into one side of one page of paper. (Rather than the two-page resume that can be printed, double-sided, on a single sheet of paper, as we recommend for most resumes.)

By using this model, Matt provides a brief chronological resume and a list of selected projects without making entirely clear when some of the project work happened. This leaves the question hanging, likely to be answered in a phone screen or job interview.

Whereas Matt's highly technical resume would be very appealing to those "in the know," many HR people and other stakeholders — such as a less-technical interviewer, and in some cases also the hiring manager — might have a hard time with it. The technical slant of the resume might be increased by the choice he makes of putting it all in one page, meaning there's no room for explanatory text, nor for using bullet points to separate out different elements of the description. Consider adding some explanation, and using bullet points, if you use a lot of technical terms in your resume.

One of the authors (Bud Smith) has written more than a dozen books, often completing them while also working at a day job. On his resume, he doesn't describe how he handled the overlap on his resume, and is often asked about it in job interviews. It hasn't seemed to be a barrier, as Smith has been steadily employed and busy writing books since finishing his bachelor's degree in 1992.

Creating Your Own Portfolio Site

The portfolio sites for the Rudders are great examples of what you want in a portfolio site of your own. Attractive, interesting, easy to digest, and demonstrating that you're plugged into the web development world as a fully capable professional.

You need a portfolio site because the nature of how we get work has changed. Often, potential employers are researching you online well before you're even aware of it.

One problem with some projects is that they're confidential — for an internally facing website, or work in progress. To solve this problem, put the project on your website, but with no identifying details. Refer to similar sites and describe your role.

A portfolio site does several things that put you well ahead of most jobseekers:

- ✓ **Brings your resume to life:** People use chronological resumes because they answer many key questions, but they're terrible for helping people understand what you really did in a job. A portfolio site demonstrates your skills and ties them to live projects that people can check out.

- ✓ **Distinguishes you from people without one:** If a recruiter has several possible candidates for a job, and one has a portfolio site and others don't, guess who's more likely to get called first?

- ✓ **Saves you from wasting time:** Recruiters are picky, and they may be looking for someone who is almost like you, but not quite. You don't want them to call you if you're not quite a fit. And, having seen your site, the recruiter will probably come straight back to you when there is a fit.

- ✓ **Solves the "confidentiality" problem:** If you fill in your portfolio site with "like this one" entries for internally facing, confidential work, you've filled gaps in what your experience looks like to recruiters.

- ✓ **Solves the "too much hassle" problem:** When a job posting or a recruiter call includes a request for work samples, it often seems like too much trouble. If you create your portfolio site up front, it's easy to apply for all positions that fit your interests.

- ✓ **Solves the "narrowness" problem:** Resumes tend to put people in a box — graphics person or coder, writer or artist. LinkedIn makes this worse because you can't customize it to fit a job requisition before a recruiter, unbeknownst to you, looks at it with that requisition in front of her. Portfolio sites show the full range of your abilities.

- ✓ **Helps with the "getting started" problem:** There's an old conundrum: You can't get experience without getting a job, but you can't get a job until you have experience. A portfolio site lets you put student work, pro bono work, and consulting work front and center, inviting the viewer to see what you can do.

Creating a portfolio site is the single biggest thing that most people in web development can do to boost their careers. You may well find that a resume gets you an interview, but a portfolio site gets you the job. Get going on starting your portfolio site — or improving your existing one — today!

Chapter 17

Getting the Interview

· ·

In This Chapter

▶ Using real-world networking

▶ Networking online

▶ Creating a stellar resume

▶ Using LinkedIn

· ·

So you're ready to look for work. You've taken classes (Chapter 13), learned the core tools (Chapter 15), and created a portfolio site (Chapter 16). How do you proceed from there?

The natural temptation for a web developer is to use an online job site to look for something suitable. However, as we explain in this chapter, online job sites are useful, but perhaps the least effective way to get a job. To put it briefly, you're better off when people are contacting you — such as executive recruiters; when people know you — such as former colleagues and others in your network; or when you simply get a promotion or internal transfer.

In this chapter, we explain all these ways of getting a job, with tips and tricks about how to maximize your chances.

Networking in the Real-World

The most effective way to do networking in the real world is simply to do a good job in your current role. Get things done on time; show respect to your colleagues and help them get their own tasks done; introduce new ideas and new technologies at appropriate times; and keep the overall project's goals, not just your own goals, in mind as you do your work.

This helps generate a friendly and productive atmosphere across your team. Team members steadily become extremely productive reference sources for each other. Whenever one of the team members gets a new job — within your current company, or at a new company — the first thing he wants to do is to hire in his favorite members of his previous team. If you play your cards right, this will mean you.

Love the one you're with

The best way to get a great new job is to be really good and widely recognized in your current job. It's very common for people to be unsatisfied, unproductive, and unhappy in their current job, and try to solve it by looking for a new job. Often, this is, if not really the best, then the "least worst" option. But it comes with many problems of its own.

When things are going poorly in your current job, you're less confident, less likely to get strong recommendations, less likely to be doing things with new technologies or that you're otherwise happy about, and therefore less likely to put forth a strong resume or interview well.

All of this turns around when you're doing well in your current job. Doing well in your current job also makes you more likely to get "headhunted" — contacted by executive recruiters — and to be contacted by managers at your current company for new opportunities.

So, ironically, the single best strategy for getting a great new job is to do well at your current job. Until you can be with the one you'll love — that exciting, high-paying new job with great benefits, where you use all the latest technologies — do your best to love the one you're with.

Being a 10xer

The concept of a *10x* employee has recently gained widespread popularity. If you can be seen as a 10xer in any role, your chances of moving to the top of the salary and opportunity pyramid skyrocket.

The idea behind 10xers was widely popularized in the famous programming book *The Mythical Man-Month* by Frederick P. Brooks (Addison-Wesley). In this classic, Brooks gives the lie to the idea that a stalled programming project could be kick-started simply by throwing more people at it — especially by throwing more mediocre people at it.

Brooks says that adding people causes an exponential increase in the time people spend communicating instead of getting things done. The best communication, according to Brooks, was inside the heads of the most talented individuals, who were ten times more productive than the least. Next most effective was informal communication within a small, experienced, talented team.

More recently, it's been observed over and over that adding just one highly talented software developer, designer, or writer to a troubled project can put it back on track almost overnight as this highly talented individual races through backlogs of project tasks and succinctly communicates their needs and helpful new ideas to relieved colleagues.

Being a 10xer is a more intense version of the idea we introduce earlier in this chapter, that being happy in your current job is the best way to ease the way into a new one. If you can be a very happy, super-productive employee — a 10xer — then you're likely to find getting your next great job very easy indeed.

Networking has developed a bad reputation in many circles as an empty exercise of people who barely know each other rushing to exchange business cards and pushing each other for contacts and job recommendations. Don't do this. Do make ongoing efforts to stay connected to, and on a positive basis with, people with whom you work closely or who do similar work to you, within your company and outside it.

Figure 17-1 shows networking tips from the state of Minnesota. They're good, top-level tips. You can find them at `http://mn.gov/mmb/careers/ applicant_help/networking_tips/`.

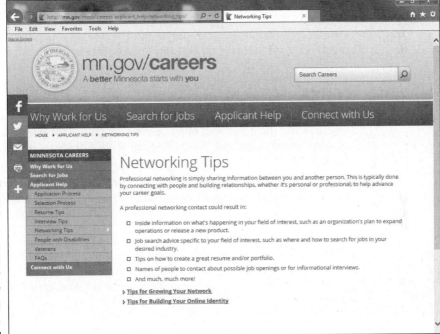

Figure 17-1:
The state of Minnesota website is a good source for introductory networking tips.

There are additional steps you can take for networking. Think of it as reaching out to wider circles of people.

People with a technical mindset — including, of course, web developers — tend to assume that you have to know someone well to be an effective networking contact for them. But studies show that looser connections can be even more effective in job searches. Definitely strive to make strong connections with your core project colleagues, but remember that it's also worth the extra effort to reach out to — and make a good impression on — more distant connections.

Here are some effective networking *targets* from closest to you to further away:

- ✔ **Your core team:** Everyone you work with on a daily basis should have good things to say about you.

- ✔ **Other teams that your team works with:** You and your team will have a reputation for being easy to work with or not, creative or not, focused on meeting deadlines or not. Strive to establish a good reputation for yourself and for your team as a whole.

- ✔ **People right across your department:** For instance, in departmental meetings or on internal discussion boards, make the effort to make useful, constructive, incisive comments every now and again. This shows that you're at the top of your game and willing to make an effort to contribute to larger discussions.

- ✔ **People with your same job description or technical focus:** Use professional group meetings and online gathering places for people in your profession, or using specific technologies, as a place to constructively work out new ideas and offer opinions.

- ✔ **Professional conferences:** Seeing and being seen at professional conferences is a big boost to your networking efforts. Snagging a speaking slot or seat on a panel every so often should be a big boost to your career.

One key tool for networking is to become known as a 10xer (see the sidebar "Being a 10xer") If you qualify, you can potentially be represented by companies that specialize in 10x employees, such as the first of its kind, 10X Management. Figure 17-2 shows the home page of 10X Management. You can find the page at www.10xmanagement.com.

Networking in your current company

Effective networking begins in your current job, and at your current company. The core effort that makes networking work doesn't fall under the traditional definition of networking at all. It's just doing a great job in your current role.

The next step, though, does start to move into the definition of networking: finding ways to let people know that the good work is happening. Casual mentions by you, followed, hopefully, by positive comments from coworkers or your manager, can accomplish this.

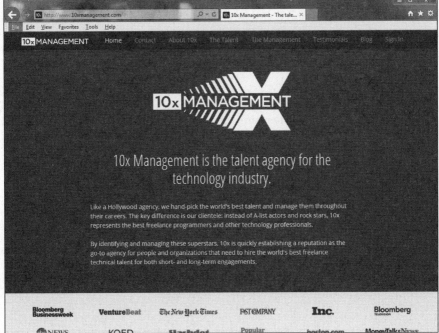

Within your company, there are specific steps you can take to network:

✔ **Say hello:** Learn to say hello to people on a casual basis. This can do a lot to make the workplace more comfortable.

✔ **Ask others about their work:** Ask other people what they do and what problems they're facing. This can give you opportunities to help and can inspire others to ask you the same in return.

✔ **Speak up in meetings:** Make helpful comments and share your opinion in meetings.

✔ **Use internal and customer service bulletin boards:** More and more companies have internal bulletin boards for employees to network on as well as customer-facing bulletin boards for solving customer problems. Contribute on these platforms.

✔ **Join non-job-related company groups:** Most companies have voluntary teams for pursuing broad goals and for skill-building, including a "green team" to pursue sustainability-related goals or an internal Toastmasters club to share efforts to learn public speaking. These are great networking venues.

✔ **Get mentors:** A mentor is a senior person who takes an interest in your career and gives you inside tips and other advice. As a web development person, consider having two mentors: one technical, for helping you build up your skills, and one organizational, for helping you look for new jobs or a promotion in your current company.

Your in-company networking is key to all your networking efforts. People outside your company will view people in your company as credible sources about you. People inside your company, but not on your work team, view people on your work team as credible sources about you. So build your network, and your credibility, from the inside out.

Networking outside your company

As we mentioned previously, the traditional view of networking is a sad effort where people meet at a semi-social event and try to use that connection to get each other to employ their networks to get themselves a new job. And this can seem most desperate outside your company, where you are likely to not already know very many people.

Three touches to sell

One of the things that's hardest for technically oriented people to understand is the confusing way that selling works — especially, the confusing way that selling works when the product is you.

First, people are inherently sales-resistant. That means that they often have to hear something several times before it even begins to break through.

Second, one source is rarely enough to convince people. They like to hear news — good or bad — from several sources before they believe it. (This is separate from the repetition issue; hearing something from the same source three times doesn't cover the "variety of sources" concern.)

Third, the usual marketer's beginning guess for number of repetitions — the number of times that someone has to hear something before he or she begins to believe it — is three.

So, in order for people to understand that you're a top contributor, they should hear this three times, from two or three different sources.

For instance, you can gently let people know that you accomplished some goal or another (one repetition); give a talk or write a paper, so that the conference or meeting or publication appears as an endorser of your expertise (second repetition); and count on coworkers or your manager to say good things about you to others (third repetition).

More is better, of course, so don't limit yourself to three repetitions. But targeting three is a good first step.

When networking outside your company, take a low-key approach. Don't appear desperate by trying too hard.

Create an elevator pitch; your name, job title, and a couple of well-known people whom you work with. Also mention the key technologies you use.

Then use it. Look for people with whom you can follow up due to shared job or technical interests. Then connect with them through a brief email and on LinkedIn, described later in the section "Following the Rules for LinkedIn."

Educational settings are great opportunities for networking, with fellow students and instructors as well. Do use your elevator pitch when needed, but also take the opportunity to go deeper. The long and in-depth conversations you can arrange to have, such as before or after class over coffee, can form relationships that help you, and your new friends, throughout your careers. And start building bonds with career services people; these can be helpful well beyond your first job out of college.

Be active in alumni groups too. Alumni groups offer the kinds of broad connections that can be extremely helpful in finding new opportunities.

Meetup.com groups, code-a-thons, and mentoring for young people are additional opportunities for mentoring, and also offer the chance to make new friendships that are personally as well as professionally meaningful to boot.

Building Your Online Network

One of the great conundrums of modern life is just how one's online life interacts with one's real life, where you actually see and interact with people in person. At best, the two realms support each other. You have a lively, interesting, real life, supported by lively and interesting interactions online.

If you're better-known, better-respected, and having more fun in your online life than in your real life, that's not a bad thing. You want to be having a positive experience in both realms, so if you're rocking it online, that's one down and one to go.

However, as a web development person, your technical interests and breadth of interest can make it easier to be a big shot online than in person. If this happens, how to bring that strong persona into your real-world life?

Use these tips to help you build a strong network in both worlds, online and off:

- ✔ **Go for a two-fer:** Try to be well-known and well-regarded in both your online and real-world lives. Don't settle for one or the other.

- ✔ **Have your online technical focus match your working life:** If you work with Python every day, but are regarded as a "wheel" in the C++ world due to your previous work, your personas aren't supporting each other. Try to spend your online time and your real-world time on the same topics. (This can mean either changing your online focus, or moving to a different job that matches your current online focus.)

- ✔ **Have your online friends overlap with your work friends:** Ask your work colleagues where they hang out online. Try hanging out there too. You can do good mutual reputation-building if there's overlap between your online and work lives.

- ✔ **Prioritize work:** When in doubt, put more energy into your work than into your online life. (And much more than into non-productive online pursuits like dating sites and online games.) Work can and should be rewarding, in many ways, and you can help yourself make it so by putting work first.

- ✔ **Reduce screen time:** Studies are showing that sitting — a necessity for logging screen time — is actively harmful to your health. All of us in web development need to move around more. So cutting screen time in favor of moving around — and even getting outside — will be better for you, even for your career, over time.

Creating a Winning Resume

There's been a lot of pressure on resumes over the last few years. Some people have advocated for the functional resume — a list of skills and skill areas, with occasional mentions of dates and employers. Others tell you that your resume has to be a single page.

However, the operative standard for a printed resume, or a resume in Word or PDF format, seems to be an old-fashioned, chronological resume, two pages long, with a summary statement at the top (optional) and educational background at the bottom (required).

If you are short on experience, consider fitting your resume on to one page, and putting your educational accomplishments at the top.

For an online resume, you simply transfer the printed resume to online format. You no longer have to worry about keeping it to exactly two pages, but otherwise, things are almost exactly the same.

Here, we tell you how to create strong chronological resume, ready to print — and then how to use it to create a strong presence on LinkedIn.

Making a Print Resume Stand Out

Your print resume needs to be a minor work of art.

Yes, the world has changed. It's highly likely that your "print" resume will hardly ever actually be printed. Instead, it will be viewed onscreen. But it's still important that it looks as if it would look great if it were printed.

Follow these rules to make your print resume stand out:

- ✔ **Format it carefully:** Your resume should look polished and professional even before anyone reads the actual words. If you need to, find a sample resume online, and then type your own information into the format.

- ✔ **Proofread it carefully:** Your resume really has to be perfect. Everyone knows this — or, at least, everyone believes it — so errors on your resume are seen as evidence of extreme carelessness and cluelessness. Make sure there are no errors.

- ✔ **Then, proofread it again:** You can't proofread your resume too many times. Then, get others to proofread it for you. Even if there are no actual spelling errors, out-of-date information can come across as an error too. For instance, one of the authors (Smith) once wrote "in progress" next to a book description on his resume — then left the telling words on there well into the next year, when he was handing people copies of that same "in progress" book.

- ✔ **List jobs in chronological order:** Start with the most recent, and go back in time. Include the company name, month, and year of the start and finish date, the city, and several lines about what you did in the job. This can be four to six bullet points per job — with as few as three for long-ago roles — three to four lines of narrative.

- ✔ **Include buzzwords:** It's crucial that you include key buzzwords in the resume text. HTML5, CSS, JavaScript, Python, SQL — these are just some of the buzzwords you want to be sure to include, wherever they apply.

- ✔ **Include a skills section:** Consider listing current skills in a separate section at the top. That makes it a lot easier for an HR person to quickly scan your resume to see if it's worth further consideration for jobs that require specific skills.

- ✔ **Include accomplishments:** List important accomplishments that you were all, or part of. Also include what you did, but "keep your eyes on the prize."

- ✔ **Include helpful dollar figures:** Words like "$5 million project" can be helpful; "I saved the company $2,123.92" are not. Put in dollar figures where you think they might help, and then check with a trusted friend about whether they actually do.

✔ **Make sure your key attributes are reflected:** If you're detail-oriented, put this in the Summary section — and then make sure that your accomplishments reflect a person who's detail-oriented. "Created a large SQL database that worked flawlessly in just two months, saving $5 million in inventory costs" is a statement that says *detail-oriented* without having to use the actual words.

✔ **You don't have to list all jobs:** In the older sections of your resume, you can cut off at a certain point, rather than go all the way back to the start of your career. Many people list only about ten years' worth of jobs to keep the resume length reasonable, reduce the presence of outdated technologies on their resume, and reduce the possibility for ageism in the hiring process.

For better or worse, anyone reading your resume will tend to guess that you were about 22 when you got your bachelor's degree, if any. There's no easy way to avoid this assumption, which for most people will be about right.

✔ **Try for two full pages:** People like a resume that fits on one single sheet of paper, front and back, chock-full of information — but without using extra-small type or narrow margins. If you're new in your career, though, don't strain to fill the space. Don't go over unless you're very senior and have a lot of accomplishments.

✔ **Print it out:** Print out your resume periodically. Make sure it looks great printed, and proofread the printed copy; it's easier to spot errors than it is onscreen.

✔ **Tweak it:** For each specific job, create a new version of your resume with the relevant buzzwords from the job description appearing in that version of your resume — especially at the top of the resume.

✔ **Get advice:** Do the best job you can on your resume, and then get an experienced friend or resume expert to weigh in. Paying a reasonable amount to a pro is worth it. Your university may have a careers services office that can help.

You are likely to use your resume again and again during your career. It's worth taking care to create and maintain a strong resume.

Following the Rules for LinkedIn

LinkedIn has several different functions. It can be a simple resume-hosting service. Or, you can add recommendations and comments, making your resume the centerpiece of a little online community focused on you.

You can also join various groups and networks on LinkedIn, building up your reputation. For technical people such as web development pros, there's a certain degree of "cool" attached to being low-key. Using LinkedIn as a simple resume hosting service might be for the best.

Here are some tips for using LinkedIn in basic mode. For more advanced tips, see *LinkedIn For Dummies,* 3rd Edition, by Joel Elad (Wiley).

Figure 17-3 shows the LinkedIn profile of one of this book's authors (Smith). Note how complete the summary is. You can see Smith's LinkedIn profile at `www.linkedin.com/in/floydearlsmith`.

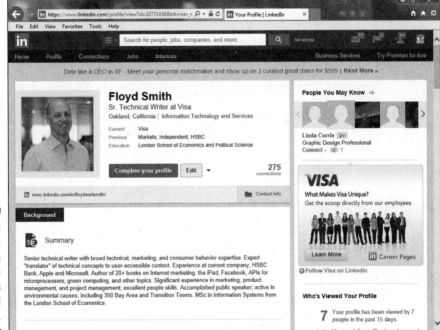

Figure 17-3:
Smith links to his LinkedIn profile on his resume and elsewhere.

Keep these thoughts in mind when using LinkedIn:

- ✔ **Make the summary count:** A recruiter should be able to tell whether you're a good candidate just from the summary. Write this carefully and be thorough.

- ✔ **Keep it inclusive:** When you apply for a specific job online, you can tailor your resume to the job description. On LinkedIn, you need to cover all the bases — a single resume has to attract all kinds of employers.

✔ **Go short:** Keep descriptions short. It's harder to read online than in print, so a smaller amount of detail goes a long way on LinkedIn.

✔ **Go long:** You don't need to trim your list of jobs to keep within a two-page (or any-page) limit on LinkedIn.

✔ **Give recommendations:** Give LinkedIn recommendations to the people you know best, or who recommend you.

✔ **Include some personal info:** List some interests outside of work. This helps people see beyond the online profile.

✔ **If you're free to travel, say so:** Many employers want to know that you're free to travel at least some of the time. If you are able to travel at all, add "free to travel as required" to your resume. If the travel demands of a job are too much, you can still back out. And if you're not free to travel, just don't mention it.

✔ **Update the Skills section:** Put your strongest skills in the Skills section. You can include up to 25, but it's best to include only those you feel most confident in. That way, you get follow-up from recruiters only on your best skills, avoiding disappointing wastes of time all around.

As with your printed resume, your LinkedIn profile may get a lot of attention during your career. Take the time to make it strong and useful.

Chapter 18

Getting and Doing the Job

So you've gotten enough education and built a portfolio site. You've had a few jobs — or you're working on getting your first job. Coworkers (or fellow students) say good things about you. And you're starting to get some interest for an upcoming job in web development.

How do you nail it down? We describe that process here.

Then comes a time when you get the job — or, you want to think a bit about the job you're already in. How do you do the job well enough to be seen as a star, one of those 10x employees (see Chapter 17) who can make, or save, a project?

This chapter answers those questions from a web-development point of view, telling you what's special about this process for graphics-based, coding-based, and mixed roles. With this information in hand, you'll be ready to boost your career, in the short term and permanently.

Getting the Interview

One of the hardest and most important journeys you'll ever undertake is the journey from sitting at your computer, looking at a job listing, to sitting in a potential employer's office, undergoing an interview.

For web developers, this journey is easier than it is for many other people. Web developers continue to be in strong demand as needs grow. And the use of many different, specific technologies within the field means that, if you have experience with the right technologies, and a solid overall background, your chances of getting a given job can be pretty good.

Most people are generally familiar with the process of applying for a job. If not, a good reference is *Job Hunting For Dummies*, 2nd Edition, by Max Messmer (Wiley). There are also *For Dummies* books on job interviewing, resumes, and cover letters.

Here are a few high points of the process, specifically for web developers:

- **The pre-submission phone call:** Before you send in your information for a job, give a call, if at all possible. Ask any key questions you have, plus the core question for any such process: Where is the company at in the hiring process? Often you'll find that the process is completed, nearly completed, or some other status that may leave you deciding to keep your powder dry and not apply for the position. If the hiring process is still open, ask about key tools and technologies.

- **The cover letter:** Always find a way to write a cover letter, even if you have to paste it along with your resume into a job application form that only accepts resumes. In your cover letter, take the three or so top requirements from the position description (as you judge them) and tie them to your experience. Also describe your availability — looking for work; employed but looking; not actively looking but attracted by this specific job description (or a personal recommendation), and so on. Be straightforward and to the point, rather than funny or cute. Proofread your cover letter to perfection.

- **The resume:** You should have a somewhat generic resume saved on your hard drive or in the cloud. For a specific job, take your generic resume and semi-customize it to fit the position. For instance, if there are specific technologies or tools required, identify the jobs where you used each one, and make sure that the technology or tool name is mentioned, with appropriate prominence, in the description for each job where you used it.

- **The follow-up phone call (immediately):** After you apply, follow up with a phone call. In our experience, this one simple step measurably increases your chances of getting the job. Ask if your information has been received. Then ask what's most important about the position and offer to resubmit your information with those points highlighted. This will really make your application stand out.

- **The follow-up phone call (two to three days later, and then weekly):** After you apply and follow up with a phone call, call again a few days later. See how the process is going and ask if it's likely that you'll move forward. If not, ask the person to whom you're speaking to consider you for future positions.

The WorkSmart site on the website for the state of California, shown in Figure 18-1, has advice on writing a cover letter. Like most such advice, this advice is a bit too formal and complicated for most web development jobs. Your cover note will often be just a short email, with a resume attached in

Word format. But even a short cover note should contain the gist of the content described on the WorkSmart site. Visit it at www.worksmart.ca.gov/tips_resume_cover_letter.html.

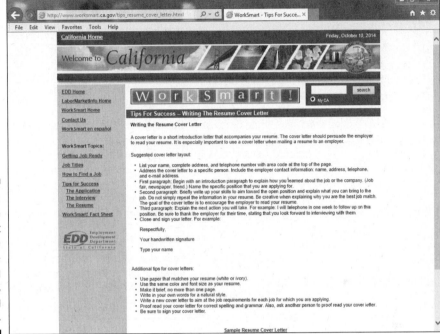

Figure 18-1:
The WorkSmart site covers job-searching basics, including cover letters.

Employers fixate (that's our view) on finding people who have used the top one or two technologies or tools that they're wanting you to use on the job. Ideally, for the employer, the desired technology and tool keywords appear in most or all of your recent jobs or projects. Not much else matters; you might be a nice person, learn fast, and so on, but if you don't have the specific technology or tool experience desired, you will often not be contacted, whereas those who do have those keywords in the right places will.

If you follow these steps, your chances of getting an interview improve.

For some reason, many companies — especially larger ones — will put up a restrictive job posting, wait months, get no candidates they can hire, and then bemoan the result. The thought of lowering the years of experience required, asking for experience with similar rather than exact matches to technologies and tool experience needed, or allowing partial work from home, for instance, doesn't seem to occur.

I. get. stuff. done.

One of the authors (Smith) had a work colleague in London, a project manager, who was very proud to say, with a long pause between words, "I. get. stuff. done." (*Stuff* might not have been the exact word she used.)

When you think of the interview process, it's good to think of the people in the hiring process as mostly having this attitude. People go to the trouble to get budget approval for new headcount, open up a job requisition, write or revise the job description, and so on because they're overwhelmed. The hiring process actually makes them more overwhelmed. You're arrival isn't going to help right away either, because it might take you a couple of months to get up to speed. (Most of this is especially true in web development, where ambitions are high and budgets, not so much.)

This is why companies are so insistent on experience with specific technologies and tools — it can shorten the time it takes you to get productive.

So the hiring process is not usually a lot of fun, nor very productive in the short term, for the people conducting it. When you think of people who you encounter in hiring, think of them as having the attitude of that project manager — they want to "get stuff done." The easiest "done" is to find some reason to say "no" to you, so avoiding that is a crucial goal for you in each step of the process.

During interviews, you might finally talk to some people who take the time to start to get to know you, and to think creatively about whether you're a good fit. Let the interviewers lead on that. Keep your answers during interviews of all sorts short, simple, and positive. This allows the interviewers to get through their routine questions quickly — and either finish quickly, which will make them feel more relaxed, or engage with you on more interesting aspects of the potential job or the hiring company, which will give you a chance to show what you know.

This is part of the reason networking is so powerful; when someone is a trusted friend and former colleague, the strict requirements on the job posting are very often relaxed. But new applicants are held to strict standards so, if no one fitting them exactly shows up, the job just goes begging.

Surviving Interviews

Job interviews can be very stressful. They have a large impact on your getting the job — assuming, that is, that the employer is truly ready to hire. If it's not, the job interview won't help much at all.

In this section, we share some web development-specific tips on the interview process.

The phone screen

A phone screen is a, usually brief, phone call between you and someone representing the company doing the hiring. This can be the hiring manager, an internal or external recruiter, or anyone else involved in the process.

The key word to remember in the term *phone screen* is *screen,* They're really trying to weed out candidates. If you're interested in the job, try to get screened in, not (as is the goal) screened out.

The person doing the phone screen is often a lower-level employee or contractor with only modest understanding of what's really needed for the position he or she is asking after. This can be a big problem in web development, where there is a plethora of technical pieces and tools, and where a manager might be just as happy if you have similar experience — but won't hear that if you're screened out first.

Unfortunately, the one thing phone screeners don't want to hear is a manager telling them, "You sent through people who don't fit the job requisition," because in that case, they've missed the whole point of the exercise. Yet web development is so fluid that it's easy to screen out people who actually are quite capable of doing the job.

So be brief and positive when talking to a phone screener. If you don't have a given requirement, give a similar alternative. "No, I don't have a bachelor's degree, but I do have an associate's degree and five years of experience." Or, "No, I don't have three years of Python experience, only two, but that's two years of Python, and I also know SQL and Hadoop." The screeners will usually pass on such comments to their bosses, if the comment is clear and simple enough to write down easily.

It's good practice to follow up after a phone screen by calling the next day to ask if you're still in the pool. You might well rise to the top of the pile as a result. You might also be given the chance to correct any negative information, an opportunity that can be invaluable.

Before you interview

Live interviews are fraught with potential pitfalls. You should do some research first. Here are a few web development-specific tips:

- **Network with other web developers:** Find out from other web developers currently at the company what the interview process is like and about working there more generally.

✔ **Find out if there are any "famous" interview techniques:** Some tech companies are famous for posing complex problems, using a fixed set of questions, asking a particular unusual question, planting one somewhat hostile interviewer, and so on. Google the company's name and the word *interviews*, and use the other approaches mentioned here to find out if there are any such tricks up this company's sleeve.

✔ **Be ready for behavioral questions:** Many companies now ask questions in the format, "Tell us about a time when you . . .." They then insert words like succeeded, failed, overcame an obstacle, and so on. Unfortunately, these questions are at least as much a test of your verbal dexterity in an anxiety-producing situation as anything. Consider writing down some of these questions beforehand and identifying three or four accomplishments you're proud of and challenges you've overcome, so you're more ready for these kinds of questions.

✔ **Look at the company's website:** If it sucks, stay away. (Unless you're being invited to help completely replace it.) It's really frustrating, and professionally limiting, to work in a web development job at a company that has a crappy website. But if it's at least decent, dive into it. Figure out what technologies are being used. Note both good and bad points, but plan to be sparing with the bad news unless it's really awful.

✔ **Check out Glassdoor:** Glassdoor (www.glassdoor.com) has a lot of good company-specific information, especially for big, technology-oriented companies. Use this information to learn about the place you're considering working, such as typical salaries, employee satisfaction (or dissatisfaction), and so on. Glassdoor can help prepare you for what your interviewers will think that you might think of their company, which is confusing, but an important thing to know so as to navigate the interview successfully.

✔ **Take Glassdoor with a grain of salt:** When you use Glassdoor, you may find that it's a couple of horror stories or snarky comments about the CEO that stick in your mind. Do not go into the interview ready to challenge your interlocutors about this. Use the negative information when choosing whether to accept a job offer, not to make yourself a "hostile witness" during the interview.

✔ **Check out your interviewers on LinkedIn:** The hiring company will check you out on LinkedIn, so return the favor. Use what you see on LinkedIn to identify items in your background that will be interesting or relevant to your interviewers.

✔ **Hit the boards:** Check out web development discussion boards for your area and see what you can learn. It can be a bit dicey to ask in an open message board for information, but a message like, "Hey, a friend" — you're a friend of yourself, right? — "is thinking of taking a job at Company X. Please PM me with any info you have," can be productive.

✔ **Use your e-resources:** Use email and Facebook in a similar way to crowdsource information and insights.

Companies and their employees get really sensitive about negative remarks posted on Glassdoor, Yelp, other online messaging systems, in emails, and so on. Find as many of these as you can, but be careful about mentioning them. If you do, ask in a neutral tone; don't badger your interviewers.

Some web-related companies are famous for giving hostile, lengthy, or tricky interviews. You need to find out if this is true before you interview. Not only to be sure you can handle the tricky part, but also because the people interviewing you will think you didn't do your homework if you didn't find this out in advance. So, be prepared.

Acing the interview

When it's time to go to the actual, live interview — probably several interviews, actually, with different people — it's easy to be nervous.

Don't be. Interviews are first and foremost about showing your interpersonal skills. For web development jobs, interpersonal skills are considered less important than for many other jobs. Yes, they matter, but they're not the single most important factor like they are, for instance, in a sales or customer support role. So relax.

Technical people pride themselves on dealing with things logically and rationally, and even on being able to handle a fairly high amount of conflict in support of doing the best possible job on a project. This means that interpersonal skills are not likely to be put under the same scrutiny as technical skills.

Your technical skills will largely be assessed from your resume and any work samples you've shared. You may be asked technical questions during your interview, but all you can do is answer those honestly and hope your experience meets the needs of the company.

It's also important to realize that many decisions about whether you're going to get a job have little to do with how well you interview. Many interviews are a waste of time; the company knows that you're not quite what it wants, and uses the interview to confirm it. Or it knows that it wants you, and uses the interview to confirm that instead. Sometimes, the company isn't even really sure if it has an opening, or the opening disappears between the time interviews are held and when it comes time to make an offer.

Figure 18-2 shows an interview with an IT specialist who works for the Library of Congress. The questions and answers are actually a pretty good proxy for a low-key job interview. Use this interview to practice for job interviewing. You can find it at `http://blogs.loc.gov/law/2012/06/an-interview-with-patrick-ouellette-information-technology-specialist/`.

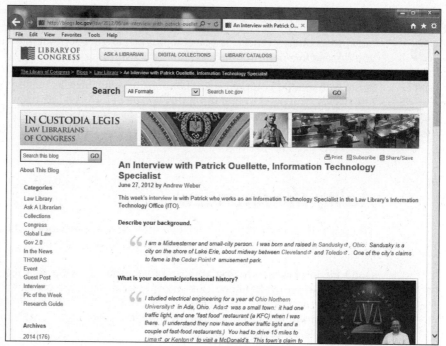

Figure 18-2:
This inter-
view reads a
lot like a job
interview.

There are only a limited number of times when an interview really makes a
"yes or no" difference as to whether you get a job, and it rarely comes down
to a single question. As long as you're friendly, positive, and honest, you're
likely to do well in an interview.

Companies sometimes make ridiculous requests of candidates — to do several
interviews spread out across different days, to add sessions after an interviewer cancels, and so on. Graciously refuse excessive requests; offer a phone
meeting instead, if needed, but don't keep traipsing back to a place that can't
organize an interview.

Here are a few web development–specific tips:

✔ **Practice, practice, practice:** We all like to think we can be heroes under
stress, but people are usually worse under stress than they are when
they're calm. Have a friend conduct three practice interviews with you.
You'll work through a lot of stuttering, hesitation, indecision, and brain
freezing that you might otherwise suffer through during the interview.

✔ **Feel free to be direct:** Web developers are famous, or sometimes even
infamous, for sharing their opinions freely. Don't go overboard in an
interview, but don't shy away from expressing yourself clearly.

✔ **Introduce yourself at the beginning of each interview:** Be ready to repeat
your basic information to each individual or group that you meet with.

✔ **Have, or come up with, a couple of questions for each interviewer:** Pivoting from defense (answering) to offense (asking), politely, takes a lot of the pressure off you — and off the interviewer, too. It makes the interview less of an interrogation and more of a discussion.

✔ **Have extra questions for your potential manager:** The most important interviewer is usually the person who will be your manager if you get the job. Even if this person is your last interviewer, and you're exhausted, or the first, and you're anxious, have a few questions written down for him or her in particular.

✔ **Speak slowly and pause between sentences:** It's very helpful to slow down your speaking during interviews. In web development, where you're intermixing graphical, technical, usability, and interpersonal concerns all at the same time, this is especially valuable. You will look thoughtful, not nervous. And no one can leave an interview remembering the stupid thing you didn't say because you gave yourself the opportunity not to say it.

✔ **Follow up afterward with a thank-you email:** Address it to whomever set up the interview. Add or reaffirm a couple of key points, shore up any weak spots in your answers, and make your availability and interest in the position clear.

The military is famous for its heroes, people who show courage under fire. But it doesn't expect it; the most important military adage relating to heroism is, "You're only as good as your training." Soldiers train over and over so they have "muscle memory" when under stress. You can do the same for yourself by having just a few practice sessions for your interview.

Becoming a Star Employee

People in all fields often look at a new job as a kind of silver bullet. A new opportunity will make them more money, introduce them to better coworkers, let them work on the latest technologies, and on and on.

Instead, a new job can sometimes be like that line in the old song from the famous rock group The Who: "Here comes the new boss, same as the old boss."

The main influence on whether a person is happy in any given situation is the person himself. There are lots of actual and potential difficulties at work, but over time, you have the biggest say in how things work for you.

This is especially true when it comes to becoming a 10xer — a star employee, as we mention in Chapter 17. A "star employee" isn't someone who's going to become a star in her next job. It's someone who is already a star in her current job.

So when you get a new job, set out to become a star employee. And if you've been in your current job for a while, figure out how to become a star employee there, as much as possible.

Figure 18-3 shows testimonials from customers of 10x Management, a firm that acts as a talent agency for top web development and other technical talent. You want to hear these kinds of testimonials with regards to your own work. Then you can get a top job yourself, or sign on with a company like 10x Management to represent you.

You can see the testimonials yourself at www.10xmanagement.com/ testimonials.

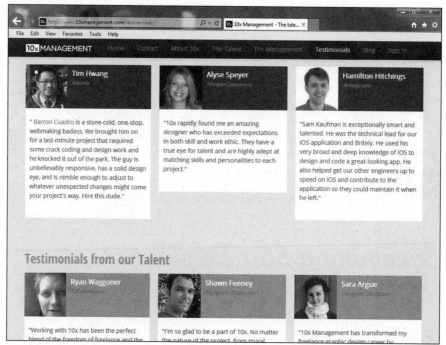

Figure 18-3: 10x Management customers love working with top talent, and vice versa.

If you're starting to look to greener pastures in your career, consider spending one year becoming as much of a star as you can manage in your current job. You're likely to become much more employable in the process.

It's true that people often develop an opinion of you pretty quickly in a new job. If you've already been at a job for a while, you may only be able to change people's opinions so much. Moving from "average" or "good" employee to "star" employee might take either several years in your current job or, more likely, at least one job change. But there's no time to start like the present.

There are three keys to becoming a star employee as a web developer: be stellar at your core skill; get more technical; and learn to communicate better and earlier.

Be stellar at your core skill

College admissions to top schools is one of the most competitive arenas on Earth. In this competition, you can divide applicants into two groups: all-rounders and angular students.

All-rounders are omnicompetent, good at a whole bunch of things: for instance, being good at math, good at English, good at sports, good at student government.

Top colleges are full of all-rounders, but here's the secret: There are a lot of all-rounders who get told "no" by top colleges.

Angular students, on the other hand, are really good at one thing. An angular student is one of the best in the entire applicant pool at chess, or calculus, or lacrosse, or writing short stories.

Top colleges are also — and, perhaps, increasingly — full of angular students, as well. But there are perhaps fewer angular students who truly excel in a niche, almost no matter how small it is, who get told "no" by top colleges.

It's similar in web development careers, when going for the top jobs. There are lots of people who are good, for instance, at the core web design skills triad of graphic design; HTML5, CSS, and JavaScript; and can write at least some Python or PHP or SQL as needed. It's quite lucrative to be one of these people.

But if you're truly expert — widely recognized, or visibly outstanding — in some aspect of graphic design; if you give lectures on how to structure your stylesheets in a hierarchy; or if you teach other designers introductory Python, then you're going to stand out further. There will actually be fewer jobs out there that are a good fit for you, numerically. But you'll get a high percentage of the jobs you apply for.

So, for the highest rewards, become stellar at the aspect of your work that you love most. You'll have more fun, and be more likely to have top pay and respect as well.

Get more technical

Most web developers come from a graphics background and are quick to call in someone technical when coding needs to get done. But the top web developers have a graphics background and can do at least initial coding themselves.

This is because people who are strongly technical tend to go into strictly technical jobs, without a strong web development aspect to them. For instance, the hottest technical job category in the last few years has been data scientist. Lots of data scientists come from a web background. But after they get the title data scientist, they're mostly not working directly on websites anymore.

So there's a lot of opportunity for people with a graphics background to get more technical and fill in the gap between the graphics and coding camps.

For most graphics-based developers, the core skill is JavaScript. If you can be strong in JavaScript, which still usually only requires revising scripts you get from somewhere else, you can be quite a threat out there in the web development job market.

Going beyond JavaScript, it can be very useful to know Python or SQL, among others. These languages get you thinking about how your website interacts with the databases that drive more and more of what happens on the web, and in mobile apps as well.

After you gain technical skills, find ways to get recognition for them. Courses, certificate programs, and projects where you're the lead for coding work are all ways to get this recognition.

Then, assess where you want to grow. You may want to be the best graphic designer you know who also knows how to handle database access — or the best Python programmer you know who's also skilled at graphics.

Communicate better and earlier

The biggest single frustration that managers, at all levels, have with web developers is that they never know — well, most of what they need to know. They don't know what a website is going to look like when the project is signed off. They don't know whether all the promised features will be there. They don't know whether the schedule will be met — or, it sometimes seems more likely, how big the schedule overshoot will be. And they don't know whether the site will be relatively bug-free, especially in the vital area of data security.

The odd thing is, if web developers on a project felt that they could be honest, they could probably answer many of these questions much earlier in the game. Management might not like the answer, but everyone would benefit from the information getting out there sooner rather than later.

So perhaps the biggest pro skill in web development has nothing directly to do with development at all. It has to do with communication. Understanding the scope of a project, or part of a project; assessing progress toward goals; calculating realistic finish dates, likely feature sets, and so on, and then communicating the information to others, especially management.

The main difficulty with communication has to do with having the courage to be the bearer of bad news, and earning the respect of others so that they'll accept it from you. Now if you're highly skilled, and willing and able to work very hard, you can sometimes single-handedly make the news less bad by filling gaps in the project yourself. But it's more important to assess, and communicate about, the gaps in a project than to try to fill them all yourself.

So as you work on your projects, don't just think of technical and artistic challenges. Think of business goals and where the technical and artistic challenges stack up against those. Assess where your project is at against those goals, and start sharing your opinion with others.

Part V
The Part of Tens

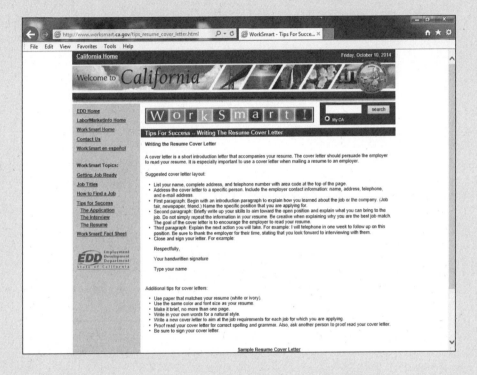

Check out www.dummies.com/extras/gettingawebdevelopmentjob for top ten tips on creating a portfolio site.

In this part . . .

- ✓ Prepare for questions frequently asked in job interviews
- ✓ Find interesting places to search for web jobs
- ✓ Decide what to do when you don't want to work for "The Man"

Chapter 19

Ten Frequently Asked Questions in Web-Developer Interviews

• •

So you got the interview! You're getting ready for a phone screen, or a series of sit-down, on-site interviews at the company location where you hope to be working soon. What are they going to ask you? How best should you respond? We've prepared a list of ten frequently asked questions in job interviews, with our helpful — or simply snarky — comments.

What Is Your Greatest Strength?

This question is always "in the air" in a job interview, whether or not it's asked explicitly. Always try to answer this question during the interview, even if you have to work the information into general discussion or your answer to another question. This question relates back to the "angular versus well-rounded" comparison between people that we mention in the previous chapter.

This is not a question to answer with a single word or a short phrase. (A disconcerting way of answering questions that many of us techie types seem to enjoy inflicting on people.)

Take the question to mean, "What is your greatest strength? Why? Please give an example of how it's shown up in your recent work or personal life." Answer each of those questions, briefly, and then stop talking.

When you provide a greatest strength, it should be work-relevant if possible. Whether the strength seems like something that's work-relevant, answer the implied question, "Why?" in a work-relevant way.

For instance, say that your greatest strength was being physically strong. This is not work-relevant for most daily tasks that you encounter in a web development job.

So you can do a couple of things. The first is that you can look within the strength for something that's work-relevant. For instance, you might be strong because you're very well-disciplined about working out. So you can answer that your strength is self-discipline. It shows up in your physical strength, but also in ways that are directly relevant to work.

Or, you can answer very directly. Here's an answer that includes all the pieces of a good answer to this question — not just the simple answer, but something about why, and a work-related example: "My greatest strength is that I'm physically very strong. That's mostly genetic — my family is full of very fit people. My main work-related strength is self-discipline, which is part of how I keep my strength up. That showed up in a recent project when we were getting near a tight deadline. Two weeks before, I started deferring non-essential activities, and I postponed a training class scheduled three days before the deadline. I was able to make the deadline with only a small amount of overtime, and with really high-quality work. I was then able to help out a couple of my colleagues who had gone over the deadline and needed the help."

What if you're interrupted?

Many of us have been taught that it's never polite to interrupt people. We think that's a bad way of looking at things, and never more so than during a job interview.

You're trying to give complete answers to questions and show your best side in response to each question. Interviewers know how much they need from you. So it's perfectly natural for you to tend to give long answers — and for your interviewers to politely interrupt you when they've gotten the kind of information they wanted, or they aren't learning much new from the direction you're going in.

The key word there, though, is "politely," and politeness is in the eye of the beholder. Complicating this subjective and important point is the fact that web development is very international and multicultural, so expectations around values like politeness can vary tremendously between a given interviewer

and a specific interviewee. Try to be forgiving of what might seem to you like bad manners on the part of your interviewer.

And don't worry about being interrupted. If you want to reduce interruptions, answer in bursts of one or a few sentences, then pause and look at your interviewer for a signal as to whether to go on. After a minute or two, stop and say, "Is there anything more you want to hear about that?" And, after doing that once, finish what you have to say and then stop — even if the interviewer takes a couple of seconds to respond. This returns control of the conversation to the interviewer.

But, whether or not you try to make your responses brief and to invite the interviewer to let you know when you're finished, a good interviewer is still likely to interrupt you at least a couple of times during the interview. Be ready for it, be gracious when it happens, and give your full attention to the interviewer's next question.

What Is Your Greatest Weakness?

This question might even be more common than our first example — but we put that one first because they're a logical pair. It's common for an interviewer to throw this in near the end of an interview, and it feels like an attempt to trip you up.

There are two things to avoid when answering this question. First, don't give a deeply personal answer. It really isn't appropriate in the workplace, and interviews aren't the time to suddenly go all Oprah confessional on people. Don't talk about how much you like prescription medications or that time you couldn't stop lifting items off the shelves of convenience stores when you were a teenager.

The second is to not try to turn the question around with a ridiculously positive answer. Some people will recommend that you offer something like, "My greatest weakness is that people love to work with me so much that it's agonizing to move to a new employer. For instance, I'm dreading the wailing, tears, and rending of garments if you hire me away from my current job."

To answer this common question constructively, think of the old saying, "Never take a problem to your boss; only bring solutions." So, think of an actual weakness that really does affect you at work. Then describe the things you do that keep it from being a problem — and which, in and of themselves, are good habits that make you a better employee.

For instance, say that you like to track a million things at once. This keeps you very well-informed and plugged in, which benefits not only you, but your entire team. However, this same tendency has sometimes made it hard for you to focus when there's a big chunk of work to be done.

So, for instance, you use an online timer to do big chunks of work in half-hour chunks. You only check email every two hours during these focused times, and you minimize meetings.

All of these techniques allow you to overcome your tendency to multitask, while still allowing you the benefits of being very plugged in and well connected.

Why Do You Want to Leave Your Current Company?

This is one of the trickiest questions for many people. Your new employer will want you to be a positive, loyal, upbeat person who can make the best of any situation. Yet it wants you to leave your current employer.

In academia, this kind of situation is called *problematization*. Which simply means, identifying the reason something needs to change, or to be done.

Don't only answer this question in terms of how great the new company is, without any reference to your current employer. That could make your employer think that you'd be willing to leave even if it does all it can — that you'll jump at the next bright shiny object. Be ready to discuss a problem or lack that is pretty strong at your current company, and one that you have reason to believe that the new company will resolve.

So identify an actual problem with your current employer that you believe will be better at your new employer. The easiest answers to this question, if they happen to be true, relate to obvious differences between the two as places of work — preferring a small company to a big one, or the opposite; strong salary and benefits versus a poor compensation package; use of newer technologies versus long-established ones; an exciting project versus a less exciting operational role.

It's common for a prospective employer to change a job description radically, offer you a different job than the one you came in for, or wait several months to offer you a job — which could be the same job, a somewhat different job, or a completely different job.

Inside information

It's great to try to get inside information before interviewing. Part of the reason is that it's important to know how people at a company see themselves. For instance, a big company may see itself as nimble; a small one as stable; a company in an established industry as innovative. If you tell people that what you love about the company is its large size and stability, and they think of themselves as the innovators in their industry, they might conclude you're in the wrong place.

Use the techniques described in Chapter 17 to find inside information — including personal networking, networking within your work discipline, networking around technologies you use, or visiting the employment website Glassdoor (www.glassdoor.com) and looking for comments. From this information, put together an idea of how people in the company see themselves. And, at the same time, leave some room for questioning; many companies have employees who are considered to have "drunk the Kool-Aid" of management's vision for the company, whereas others are skeptical.

All of this will be invaluable to you in deciding whether you want to work at a company — and, if you do, in helping you reply to interview questions using your interviewer's own frame of reference. With this extra effort, you're more likely to be able to walk in the door that you want to walk in through, and to be happy staying there a good long time with your new employer if that's what you want.

With that in mind, consider not tying all your excitement about leaving your current company, and coming to the new one, in terms of a specific role, a specific coworker, or a specific technology. (Unless the technology in question pretty much dominates the workplace at the new company.) Instead, mention these things where they're relevant, but look for things you like about the company as a whole to talk about as well.

Tell Us about an Accomplishment You're Proud of

This question is a version of "What is your greatest strength?" which we discuss previously. It's pretty easy to answer, if you're prepared.

Think of an actual accomplishment you're proud of — and make sure it's work-related. If you answer, "my children," or something similar, you might really put off a work-oriented interviewer. (You would certainly put us off.)

Again, this question is not one to which you want to give a one-word answer or a short phrase. Talk about the accomplishment; how you made it happen; what skills you showed; and relate it to something you expect to do or face at the company where you're interviewing.

Tell Us about a Problem and How You Handled It

This question is a version of "What is your greatest weakness?" which we also discuss previously. Like that question, it's pretty easy to handle, if you're ready.

Describe a work-related problem and how you resolved it. Also describe the skills you showed and relate the issue to something that you know of at the company where you're interviewing.

Your interviewer will probably think of several relevant issues at the workplace that you won't yet have had the opportunity to learn about. You might even ask the interviewer if he or she has had a similar experience to what you've described; the answer could be quite informative.

Why Do You Want to Work at Our Company?

Use the information and approach that you developed to answer the previous commonly asked question, "Why do you want to leave your current company?" to prepare for this one.

If you're asked this question directly, have perhaps three reasons ready. They should cover opportunities for growth, cultural fit, or technical interest.

If you're well-prepared, this question is a softball, and you can knock it out of the park if you're ready. Here's an example of a solid answer to this question:

> *"I looked into your company a bit before coming here today. I hear that you treat people well, and I'm looking for an environment where that's valued.*
>
> *I'd like to develop myself into a management position at some point, and I think the supportive environment here would help. I also understand that the company is growing, so that provides more opportunities for people like me to grow with it.*
>
> *Finally, the technology set you use is the one that I've become comfortable with because I believe it's the right solution to the technical problems that you face on this project. I look forward to showing what I know, and learning even more about it."*

Alternatively, if the employer is using a technology set that's new to you, a good answer could include this: "Finally, the technology set you use is new to me, and I look forward to learning it in depth. I believe it's the right solution to the technical problems that you face on this project, and for similar problems as well."

Where Do You See Yourself in Five Years?

The length of time cited in a question like this might be 10 years, or even just two to three years in a fast-moving environment like Silicon Valley. The idea behind the question is just to get a feel for how you think of yourself going forward.

What makes a question like this difficult to answer, if you're surprised by it, is the invitation inherent in the question to think beyond the job actually being offered to you. Here you are, trying hard to get a job offer, and your interviewer asks what you would want to do next if you got the job. A tricky question indeed!

Also inherent in the question — and a very lively topic for web developers — is whether you see yourself on a technical track, growing in ability and knowledge. Alternatively, do you see yourself on a management track, focusing on herding the cats: that is, managing the people on a web development team? And do you see yourself doing that at the company you're applying to, or elsewhere?

This question is only likely to be useful to you if you think through your answer beforehand. Decide if you're interested in a management track, or a technical track, at this time. Include that focus in your answer.

Also identify what really gets you going in the job that you're applying for. It could be delivering improved functionality; making things look great or work great; innovating technically, either in the visible delivered website or in the tools and techniques used to make it; and so on.

If you figure out what it is that really drives you, considering this question might be a big help to you in your career.

However, whatever new insights you encounter, if you're like most people, you should be quite tentative in your answer. There are big potential rewards in both the technical and management tracks in web development, and many jobs that blend elements of each. You are quite likely to trim your sails to suit your cloth — to be opportunistic about opportunities that present themselves to you. During a job interview is exactly the time you're least able to understand, and least interested in sharing, what your opportunities over the next few years will be.

Sometimes interviewers ask you about your future because of difficulties with a previous or current employee who was too ambitious — or, conversely, who refused to take on the manager role when it was offered to her. They may be seeking to grow their manager ranks, or be flattening out hierarchies and shedding managers. It's easy for there to be a hidden agenda in a question like this, and very hard to meet it. So keep your answer low-key and tentative so you can get the job and then figure out what's up.

So a good answer to a question like this goes something like the following: "Well, the thing I love most about web development is the opportunity to make life visibly better for users. I can do that either by getting better and better at my job, or by managing other talented people to create great new sites and site updates. Right now, the challenge of managing appeals to me, but I'm hoping to start a new job here soon. If I get this job, I'll work hard to excel in it, and see what opportunities arise a few years down the road."

Are You Willing to Relocate?

This is a strange question to suddenly bring up in an interview; the job ad or phone screen should have asked you about this previously, if relocation is truly a possibility with this role.

If that's come up earlier in the process, you should have a pretty good idea of what's behind the question, and gotten a start on answering it. If so, just repeat your previous answer — or give your new answer, if it's changed.

A common reason for this question to be asked, relatively late in the game, is if you're interviewing in an office of a company whose headquarters is somewhere else. It's common for talented people to "move to headquarters," and, if your interviewers are starting to get serious about hiring you, they may now want to ask this question.

Less commonly, your company might want to dispatch some people from headquarters to a regional location, or move people from one region to another.

Strategically, you want to keep your options open on a question like this, without suggesting that you'd abandon the office you're interviewing in — and the people who are currently considering hiring you onto your team — on a moment's notice.

You may believe at the moment that there's nothing that would ever inspire you to move, and in some situations that's true. If so, you should say that you're highly unlikely to want to relocate. But many people have ended up voluntarily relocating, for the right offer, when they might have thought that they would never relocate — right up to the time when they decided to take the plunge.

Given these uncertainties, it's not dishonest to leave your options open. If you tell the truth, but without saying a strong no (if there's any wiggle room in your future plans at all), you give yourself the best chance of getting the job, and possibly having some exciting opportunities open up down the road.

On the other hand, if you'd be perfectly happy to relocate, you don't want to sound too eager. The current hiring managers might want you around for awhile before you consider looking off to greener pastures.

If you consider yourself unlikely to relocate, but are aware that a great offer might tempt you — a pretty common situation — an answer like this one is appropriate: "I'm not looking to relocate anytime soon, and I really like this area. However, I'm pretty excited about future opportunities with this company, and if the right offer came up down the road, I might be willing to consider it."

Why relocate?

There are certain gravitational pulls that make everyone more likely to relocate to some places — and others that only affect certain people.

One of the authors (Smith) got tired, early in his career, of getting to know colleagues in Silicon Valley, only to see them move away after a few years. He developed the habit of asking each colleague where his mother lived. It was common for the colleague to end up moving to that city after either doing well, or more or less striking out, in Silicon Valley. Several married friends who had children ended up moving away soon after — often close to wherever the wife's mother was located.

The draws that tempt a great many people tend to be oriented toward greater career opportunities, and include moving to Silicon Valley (especially in web development); moving to a world-class city, such as New York City, or a state or national capital city; moving to headquarters of the company that's interviewing you (which is probably in a world-class or capital city); or moving overseas, if perhaps only for a few years.

There are also more or less random draws, when considered across a large pool of employees, such as where your family's from; where your spouse or partner's family is from, if you're married or in a partnership; where you or your spouse went to college; or where a star former boss or mentor has moved on to.

Take account of the city you're in when you're interviewing; whether the location you're interviewing in is headquarters; and whether there's an attractive city or region, such as Silicon Valley, which has already siphoned good people away from your current location.

Then figure out if that's a path you may want to tread yourself, and plan accordingly. Don't tip your hand, though, and be wary of questions designed to draw you out on the topic. You want to keep your options open: You never know what will happen in the company where you're interviewing if you get hired.

Are You Willing to Travel?

Like a willingness to relocate, this is a strange question to suddenly bring up in an interview; the job ad or phone screen should have asked you about travel previously, if it's any part of the job at all.

If you can't travel at all, due to family, health, or other considerations, say so. You don't want to take a job and then lose it soon after because you can't meet a basic job requirement.

If you dislike traveling, or it's inconvenient for you, say that you're willing to travel up to about one week a month. This is a level of inconvenience that many professionals have to put up with, and it does have some perks, such as seeing new sights, meeting new people, and paying for some of your meals and gym time with the company's money.

If the job requires more travel than that, and you haven't been alerted to that fact before the interview, think carefully. It doesn't show very good planning, or care for your interests, for a factor this big to first come up during the interview.

Don't stretch much on this question just to get a job — you have to want to keep the job after you get it, and travel is a major factor in causing work/life imbalance. When it comes to willingness to travel, say what you mean, and mean what you say.

Do You Have Any Questions for Us?

This is a sensible question, and shows an interest in your views by the company that's potentially hiring you. But it often leaves people flummoxed, and is almost a trick question.

Many people, on hearing this question, want to be polite, and say no. This is a big, but forgivable, mistake.

Other people, on hearing this question, and perhaps feeling nervous, ask questions that are important, but not really appropriate to an interview, such as how much vacation they get, how much overtime they'll be expected to work, how much they can work at home, and so on. These are questions you should ask outside the interview situation, not bring up because someone happened to open the door to them during your job interview.

You want to have some questions ready for this — two or three is a good number. Here are some questions that may be relevant to you:

- ✔ Tell me more about the tools and technologies used here.
- ✔ Is this a new position, or are you replacing someone who's leaving?
- ✔ Why did you open this position now? (Or, can you share about why the previous person is leaving? Be aware that you might not get a truthful or full answer.)
- ✔ What brought you to this company?
- ✔ What makes you happiest about working here?

Note that these are either strictly factual, highly relevant questions, or easy and positive ones. They all show an interest in the environment that you are, the interviewers hope, interested in moving into.

Ask two or three questions, and then stop. You don't want to get into any areas that are clumsy, personal, or embarrassing for anyone involved, including yourself — and open-ended questions like this one make that surprisingly easy to do.

Practice and prepare

We suggest that you prepare for your interview by writing down these questions, plus a few others that might be pertinent to the particular job you're applying for.

Write brief answers to each question, and then practice with a friend. Ask the friend to throw in a few questions of his or her own, and perhaps even to zing you with a ridiculous question or two. Three 30-minute practice sessions is probably enough warm up for most interview situations.

You want to get to where you're answering questions comfortably and sensibly, with reasonably consistent answers from one practice session to the next.

After you've practiced to this extent, not much will mess you up. You may get asked entirely different questions, and it won't matter too much; the confidence you develop from successfully getting through a practice session, and the themes in your experience and interests that develop, will be enough to get you through.

Before the interview, you may want to create a crib sheet — perhaps up to one page of notes and key themes. It's acceptable, during an interview, to say, "I think I made a note on that topic, and I want to give you my best answer. Just a moment." And then look at your notes.

You'll feel much more relaxed, and are quite likely to perform better, with this level of preparation. If that's the case, you'll also feel much better in the anxious wait between interviewing and finding out if you got the job.

Chapter 20

Ten Interesting Job Search Websites for Web Developers

· ·

Searching for a job online can be kind of fun — or kind of awful. You can do it playfully, dreaming of a job being great, or worriedly, feeling a bit desperate for something to come through and get you off of the unemployment rolls, or out of a difficult situation at your current job.

These sites, which are especially helpful for web developers, are interesting alternatives to the large sites — the large job search sites such as Monster (www.monster.com) and Indeed (www.indeed.com).

One great way to go through the large sites is to use SimplyHired.com, which aggregates results from most of the large sites. With SimplyHired, you avoid duplication and wasted effort.

Dice.com

Dice.com (www.dice.com) is an ideal site for technically oriented jobs. Easy to use, fast, and limited to technical jobs, Dice is the most time-efficient site we've found for finding a job — especially contract work — quickly, without a lot of muss and fuss.

Dice.com started in Silicon Valley, and it's still strongest and deepest there, but it's built up strength in many other locations as well.

Dice, as fans call it, is very specific and to the point. For most of the jobs listed, you need to match the specific skills, technologies, and tools listed. Most of the recruiters are just trying to find a quick fit. The jobs are often just average in pay.

However, if you're in a hurry to get a decent, if not necessarily spectacular, job, or you want to quickly check what's out there in your field, and in your region, Dice.com is a great place to go first.

Elance/Odesk

We're kind of cheating by combing Elance (www.elance.com) and Odesk (www.odesk.com) into one entry. However, although the sites are different, they overlap in a lot of ways. Not least is the fact that Elance, the company, recently acquired Odesk, which at that time was a separate company, and made them into one big company.

We're also cheating by listing Elance and Odesk at all. These are really not job search sites. What they are is project boards, where potential clients post jobs they want done. You bid on jobs, take them, manage the project through the site's tools, and get paid through the site as well.

There are several different approaches to doing well on Elance and Odesk, and each site has its own feel. (These differences may erode, however, as Elance "rationalizes its operations" — that is, combines functions internally and lays people off as a result.)

Check out these sites. You can start building a reputation on one or both sites by doing a few small jobs while you're employed. Then you can up your presence on either site, or both, and make it into a nearly full-time or full-time gig.

We Work Remotely

Many Web developers are frustrated because the dream of living wherever you want and choosing the best jobs from a wide geographic area hasn't come true for most of us. A surprising number of jobs — the vast majority — still require you to come into the office most days.

We Work Remotely (www.weworkremotely.com) is an alternative. This site lists jobs where you aren't required to come into the office much: in fact, in most cases, never.

Competition is stiff for We Work Remotely jobs, but the site is worth checking out if you're talented, but live off the beaten path for web development jobs.

Startupers

Startupers (www.startupers.com) is specifically for finding jobs in startups. You'll see a lot of jobs in Silicon Valley, but others in New York, Boston, and other tech hubs as well.

This site is engineering-heavy, but there are visual developer-related jobs as well. There are only a few listings per day; you're not likely to find a job in a hurry here, but it's fun to keep an eye open while you're in a long-term job, and you could easily find something interesting for a friend or colleague.

If you've ever dreamed of working in a startup — and, if you don't already live in a tech hub, you're willing to relocate — Startupers is a great site to check out.

Angel List

Angel List (www.angellist.com) is another specialized job board for startups. This one contains angel-funded startups looking for people who are, in many cases, willing to take stock options in return for a lower-than-usual salary.

If you're a star, some of these companies may be willing to consider part-time or full-time remote work as well.

Angel List is another place where you don't necessarily spend a lot of time if you're pounding the pavement, virtually speaking, looking for a job in a hurry. But, like Startupers, it's another good site to keep an eye on over time.

Authentic Jobs

Authentic Jobs (www.authenticjobs.com) is for creative types who want to "make a better web" — which means you! It tends to be engineering-heavy. Take a look — if you have the kind of skills that companies that post on Authentic Jobs are looking for, this one is worth coming back to.

Krop

Krop (www.krop.com) is a creative job board with positions that lean more toward designers, although there are positions for software developers here too. As with Authentic Jobs, check it out. If you're in its target demographic, you'll keep coming back.

Stackoverflow Careers

A *stack overflow* is something that happens when you're programming and you try to store more information in limited, temporary storage — the stack — than will fit. Stackoverflow is a site for programmers to ask each other questions and get answers. The Careers (www.careers.stackoverflow.com/) area is where these same people go to find jobs.

You're more likely to find a job on Stackoverflow Careers if you first become a contributor in the main Q&A part of Stackoverflow.

Coroflot

Coroflot (www.coroflot.com) is great for visual designers and related creative roles, whether freelance or full-time. You can narrow your search using scores of check boxes for specialty areas, including 3D Modeling, Account Management, Advertising, and many, many more.

LinkedIn.com and Glassdoor.com are information-sharing sites of different types. Both have added job search capabilities, and LinkedIn has jobs posted on company pages and in the many, many LinkedIn groups related to web development.

Chapter 21

Ten Red-Hot Roles for Web Developers

• •

*W*eb developer jobs are nothing if not flexible. It's great to know which roles are hot. Not only is it fun — like following races in politics or sports — but you can aim your own career in the direction of any hot job that attracts you. What could be more of a blast?

Some of the roles listed here, such as visual designer, include jobs for entry-level people straight out of school or a training program. Others, such as art director, require years of experience. If you're just starting out, and one of these high-level roles appeals to you, use it as a target as you add skills and gain experience.

The following roles are listed in no particular order, based only on our flexible and varying ideas of what "red-hot" might mean to us and to you.

Visual Designer

This is one of the most common jobs in the web development world. How can it also be one of the hottest?

Well, the traditional title for this role is graphic designer. The two terms are often used interchangeably. However, used properly, the term visual designer means something somewhat different. It emphasizes the effect of your designs and assumes that your designs can travel with integrity across platforms: not only all sorts of electronic devices, but print, billboards, T-shirts, and a whole wide and wild range of destinations.

If an employer differentiates between graphic designers and visual designers, or hires visual designers and artists but not graphic designers, it is making a statement — a statement that partly means "we're up to date" and that partly shows that it gets the difference. So, visual designer is a hot web development career and should continue to be for quite a while.

SQL Web Developer

This is a "hard" developer job, in a way. As an SQL web developer, you create databases, write code to interact with them, and work with others on most of the web-specific parts of the job.

What makes this accessible is that SQL database programming is, for many people, not as complex or confusing as "real" programming in languages like C++ or even Python. Yes, table joins can be confusing, but a lot of the rest of it is not that hard for people who can handle, say, introductory-level calculus or statistics.

This is a growing job category with a lot of promise. Eventually, there might be more focus on grid databases and advanced development and runtime environments like Hadoop. But an SQL database will be the standard for a great many websites for a long time to come. This is a great role to consider from many spots in the world of web development.

Interaction Designer

An interaction designer is a specialized relative of the user experience, or UX, developer. Interaction designers get down into the nitty-gritty of what makes people click and what helps them get tasks accomplished.

Human-factors work, which is the overall world you have to spend time in to succeed as an interaction designer, is just plain cool. From jet-fighter cockpits to video-game interfaces to e-commerce click-to-buy front ends, really understanding what makes humans tick under different kinds of pressures is just plain fun.

This is also one of the "hardest" — that is, most technical and most metrics-driven — jobs that a person with "soft" skills like graphic or visual design can hope to get into without learning programming. The metrics focus means you can show your value, which means you can justify a hefty paycheck. (And for your colleagues, too, if you're generous.)

So consider interaction design as a career choice if you like the idea of making a real and measureable difference.

Mobile Developer

Most traditional web development jobs have an analog in the world of mobile development. It's a short journey from web development to mobile development — so short that mobile development can be considered as a subset of the web development world.

Mobile development is intensely competitive, and you have to make your point and make your users happy in a much smaller screen space than on a personal computer screen. Many people, however, consider these kinds of constraints fun and rewarding.

The only thing you need to do to get into mobile development is get a role on a development team that ships something on mobile, hopefully something that's moderately successful. And you're off to the races.

You can even jump-start this career by creating your own app, using one of many toolkits out there of the "just add water" variety, such as Sencha Touch (visit www.sencha.com). The app you develop can be a real app, intended for sale or free distribution through an app store, or just something for your portfolio. This accomplishment should be enough to get onto a commercial web development team and move your new career forward from there.

Art Director

What fun! Being an art director for the web is probably about as much fun for being an art director in print, or for commercials, or any other area. That is to say, a lot.

As an art director, you get to think big about how design and all the other elements of the website experience work together to help customers, reinforce your brand, and support clients' or users' goals.

You can approach becoming an art director from just about any position on the design side of the web development careers spectrum.

One suggestion, both to help you get the job, and to help you enjoy it more if you do get it: Consider getting your PhD, from as demanding and reputable a university as you can manage. In this case, getting the PhD after you've been working in web development for a while might be especially advantageous, as your real-world experience and your academic work can feed off each other. (Also, solid work experience is likely to help you qualify for a better doctoral program than you might otherwise be able to get into.)

Then, after you get the art director position, you can teach and consult as well. What fun! If either of us, the authors, had any artistic talent at all, we'd be there.

Full Stack Developer

If we were on the software side of web development, we'd try hard to avoid getting sucked into non-web software development roles. Sure, they pay well, and you avoid all sorts of hassles, but you miss out on the direct interaction with real users and the rich project teams full of characters that are a feature of web development.

As a full stack developer, you can stay firmly in the web world. That's because your expertise is making all aspects of web software, from front-end software such as JavaScript to back-end software such as C++ or Python, work together to make the whole site work smoothly. That means you have your fingers in just about every issue that makes modern websites interesting.

The key to becoming a full-stack developer is becoming good at all the different technologies that make up a software developer's world in web development, without abandoning the range of technologies in favor of any one discipline (such as database programming) or technology (such as Python). You really do want to be a jack-of-all trades and a master of none. (If you focus enough on one technology to master it, you're in danger of losing the breadth of vision implied by the term *full stack developer.*)

Product Manager

One of us (Smith) has been a product manager a couple of different times, once for web-savvy software — Apple's QuickTime — and once for devices enabled by web connections, in-car GPS devices. It was a lot of fun both times.

A product manager is a kind of business unit manager for a product or service. In the web development world, you can move up to product manager — it's usually considered a promotion because there's a lot of responsibility — from any number of other spots. You just need to be good at your initial job and show some business savvy.

Product managers often have MBAs, so if you want this job, consider getting one of those. It's a good career, but you won't necessarily be in web development anymore; after you're a product manager, you can end up managing all sorts of products.

Project Manager

Project managers make the trains run on time. Project managers typically work closely with product managers because they both want schedules met and features to work as promised.

Typically, a project manager has spreadsheets or Microsoft Project project plans for every part of a project, and does all he can to help make sure that the project meets the deadlines in the project plan.

This job is conceptually simple, but really, really hard. Web development professionals tend to be poor estimators, so rolling up these bad estimates into schedules produces unreliable results. Then, customers or clients tend to want changes as a project progresses, but no one wants to increase the budget or move the target date out.

Despite the job's high degree of difficulty, project managers seem to enjoy their work. They enjoy it even more when they join a professional organization, such as the Project Management Institute, and get a professional certification, such as the PMP, or Project Management Professional certification.

To an even greater degree than a product manager, a project manager can be made from almost any professional on a web development team. If you want a different job on your current web development team — or if you want to get into web development, but lack the requisite talent or skills or experience — consider coming in as a project manager.

Program Manager

Despite the title, a program manager doesn't necessarily write software. Instead, a program manager can be the boss of a group of product managers, the boss of a group of project managers, or the directly responsible individual, as Apple used to call it, responsible for all aspects of a project.

Program managers are often former product or project managers, but they can come from other spots too, and from outside web development as well. Useful qualifications to be a program manager include a technical bachelor's degree, an MBA, and a PMP certification.

Program managers breathe pretty rarefied air, making big decisions and making big money while they do it. If you enjoy managing people and bearing a lot of responsibility, consider working your way toward the program manager role.

Webmaster

As the songwriter wrote, "Everything old is new again." As a job title, *webmaster* has always kind of sucked. It was a generalist term used by those who didn't really know what they were talking about, a kind of verbal Hail Mary pass uttered in hopes that someone would come along and "solve" the web for some hapless company.

However, webmaster today means two things, both of them great. The first meaning is for someone who will, well, "solve" the web for some hapless company. These days, when most business professionals "speak web" to a high degree, it can be a lot of fun to work in an environment where that's not the norm. You can do a lot of fun, informal teaching about what the web can do for an organization these days.

The second meaning of webmaster is an arch, ironic use of the term by people who know that it's vague and imprecise, but are looking to hire sharp web people without pigeonholing them too much. It can be really fun to work for a company that exhibits this degree of understanding of the current web and its own situation.

So don't turn your nose up at the job title *webmaster.* Check it out. There might be an interesting situation behind it.

Index

• U •

UI (user interface) designer, 35

`<ul>` tags, HTML, 114

undergraduate degrees. *See also* four-year degrees

two-year, 165–168, 173

value of, 164–166

underlining, in text for web, 111

university programs. *See also* education for web development careers

personalizing, 174–180

for web development tools, 190–191

updates (book), 4

URLs (Uniform Resource Locators), user-friendly, 20

U.S. Bureau of Labor Statistics (BLS)

educational level needed, 66

management jobs in computer science, 175

Occupational Outlook Handbook, 164, 169–170

projected growth in web development, 70–71

salaries, 68

statistics on website of, 64–65

web developers, description of, 65

work environment description, 65

U.S. Department of Agriculture website, 139, 141, 142

U.S. Department of Defense website, 139–140, 142

U.S. Department of Energy website, 149–150

U.S. Department of Health and Human Services, 109

U.S. Department of State website

goals of as implemented in look of site, 139–140, 142

salary negotiation advice, 170–171

U.S. Department of Veterans Affairs (VA), 193

U.S. Environmental Protection Agency (EPA), 143

U.S. Federal Agency for Healthcare Research and Quality, 200

U.S. Federal Communications Commission, 95

usability

lists as improving, 115

tips for, 121–122

usability professional

defined, 30

jobs related to, 35

overview, 34

usability.gov website, 101–102, 147

useit.com website, 125

user interface (UI) designer, 35

user needs, grokking, 146–148

user testing

defined, 35

grokking user needs, 146–147

importance of, 34, 148

Utah

Dreamweaver tutorial from, 207–208

Web Development 1 course in, 77–81

UX (user experience) designer. *See also* visual designer

job description, 35

overview, 23–24

• V •

VA (U.S. Department of Veterans Affairs), 193

vector graphics tools, 198–199

Veronica, 98

visual designer. *See also* graphic designer; UX designer

as hot career, 275

job description, 31–32

priorities for, 27–29

versus web designer, 32

• W •

W3C. *See* World Wide Web Consortium

wages. *See* salary

Warning! icon, explained, 4

We Work Remotely job search website, 272

weaknesses, interview questions about, 261

About the Authors

Floyd Earl Smith is a leading Silicon Valley technical communicator and author, with more than 20 books to his credit. His career includes a long stint at Apple in the 1990s, as well as work for Microsoft, IBM, AltaVista, AOL, and financial institution HSBC. Floyd's best-sellers include *Creating Web Pages For Dummies,* 9th Edition; several editions of *AutoCAD For Dummies*; and *Internet Marketing For Dummies*. In addition to his writing work, Floyd is active in 350 Bay Area, a Northern California nonprofit working to reduce greenhouse gas emissions and limit climate change.

Kathy Taylor is one of the leading executive recruiters in Silicon Valley, boasting a success record of more than 95 percent on searches. She concentrates on startups and emerging growth companies, serving as the go-to person for many VCs (venture capital firms) in Silicon Valley. Kathy served for ten years as head of TalentPlanet, a boutique executive search from specializing in the C-suite (CEOs, CFOs, and so on), as well as top positions in sales, marketing, and business development. Productivity expert Hugh Culver says of Kathy, "If you get a chance to work with Kathy, don't let it slip by!"

Dedication

Kathy and Floyd dedicate this book to the many talented people who continue to build a new world online that's more open, interesting, and fun than what came before.

Authors' Acknowledgments

Kathy and Floyd would like to thank Wiley for the opportunity to write this foundational book in the *Getting a Job For Dummies* series now pouring forth from the presses — physical and digital — of this iconic imprint.

We appreciate the effort of Steve Hayes to start and finish the project with us; of Andy Cummings to step in when Steve was pulled onto other projects, helping to keep things on track; and, most especially to project editor Linda Morris, who stuck with us as our trickle of writing early in the project finally crested to something resembling a flood. Our technical editor, Brian Benedict, made incisive comments that improved the book.

We would like to conclude by thanking our talented and knowledgeable agent, Carol Jelen, an executive at top digital and print agency Waterside Productions.

Publisher's Acknowledgments

Executive Editor: Steve Hayes

Project Editor: Linda Morris

Copy Editor: Linda Morris

Technical Editor: Brian Benedict

Editorial Assistant: Claire Brock

Sr. Editorial Assistant: Cherie Case

Project Coordinator: Patrick Redmond

Cover Image: ©iStock.com/sydmsix